UNDERSTANDING VISION

UNDERSTANDING VISION

R.J. Watt

*Centre for Cognitive and Computational Neuroscience and
Department of Psychology,
Stirling University,
Scotland*

ACADEMIC PRESS
Harcourt Brace Jovanovich, Publishers
London   San Diego   New York
Boston   Sydney   Tokyo   Toronto

ACADEMIC PRESS LIMITED
24–28 Oval Road
London NW1 7DX

US edition published by
ACADEMIC PRESS INC
San Diego, CA 92101

British Library Cataloguing in Publication Data
Watt, R.
  Understanding vision.
  1. Man. Sight
  I. Title
  612.84

ISBN 0-12-738500-2
ISBN 0-12-738501-0 pbk

Typeset by P&R Typesetters Ltd, Salisbury, Wilts, UK
Printed and bound in Great Britain at The Bath Press, Avon

To Sarah, Samuel and Andrew,
scrutineers of understanding

The eye cannot say to the hand, 'I don't need you!' And the head cannot say to the feet 'I don't need you!'

1 Corinthians 12:21

Contents

Preface   **ix**

Acknowledgements   **xiii**

1. What is Vision?   **1**

2. Vision: Images to Action   **13**

3. What are Images Like?   **24**

4. Image Algebra   **57**

5. Image Description   **97**

6. Visual Description   **133**

7. Visual Interpretation   **161**

8. Studying Human Vision   **191**

9. Psychophysics and Image Algebra   **217**

10. Psychophysics and Visual Descriptions   **245**

11. Psychophysics and Visual Interpretation   **270**

12. Postscript   **293**

   Index   **299**

Preface

I have learnt a great deal from writing this book. I have thought about the nature of what I, as a scientist, am seeking from my own work. The questions that I have had in the forefront of my mind whilst writing this now colour all the work that I do. I am less and less satisfied with the quality of explanation that is usually offered for observations about vision. I am less and less satisfied with the directions in which the research is being led, and with the assumptions on which it is based.

The questions that this book sets out to examine do tend to read pompously. What is the nature of vision? How can I claim to have real evidence about our own human vision, free from contamination by my preconceptions? How will I know when I have a satisfactory account of vision? What concepts will be in the eventual explanation? Of course, questions themselves are rarely pompous, it is the answers, and more importantly, the manner of the giving of the answers that makes for pomposity. In writing this book, I have worked out answers that satisfy me, personally and scientifically. My answers can serve to introduce the subject to newcomers in a comprehensive manner. But I think that they will also be of interest to many colleagues. I expect that they will stimulate these colleagues to work out for themselves what their answers to these questions are. Hopefully, some will agree with me, and hopefully some will disagree. Understanding something as intrinsically human as vision must be a personal, individual and diverse affair.

Scientists tend to work in a cycle of phases, sometimes knowing where their research is leading and what kinds of answers they are looking for, and sometimes not knowing. The field of vision has seen a great deal of work done over the last few years, but most of it has had relatively short-term goals. On the side concerned with human vision, there have been many interesting phenomena examined individually in great detail; in machine vision, a number of very elegant solutions to particular engineering problems have been found. On neither side have there been great conceptual advances. Each side seems currently to be obsessed with a view of vision as creating a reconstruction of the scene from an image or an optic array. As I sit here, there is a breath-taking view of mountains and lochs outside, just beginning to show signs of spring. The clouds pass over leaving dappled patches of sunlight; snow high up gleams brilliantly in contrast to the dark rock and brown heather. I think that I am experiencing a reconstruction of the scene, introspection supports the idea, but there is no proof. As I gaze and think, I am far from convinced that any of the actions or decision that I might take imply that the scene has been reconstructed or needs to be. The information that is necessary for competency in my actions is more basic. I am unsure how well founded the current obsession with scene reconstruction might prove to be.

By making attempts at interdisciplinary collaboration, each side has learned something from the other. Usually this has been the worst habits of the other side. People working on machine vision have picked up the idea that psychophysics is concerned with creating demonstrations of perceptual phenomena and then using introspections on these phenomena as evidence for a particular view of how human vision works. Read any of the journals that publish machine vision material and you will find articles that are written as if they are the last word on how human vision detects edges, or segments texture, or measures surface reflectance. They are usually written in apparent ignorance of the facts that are known and are invariably based on a weak, very suspect model of how human vision can be studied. On the other hand, people working on human vision have picked up an idea about computational vision that is as distorted in its own way. Typically, it is held to be a distinct advantage to have a fully implemented computer model of some hypothetical process in human vision. If the result of applying this process to the experimental stimuli results in the same data that subjects give, then this is taken as strong evidence for the model. The trouble is that there is rarely any examination of where in the model the pattern of results is stemming from. Without this level of analysis, it is difficult to assess objectively the worth of the model. Moreover, there is rarely any attempt to discover whether the proposed computational model might be useful in helping us to see. Partly this arises because the process of seeing involves many components, and the relationship between the components is not well understood. For example, the psychological study of reading makes some strong assumptions about what information vision can deliver: individual letters and their order and identities. Perhaps these assumptions are valid, perhaps they are not. It is not known.

These problems are becoming particularly aggravated at a time when there is pressure on those in research to become "interdisciplinary". A pressure on research of this type should not replace the more traditional values of scientific evidence and hypothesis, and yet all too often it seems to have done so. Despite their relatively long histories, it is still very uncertain how psychophysical and neurophysiological data ought to be related, because they work at very different levels of organization and implementation. It seems to be relatively widely held that physiology is the "truth" and incontrovertible, whereas psychophysics is an "interpretation". This is the theory behind the frequent claims, usually by neurophysiologists, that psychophysical models should be plausible, justifiable, and explicable in neurophysiological terms. This implies that the models of psychophysical results are somehow more negotiable than the models of neurophysiological data. Common sense suggests the opposite: data taken from a complete, fully working system could be expected to have more "validity" than data taken from a small part of a system that is not working. In principle, however, each approach has its own discipline, and neither has the right to make any restriction on or lay claim to a privileged interpretation of the work of the other. It is not surprising that the relationship between machine vision and human vision is so ill understood.

It was with this background that I set out to write a book that would usefully expound psychophysics to machine vision students and experts, and would expound machine vision practices to those studying human vision. The book was to be a quick snapshot view of the subject as I perceived it at a time of flux. The first draft was written quickly, in six months. It was immediately apparent however, that the product was an account of a set of (then) current obsessions, rather than anything with insight. I felt that this was very unsatisfactory and spent the following four years completely rethinking and rewriting.

The original draft was unsatisfactory because it had no real horizon. In this respect it probably did reflect the state of research into vision at that time: there were few long-term goals, but a great many short-term goals. I would claim that this version has a horizon to impart perspective. The major thrust of the book is to consider *competent visual systems*. A competent visual system is one that can do what it has to well. In order to design or understand a competent visual system, we must have a specification of the task or tasks to which it must be turned and the environments within which it must act.

The book is laid out to a plan that I have found useful in writing, and I believe to be helpful in reading. The first and last chapters are general in nature and will present no difficulties of comprehension to anyone. The second chapter is then an overview of the framework for understanding vision that I have built. The ideas of competent visual systems are to be found here. The third chapter contains a consideration of the nature of light, of things in scenes, and of optical images. This is rather technical in parts, but the timid reader may rest assured that skipping the tricky bits will not seriously hamper further reading. Chapters 4 to 7 then describe a theoretical framework that can be used to understand vision in the terms of basic logico-formal methods. The treatment is initially mild, but each chapter ends with a summary which is more formal in its language.

At Chapter 8, a new section of the book starts. Chapter 8 describes general methods and strategies for approaching human vision through psychophysics. These are then applied in Chapters 9 to 11 in examining in detail a range of different experiments that have been conducted and reported. This part of the book implies some familiarity with the earlier chapters, and is best read after at least Chapters 1 and 2. The experiments have been chosen for the extent to which they illustrate techniques as well as the extent to which they offer real and useful insights into human vision.

For most chapters there are reference lists. These are basically selected to give the interested reader an entry into a rather large literature. Since the framework that I have adopted here is a new one, it is rare for any reference to "belong" to one particular chapter, and I have adopted the strategy of placing them where they are most relevant. Sometimes this is appropriate but sometimes the result is a little unsatisfactory.

Most chapters also have a few exercises. These are designed with a view to two different possible reasons a reader might have in looking at them. At one level they provide a check that the material of each chapter has been assimilated and understood. But beyond this, they should also offer some lines of independent enquiry that readers can follow, beyond the scope of this book. Some exercises will be rather difficult to do without access to a reasonably powerful computer and some software for mathematical programming and for image processing and analysis. I have used several different packages in producing the illustrations for the book, and would gladly offer advice to anyone on the choice. This type of information can go out of date very quickly, and so I have not published any details.

The real art in understanding vision is to get out and do it. I would urge all readers most strongly to go away and try to implement visual processes, to run experiments on themselves and others, and to examine carefully the logic of what they are doing.

R.J. WATT

Acknowledgements

This book would not have been produced without the direct and indirect assistance of many, many people. It is a product of an international research tradition into vision, and owes much to all those who practice this tradition.

I started it whilst working as an employee at the MRC Applied Psychology Unit, Cambridge, UK, and it is no exaggeration to say that there are few places where the scientific environment is so strong. I learned a great deal about explanation and about cognition whilst there, and I doubt very much whether I would have been able to undertake this project without that start. I thank the director, Dr Alan Baddeley, and the staff for that.

I completed it here in Stirling, supported by a BP Royal Society of Edinburgh Research Fellowship and by the University. Moving to Stirling gave me the opportunity to break and rethink what I was doing. The final form of the book and the structure of the understanding that it describes owes much to my new environment. The Principal of the University and the President of the Royal Society of Edinburgh are both thanked for making my move here possible.

Software has been developed during the course of writing this book with the support of a grant from the SERC Image Interpretation Initiative. This software has been used to test some of the ideas and to produce many of the illustrations.

Next, I wish to thank the two editors who have had most to do with this project. Rosie Altoft started me off, and restarted me after the failure of the first draft. Andrew Carrick has encouraged me thereafter. Both have provided the support and help that I needed.

Finally, I must thank those who have sustained me whilst writing this book. Chief amongst these are my family, Helen, Sarah, Samuel (and latterly Andrew), without whom, I am sure, my sanity would have been done before the book was. The owl whose early morning hooting fills Coilhallen Forest, where I live, and has called me to work each day is now requested to desist.

1

What is Vision?

Let's start with questions. Several years ago a local priest paid my family a visit and in the course of conversation asked what my job was. I explained that I was involved in research into human vision, to which the priest replied that he thought that it was already well understood that the eye works like a camera and wondered why further research was necessary. I had to explain that a camera does not see. We have so many deeply rooted preconceptions about our sense of vision that offer answers to the most important questions about vision. These ingrained images are a hindrance because they are probably wrong. In this first chapter, I am inviting the reader to shed at least some of the strongly held assumptions, by asking some questions. First, to get started, a couple of thought pictures about vision.

Imagine sitting at a desk in total darkness and wanting to know what is on the desk. You would extend a hand out until it touched something, then you would feel around about to get a sense of the shape of the surface you had touched. You would be trying to find edges, corners, creases. Once found, each would be followed until something else interesting was touched upon. You would not start at the far top left corner and move across to the extreme right then down a little, back to the extreme left, down a little, back to the extreme right, down a little and so on. This is how a mindless robot might do it. Your way is a way in which the information that you obtain structures your search intelligently; the robot is doing it in an unstructered fashion. When your hand touches something on the desk, it explores the immediate vicinity because it knows that what it finds in this neighbourhood will be related to what it has just touched.

Now contrast the ways in which a camera and an artist might record a scene. The camera never lies, and we tend to think of it as a metaphor for our eyesight. In truth, we would be nearer the mark if we were to look to the artist, painting first with his coarse brush and then building within and over these broad strokes with finer details. This is a paradox: the speed of the camera seems more akin to the dynamics of vision than does the painstaking care of the artist. But this is an invalid comparison: the camera hasn't seen anything, the artist has. The artist notices that adjacent points in the scene tend to look alike, and that this is more true the less detail he attends to. The artist has found the patterns, many rather regular, that exist in the scene, and the brush strokes represent this discovery and understanding. The camera lens forms an image all the time, and for most of the time the process of image formation is completely pointless. The artist, on the other hand, paints his image always for a reason. The camera is a passive device, always producing the same image for the same scene; but the artist will never produce the same image for the same scene. The artist is an active device: the scene is moulded both to the physical frame of the canvas and to the psychological frame that is the artist's vision. The artist's attitudes and feelings about himself and his environment interact with his task of recording a visual experience.

1.1 How Can We Test For Vision?

It is surprisingly difficult to decide sometimes whether an infant can see or not. Some babies do not learn the social skills of eye contact and response very effectively. If this is coupled with an inability to pursue a bright light with their eyes, it seems to the parent that the child is blind. Whether such an infant is blind or not is a moot point, because it is occasionally found that appropriate training can give the child what the parents are happy to accept as sight. Why is it a moot point whether blindness can be inferred? The reason is that we implicitly recognize two sides to vision. On the one hand vision leads to certain patterns of behaviour that can be publicly observed, but on the other, vision is private. If we don't observe the behaviour that we expect and we can't ask about the experience, we cannot decide whether a baby can see or not.

I think that when we are discussing the vision of a person we tend to take the experience as the critical factor that determines whether someone can see or not. This is quite bizarre. How could I ever discover what someone else's visual experience is like? I don't even know what it means to compare my experiences with those of another person. Generally we can agree about the words that we use to describe these experiences, or rather, to describe their physical causes. Imagine that we did not. My son and I disagree about the colour of the Invicta steam locomotive at Canterbury: he says that it is red; I, that it is orange. Do we have different experiences or different understandings of the colour names? Even though there may not be agreement between the reports of different individuals, we would expect each person to be consistent. Consistency implies that the sensation and the physical cause are closely coupled. Does this matter? I don't know. My daughter and I disagree about the colour of Mahler's 1st Symphony, but we are not even consistent when we talk about it. The experience depends on other factors such as mood. In neither case do I conclude that there is something wrong with the vision of my children or myself. I hope that this discussion has persuaded you that talking about experiences and sensations is not a very good test of vision.

How about observable behaviour? There are many aspects of human behaviour that would leave little doubt that the person concerned was seeing. Reading a newspaper, handwriting a letter, and driving a car all require vision. Yet none of these requires vision alone; they each rely on other skills as well. Just because someone could not do one of them, we should not conclude that they could not see. Could we perhaps simply look for any form of observable behaviour that is contingent on light in the environment? We now run the risk of deducing that trees can see because they move their leaves to keep them aligned with the sun. Trees do not have vision. Why not? Has the reason to do with the complexity of their behaviour? To slowly move a leaf seems very simple, but plants also show profoundly complex patterns of light-contingent behaviour. The popular houseplant *Euphorbia pulcherrima* flowers when the night length reaches a critical number of hours. A few minutes of artificial light at midnight can prevent it from flowering: the plant has recognized that the conditions are not right for the complex behaviour of flowering.

Light is a messenger. We do not see light; we see the world as it is revealed by light. People have vision when they can see *things*. What are the things we can see? As a starting point, we see the surfaces in a scene: changes in the density and characteristics of matter in space. Surfaces are important determinants of our behaviour. Some we must avoid colliding with whilst others we must try to touch, grasp or lift. In order to decide which behaviour is appropriate, we have to know what the surface is. In order to know how to move, we have to know where the surface is.

Let us return now to the original question of deciding if someone can see. I have suggested that if someone has the power of sight, then it will bear fruit in their behaviour. This allows us to decide the issue: do they behave with *knowledge* of *what* surfaces are in the scene and *where* those surfaces are? As a test for vision this is quite good. It lays down several fundamentals. In order to know where surfaces are requires that an optical image be formed of the scene. It implies that the image can be processed to reveal information about the individual surfaces and to analyse their properties. It also makes the point that vision involves the creation and use of knowledge about the specific scene. If I sit motionless, producing no observable behaviour, I have not stopped seeing. But I am doing more than just having experiences. I am retrieving information from the optical images in my eyes and storing it as knowledge about the scene. I am preparing for potential alternative behaviours.

1.2 What Do We Need Vision For?

To see what to do, of course. And how to do it.

Vision allows me to decide what actions to make. I am thirsty, and I see on the table many things. One of these looks like a cup, and so I can decide to pick the cup up. Once I have decided on a particular course of action, such as picking a cup up, vision is then necessary to guide my hand as it moves. Vision is crucial for the successful outcome of many behaviours of this type.

Vision can also be useful for prompting behaviour. I look out the window and notice that the mulberry tree is beginning to show some dark berries. I am diverted from what I was doing (writing this paragraph) to go and try a mulberry. The behaviours of walking out, reaching for a fruit and picking it are all visually guided. The overall response to the tree was suggested to me visually: I wasn't actually hungry. Many things in our environment have this property of suggesting behaviours that we might not have deliberately planned. It is a good idea to keep an eye out for possibilities.

Let us start with some notional universal limb that we are going to be called upon to move around and touch things with. It is placed in a scene that has many things lying around. It is connected, somehow, to a vision system that must issue commands to control the actions of the limb. The vision system receives instructions from some outside agency, such as *pick up the pine cone*. It is equipped with enough knowledge about the thing to be able to understand what it is. This allows us the use of a shorthand description of the potential targets.

(i) Touching Something

We can issue a command to touch a ball which is in front of the limb. A visual system then has to provide information so that the limb can be moved successfully. The movement needs to know where the ball is, that is, in what direction from the limb. In order to deliver this information, the visual system has to do certain operations. It needs to identify the image of the object of the action, the ball. It then needs to measure its visual direction and this has to be related to the position of the limb. The rudiments of any functional visual system are the ability to identify and select out the important information in an optical image, and to characterize some elementary properties of the relevant part of the image.

The important information is defined by some unique property and all we need to do is devise some transform that is only sensitive to the presence or absence of that property. The location of the object part in the optical image is a clue to the visual direction of the object from the sensor. The fact that it is visible means that there are (usually) no intervening obstacles. In order to move a limb to it, we then just need to convert the visual direction to a series of action commands.

(ii) Grasping Something

We can now consider how to grasp something. Our universal limb has grown opposable fingers on its far end that need visual information for guidance. In order to grasp a ball they need to be placed either side of it at a place where they can get sufficient friction to clamp it. They then need to be closed to a specific grip force. Experiment with a ball yourself to find out a little of how the mechanics of the grip are constrained. The grasp is most successful when the fingers are placed opposite each other at the ends of a diameter. This means that the forces that they are applying to the ball are equal and opposite so that there is no net force on the ball that will make it move away.

The conditions where this criterion is met depend on the shape of the surface of the object. Just where to hold any arbitrary lump of matter depends on the shape of the lump. Vision is obviously a good potential source of information about the shape of an object.

(iii) Lifting Something

A further sophistication that we can consider is then to lift the object. In this case, we need to be able to grasp the thing as above, and then apply the appropriate force to oppose the force of gravity. This further constrains the nature of the grip which has to be placed roughly around and beneath the centre of mass of the object. Try picking up a few tools, such as a hammer, to see what the new constraints are.

In order to satisfy these new constraints, we must form some estimate of the inertial mass of the object and the location of its centre of mass. Neither of these properties are fully specified by the visual image on its own, although the visual image will contain evidence that is useful when, for example, we "know" the relative densities of the metal and wood in a hammer. Vision is a good source of evidence about the types of force that are needed to lift things up.

Equally important is information about the quality of the surface. Is it rough or smooth? Is it hard or soft? Are there sharp corners and creases that can be used to get a good grip? Once again, vision is a good source of information of this type.

(iv) Catching Something

The next degree of complexity is to consider how to catch something. This is rather akin to grasping and lifting something, except that the object is moving. We now need to have information about the velocity of the object in addition to its visual direction from us. The manner in which the image of our object changes as time passes will give visual evidence about its course in space and the speed with which it is approaching or receding.

(v) Locomotion

If a device is going to move itself towards an object, then there are a number of further complications. The direction in which to move to reach the object is not as well specified by location in the image plane, because movements may not be as free. A device which is restricted to moving along the ground can be steered left or right to varying degrees, but must otherwise follow the surface. Following the surface may not be a trivial exercise if it is rough or steeply inclined. The selection of a route to follow is an important component of locomotor behaviour.

Movement of the sensor, the camera or the eye, has consequences for the optical image. Everything in the image changes, in ways that depend on what is present in the scene. Following the image of the object over the image plane is a good way of judging how close it is getting and thus when to stop moving and start reaching out.

(vi) Planning

Many of the things in our world suggest courses of action that don't otherwise have to be designed into the system. If we are looking for somewhere to rest, we don't necessarily have to issue a set of commands to search for a chair. There are other possible resting places, and a visual system that could analyse the physical properties of the things in the scene would be capable of identifying the suitable surfaces.

Pursuing this idea further we can imagine a different type of device that was programmed with a wide battery of possible, fruitful behaviours, each contingent on the presence of certain triggers in the optical image of the scene. Just what it did would then depend on what was possible. Since it is likely that many courses of action could be possible, it would also need some way of arbitrating between different suggestions. The main visual requirements are that the useful properties of the things in the scene be made available. For example, a shiny inclined surface would be described as having less adhesion than a rough one and would then suggest climbing much less weakly. Conspicuous fruits would suggest eating; a stone might suggest throwing and so on.

(vii) Alerting

Another very different reason for having vision is as an early warning system. As well as providing the means for carrying out actions in the environment, vision lets us see what possibilities there are. It is easy to imagine a device that has a great dread of wolves and a great taste for lambs. It could be designed to examine the image alternatively for wolves and then for lambs. Depending on the outcome, the device could set into operation an escape program or a predation program or in the absence of both objects a random walk. But suppose the wolf was to assume a disguise, so that it no longer looked much like wolves are supposed to. The simple device would be foxed and at considerable risk.

A more successful design would form some crude evaluation of everything in sight and draw attention to any unusual or suspicious manifestations. Leaving aside how such an evaluation might be possible, this design would be more robust because it had a degree of responsiveness to the environment. A lump of matter rapidly approaching the device could be detected, analysed and avoided, without it first having to be identified as a wolf.

1.3 Can We Trust Vision?

An optical image, like a photograph, is a two-dimensional pattern of light, in which different places have different intensities and colours. The optical process collects light from the three-dimensional world to form this image. We can discover, for any particular point in the image, just where the light came from by tracing a straight line back through the lens and out into space until a surface is found. The light came from this point on this surface.

The intensity of light that is received from any particular point on a surface depends on both how dark or light the surface is and how brightly illuminated it is. One vision problem is that the nature of the surface is what interests us, but we cannot discover that without knowing how it is illuminated. We would receive the same amount of light from a dark surface brightly illuminated as from a bright surface dimly illuminated.

The light has no information about the distance it has travelled since that surface, so we cannot know directly how far away the surface is. It would be very useful to have this information available, and not just for the obvious reason of avoiding colliding with things. Hold your hand out in front of you at arm's length and note how much of the scene is obscured by it. Now move your hand towards you and watch how more and more is hidden. What is happening is that the image of the hand is growing in size, even though the hand is fixed in size. The image size of the hand does not tell us how big the hand is, unless we also know how far away the hand is. Of course, it also follows that we don't know how much of the scene is hidden from our view. A small, near object can obscure as much as a large, distant object.

These two examples of image brightness and size, and many others like them could be taken as proof that vision is therefore impossible. To do so is not entirely fair. It is certainly true that any given optical image could have been formed from an infinite number of scenes. In practice very few of these are plausible in the world that we inhabit. The serious question is therefore whether it is possible reliably to select the most plausible solution to the vision problem.

The world obeys physical laws. Things fall under gravity; everything has to accelerate under a force to change speed; solid matter cannot pass through solid matter, and so on. There are also some general trends in nature. Matter tends to be clumped into fair sized things rather than existing in diffuse dust clouds; lighting tends to be fairly uniform in a scene. These all lead to powerful rules for deciding what is a plausible interpretation of an image.

This means that vision can be trustworthy if it is based on sound knowledge about the way the world really is constructed. You will have realized that this is leading us back to the question of why you want vision. If you can state what you need to know about the scene, then it is probable that you have also stated, implicitly, the general knowledge that is required. The need to see is the need to choose a pattern of behaviour from a set of alternative responses to alternative possible things or events in the scene. If the choice is properly defined then the possible alternatives are also defined. This makes it just a question of whether optical images can provide the necessary information to make the choice.

1.4 How Can We Describe Vision?

Imagine being asked by someone who had been blind from birth what vision is. How would you answer? This is rather like trying to describe the sea to a Tibetan: there is no guarantee that any of the words that you might try to use will convey the correct, or indeed any meaning. There are two ways in which the problem can be approached. You might try to find analogies that could help. For example, vision has some of the characteristics of touch. Both are concerned with things in the environment, where they are and what they are like. Later in this book I shall use the term texture as if it describes the visual character of the surfaces of things. In ordinary use, it rather better describes the feel of a surface. Of course, touch is a slow process and to convey the great speed of vision, you could compare it with the sense of hearing. This might work, provided that your senses of touch and hearing are the same in their structure and effect as they are in the person you are talking to.

The second approach is to deliberately construct a set of words with meanings that are well understood or that can be well defined. We can obviously start with matter, bodies of matter and surfaces of bodies. These are our physical world (an alien that did not have these concepts would inhabit a universe so markedly different from ours that there would probably be little or no point trying to describe vision). We could also start with a description of light as radiant energy that interacts with matter at surfaces. We might then explain that because of the way light is reflected at surfaces, when some of it enters an eye it carries indirect information about the surfaces in the scene. This indirect information can be used to support our actions in the scene because . . . Here we hit a snag. How does the information within a light pattern get transferred into behaviour? What language are we going to use to describe how this happens?

Representation is the important concept here. The light image can be represented by a matrix of numbers, with each one standing in place of the light intensity at the same point in the image. Remember that we are doing this, not the brain: it has its own way of representing the light image. There are lots of things that we can do to numbers, and as we shall see in the chapters that follow, some are very useful in the context of vision, but representation is an even more powerful concept for describing how an image is processed by the visual system.

It is not easy, or appropriate, to describe actions that are contingent on vision by a matrix of numbers. How can you specify the act of picking up a cup of tea with just numbers? The problem is that numbers are really only useful for describing quantities: the intensity of light; the mass of the full tea cup; the distance and direction of the hand from the handle. Numbers are not useful for describing discrete concepts such as cup and handle. Of course, given a finite set of permissible concepts, it is possible to use a finite set of numbers as a code for the concepts. But the numbers will not be used in the same way. We can code cup by the number 7, and tea by the number 21. How will we describe a cup of tea? Not by $7 + 21 = 28$! Why not? Because 28 is also 2×14 and $3 + 25$ and $9 + 19$. The rules of algebra define certain equivalences that are not appropriate for manipulating these concepts. Numerals are a set of symbols that can be used to represent quantities. Algebraic signs are another set of symbols that we use to manipulate numerals. These symbols are just marks on paper that we require to conform to certain rules: to conform to a specified grammar. We can easily invent other sets of symbols and grammars.

There is however one property of the numerical representation of the image that we should aim to keep whenever possible. The intensity at any point in the image can be represented by a number; there are no regions that cannot be represented. Imagine that we take the symbol ⟨edge⟩. We can append values to this symbol to record edge length, orientation, curvature, sharpness and so on. However, we cannot apply the symbol throughout the image because there will be many places that will not be the locations of edges. If we add the symbols ⟨line⟩ and ⟨patch⟩ to the representation language, then it is complete in the sense that any place in any image can be represented.

We can have several different sets of symbols. The example set based on ⟨edge⟩, ⟨line⟩ and ⟨patch⟩ is sufficient to describe an image. We can devise another set using symbols such as ⟨crease⟩, ⟨occlusion⟩ and ⟨surface⟩ to describe the visible parts of the scene. There will be some high level representations, such as those which classify things in view according to a semantic category such as ⟨chair⟩, ⟨books⟩, or ⟨person⟩. At this level it is no longer possible to guarantee that everything visible in the image can be represented.

Return to the original question. How can we describe vision? Vision is the extraction and analysis of information from an optical image in preparation for, and execution of, behaviour within the scene. The behaviour part can be viewed as a set of commands to effector organs. These can be represented by an appropriate language or set of symbols plus a grammar. Our description of the process of vision can then be seen as a set of different languages each producing its own description of the visual information. Some are image oriented; some are scene oriented. Many of them will use representations of the image as their source of information rather than the image itself.

1.5 How Can We Understand Vision?

There are many ways in which something as richly complex as vision can be understood, and many levels at which it can be described. When we are looking, patterns of light enter our eyes, something happens to those patterns and we see. It is very tempting to imagine that we see things and that this means that the outcome of visual processing is a list of the things within eyesight: what they are and where they are. I can quite sensibly say, with natural language that I see a chair and where the chair is. This implies that within my head there is a "visual system", the output of which is a representation of the objects within the field of view and their spatial relationships.

How might we define the term object? We could take a person and place him in front of a table, on which we have placed several things: a pot plant, a spoon, a toy train and so on. We then ask the person how many objects he can see on the table. I expect there would be very broad agreement about which things constitute one object under these circumstances.

Suppose now that I invited the person to walk around the garden with me to see how many objects there were out there. This would be more difficult. Leaves on a tree might belong to the "tree object", unless they were lying on the ground. Is it the connectivity that defines this relationship? Clearly not because the tree is connected to the ground as are all the others: but each tree would surely count as an independent object. What is the difficulty?

I believe that the problem lies in the difference between the many artefacts that we surround ourselves with and natural things. Most artefacts are distinctly different from natural things. Most artefacts exist for relative specific functions, which means that we use them in specific ways. They are the objects of only a very few actions. They constrain our behaviour into a very small number of possibilities, unlike trees. A spade is visually equivalent to the action of digging; ⟨dig⟩ and ⟨spade⟩ are the same entity. A tree can be climbed, avoided, harvested, etc. A tree is not the object of one action, and has no visual equivalence with any one action. It is not an object until we have decided what we are going to do. If the output of vision is the selection, preparation or control of a behaviour pattern, then when that is directed towards an artefact, the artefact itself is virtually equivalent to the behaviour. There is no similar near equivalence between most natural things and the behaviour patterns that may be directed towards them.

We see things because it is necessary to do so, not just because they are there. Human perception is a skill and an art: as you read this page, your eyes are moving from word to word according to a set of rules that you have had to learn. Look at this part of the page, but experiment with the different ways you can do so. Observe the word MIRAGE closely, notice perhaps for the first time the exact shape of the letter G; compare the heights of the different horizontal strokes in the word; look at the wedges of light paper between and within the letters. The spelling of the word may even begin to seem a bit odd while you do this. Now look for the rivers of light than run right down through the text on this page; next, without moving your eyes off this sentence, look at the back of your hand. The page looks subtly different whilst you do this. It is this rich diversity of ways of seeing that make the understanding of human vision such a fascinating intellectual goal.

As a species we are very conscious of our vision, many of our ways of doing things are by sight and it is no surprise to learn that a lot of effort is being spent on attempts to mechanize some of the tasks we do with our eyes. Face recognition, inspection of machinery, reading, navigation are all many tasks that might be undertaken by machines with a sense of vision. There is always an intellectual challenge in machine vision: as soon as a light image is transferred into a set of numbers in a digital memory it is obvious how many different ways that it can be manipulated, examined and represented. But all of these are precise, and generally what the machine vision designer wants is something that is not easy to define in exact terms.

Suppose that you have digitized an image of the back of your hand and it is the task of the computer to discover whether you are wearing a wedding ring. What are you going to ask the computer to do, what to look for, and where? Precisely, of course, in each case. It's worth spending a few minutes thinking about this little puzzle and noting down some of the difficulties. Ask yourself why there are these difficulties. What solutions can you devise? For example, one immediate difficulty is knowing where to look, because the hand could be anywhere in the image. In order to know where to look you need some way of identifying a hand in the image.

The point of an exercise like this is that you will quickly be able to think of specific solutions to the problems as they arise. Eventually you would be able to devise a way of doing the task: this would be called an algorithm. Now suppose I produced a picture of one particular tree and a book of trees and asked you to identify the tree species by using a computer vision system as before. This is a more difficult puzzle but one which is, in principle, soluble. How much of your previous work on the hand would be useful in this new situation? Clearly we could continue in this way setting puzzles and finding solutions and slowly accumulate a lot of useful algorithms. There will be a number of processes within these algorithms that are very commonly used; there will also be some highly specific knowledge about specific bits of the world.

At some stage during this exercise it will cross your mind that there should be a way of organizing the way in which algorithms are stored so that the commonly used parts can be taken from one to another. A library of useful processes would be of great benefit. Similarly, some way of organizing how specific world information is stored would make sense. Designing the structure of these two stores is an interesting problem because it will force us to examine the logic of what we are trying to do. If it is simply an attempt to save some repeated labour, then any type of store will suffice. However the possibility of a rather general purpose vision system is also raised. Suppose we could create a library of effective, useful processes and a store of world knowledge and then devise a way of automatically selecting the relevant bits for any new task that might be set.

This is where our interest returns to human vision again, because when we look at something our system has decided what it wants to know by seeing and has put together a package of processes that will accomplish that goal. The library of processes within the human visual system exists so that a valid compilation can be created whenever a new demand is placed. This is a quite fundamental issue in understanding vision, but one that has not been tackled to any great extent.

The cross-fertilization between the study of human visual perception and the practice of machine vision should encourage rapid progress in each. Machine vision is a good reminder that there has to be a purpose for sight: you don't write a computer program unless you want to compute something and you won't understand it unless you know why it was written. Human vision is a good indication of what is possible, and perhaps what is not: we cannot see the invisible.

1.6 Coda

In this first chapter I have asked questions. The intention has been to set the reader thinking about vision, perhaps afresh. We are all so adept at seeing that it is difficult not to be burdened with heavy preconceptions about what we see and how we see.

Vision is *purposeful*: define the goals of vision, why you need to see, and it is clear what type of visual processes should be sought. Vision is also *opportunistic*: it uses light that is already in the environment. But that light source of information requires some processing: it does not deliver the information that is required in a form in which it can be used. If we examine how the information is delivered, then we shall at least be able to find what has to be done. Visual representations and symbols are mental constructs: one might as well look for them in the scene or the behaviour of people as look for them inside the head. However, for our purpose of understanding vision, they are invaluable because they reflect the way in which vision is descriptive of the scene. Vision is *cognitive*.

References

Suggested Further Reading

Gibson J.J. (1966) "The Senses Considered as Perceptual Systems". Houghton Mifflin, Boston.

Gibson J.J. (1979) "The Ecological Approach to Visual Perception". Houghton Mifflin, Boston.

Gregory R.L. (1970) "The Intelligent Eye". Weidenfeld & Nicholson, London.

von Helmholtz H.L.F. (1910) "Treatise on Physiological Optics" (trans. J.P. Southall, 1925). Dover, New York.

Kanisza G. (1979) "Organization in Vision". Praeger, New York.

Marr D.C. (1982) "Vision: A Computational Investigation into the Human Representation and Processing of Visual Information". W.H. Freeman and Co., San Francisco.

Vurpillot E. (1976) "The Visual World of the Child" (trans. W.E.C. Gillham). George Allen Unwin, London.

Wertheimer M. (1938) "Laws of Organization in Perceptual Forms". Harcourt, Brace and Co., London.

Exercises

1. Keep a visual diary for a short while: note down everything that you do that requires visual information. Now try to classify the activities that you have recorded. What rules are you using to do this?
2. Collect a number of naive opinions of what vision is about, and then examine them to find out what assumptions they are making. These naive opinions are part of a general mental model of visual perception.
3. Give some thought to what conscious experience might be doing in our visual perception.

2

Vision: Images to Action

In this chapter I will describe a classification of vision into different types of operation. I start with a simple type where the outcome of visual processing is just a movement in a given direction based on image properties. There are then two ways in which this may be made more sophisticated. The first is where certain structures in the scene are deduced from the image and used to control behaviour. The second is where the three-dimensional layout of the scene is derived from the image allowing much more complex behaviours to be planned and executed. Although I shall describe these in a sequence of progressive sophistication, it is important to realize that all three can co-exist in one "visual system". This sounds simple, but of course there are hidden complexities in keeping all three co-ordinated.

2.1 Image Summaries: Images ⇒ Action Descriptions

Let us start by building a device with very modest visual requirements, simply to approach brightness[1]. The output from vision for this task just needs to be a direction plus a sign, such as "course on a bearing *10° left* of straight ahead and move *forwards*". I shall call a sentence of this sort an *action description*. If the device is succeeding in approaching brightness, then the projected image of the bright region will be expanding in size, and so the image should be getting brighter overall. The mean brightness level should be rising, and the device can use the sign of the change in mean brightness value to control the sign of movement, forwards or backwards. It has also to steer itself left or right, and it can make a qualitative decision by comparing the left half of the image with the right half of the image: the brighter side is the one to steer towards. The device can compute the mean brightness on the left side, B_{L}, and the mean brightness on the right side of the image, B_{R}. The decision of our device can then be written down

---

[1] In this section I use the term brightness to refer to an unspecified product of the intensity of surface illumination and the intrinsic lightness of the surface. Brightness increases and decreases with either.

as three conditions:

If $B_R < B_L$ then   Left $\Rightarrow$ Direction

If $B_R = B_L$ then   Ahead $\Rightarrow$ Direction

If $B_R > B_L$ then   Right $\Rightarrow$ Direction

Now we can code the directions by signs: $-$ for left; $=$ for ahead; $+$ for right.

If $B_R < B_L$ then $-$ $\Rightarrow$ sign(Direction)

If $B_R = B_L$ then $=$ $\Rightarrow$ sign(Direction)

If $B_R > B_L$ then $+$ $\Rightarrow$ sign(Direction)

We can rewrite the conditions as:

If sign$(B_R - B_L) \Rightarrow -$ then $-$ $\Rightarrow$ sign(Direction)

If sign$(B_R - B_L) \Rightarrow =$ then $=$ $\Rightarrow$ sign(Direction)

If sign$(B_R - B_L) \Rightarrow +$ then $+$ $\Rightarrow$ sign(Direction)

or more simply:

$$\text{sign}(B_R - B_L) \qquad \Rightarrow \qquad \text{sign(Direction)}$$

The greater the difference between the two brightnesses, the more strongly our device should turn in that direction. So, the next step is to code the direction by a value, rather than just a sign, so that the degree of turning can be decided. We could write quite simply:

$$\frac{B_R + B_L}{B_R + B_L} \Rightarrow \text{Direction}$$

The part of this expression underneath simply ensures that the value ranges from -1 to $+1$. If we set *direction(Left)* to -1 and *direction(Right)* to $+1$, then we can rewrite the expression as:

$$\frac{B_R \times \text{direction(Right)} + B_L \times \text{direction(Left)}}{B_R + B_L} \Rightarrow \text{Direction}$$

The expression underneath in this fraction is just there to make sure that the *Direction* we actually get out have sensible values. So, for example, if B_L is equal to zero, then *Direction* will be equal to *direction(Right)*.

Finally, we can use finer grain directions and mean brightnesses on the left hand side of these equations, splitting the image up into far left, near left, far right and near right, for example. In practice, we can split the image up into the smallest possible areas which we shall identify by using the subscript i, in which case the mean brightness term becomes simply the brightness at a point, B_i, and the direction term becomes the direction of the point, which is *direction(i)*. The expression for the direction then involves the sum of all the products of the brightness and direction at each point, and this large sum can be written with a convenient piece of algebraic shorthand using the summation symbol $\sum$:

$$\frac{\sum B_i \, \text{direction}(i)}{\sum B_i} \Rightarrow \text{Direction}$$

The quantity that is being calculated in this expression is known as the *centroid,* and is a weighted mean position.

   This device illustrates how an image can be converted into a motor command, via an *image summary.* The mean value and the centroids are statistics that summarize certain properties of the image. This technique allows us to convert the image, which is in one mathematical format, into an action description, which is in another format that is more appropriate for the types of command that vision is called upon to deliver.

2.2 Image Algebra: Images $\Rightarrow$ Images

Consider another example. How could we build a simple device that would avoid places of high brightness? There is a complication to this specification. The device cannot retreat from the brightest place, because that would mean invariably moving backwards in a direction that it cannot ever see. Perhaps it could approach the darkest place, but what should our device do when a very bright place is next to a very dark one? If it approaches the dark one it is also approaching the bright one. It cannot just approach the darkest place; it needs to approach the direction where, on balance there is the least brightness.

   Suppose that each point in the image has been assigned a value representing its brightness. Let us imagine that a particular direction is being considered because the image in that direction has a region of darkness. Before going that way we want to check our wisdom by examining the directions nearest to our chosen direction to see if there are any particular high values of brightness amongst them. We might then look further afield, although the further afield we look, the less important any high brightness values would be. We want to give importance or weight to each brightness value in accordance with how near it is to our considered direction. We can do this by multiplying the value by a weighting function that gets less in value the farther it is from the direction that we are considering. The risk of our choice is then reflected by the sum of all these weighted values: a high "risk" sum is bad; a low one is good. Ideally, we want to find the direction that leads to the smallest sum and to do this we must obtain the "risk" sum at all points. We simply apply the same weighting function at each point in turn. Then all we need to find is the point in this transformation of the image that has the lowest value. To do this part we can just apply the mechanism of our first device, albeit not working on brightness values directly now. The process that I have just described for calculating a weighted sum is called *convolution,* and is a standard part of image algebra with many different applications, depending on the spatial form of the weighting function.

Another device illustrates a second powerful image-processing tool. Consider a device that is specified to avoid regions of unfamiliar brightness. Some brightness values in an image are common and some are rare. We can plot a histogram of the frequency of occurrence of each value that will show us which are the common values and which are the rare ones. Such a histogram provides a table for converting brightness values into a measure of scarcity or unfamiliarity. We can replace each image brightness value by a new number which gives the rarity of that particular brightness. It then remains to apply the mechanism of the second device to select the best direction, except that the image that it is dealing with has unfamiliarity values not brightness values. This transformation from image brightness to unfamiliarity illustrates another general technique in image algebra, known as the class of *unary operations*.

Suppose now that we are building a device that has more than one specification. It should approach shadows *and* avoid unfamiliarity. Each requirement produces its own preferred direction of movement, but which should the machine follow? In some way it has to set its priorities. It could adopt the strategy of pursuing darkness when this means following a course that has a "risk" value that is no more than, say, twice the smallest. There are all sorts of interesting possibilities, but they all depend on assigning a priority structure. This can be done dynamically: follow the darkness direction whilst mean luminance is dropping, but switch to unfamiliarity otherwise.

Image algebra is adequate for many situations where the attribute of interest can be made explicit by creating an appropriately transformed image. When the attribute of interest can be expressed as a function of brightness or brightness comparisons across the image, such as seeking darkness or avoiding novel lights, then this condition is met. In other words, the object must be conspicuous.

2.3 Images ⇒ Image Descriptions

We now wish to orient a device towards an object that will appear as a thin bright line in the image. It is possible to devise an image algebra transformation that will place high values where thin bright lines are found in the image, and usually place low values elsewhere. The thin bright line is then marked by the highest value in the transformed image. Suppose now that our device needs to look for the thin bright line that has the highest positive curvature in the image. We could produce a transformation that gave a higher positive value the more curved a line was. But what value should it place in the image where there are no lines? In principle, all the numbers could already be in use. We have found a fundamental limitation in image algebra. We need a way in which the image can be split into parts so that each part can be independently described. Each part might then be chosen so that it contains one line, and the description could then give the line curvature explicitly. From the set of such descriptions, that with the greatest curvature could be selected.

What do our simple devices do when faced with an image which contains two likely targets. If the transformed image has two places with high values, then the centroid will lie between them. This is a fundamental limitation on image summaries. We need a new way of analysing the image, and a new way of describing the information in an image. We need a way of creating a set of descriptions of small parts of the image, rather than one description of the entire image. This means that we need a way of splitting the image into regions and then we need a structure to hold all the independent descriptions.

Each part of the image is described in a descriptive sentence; all the various sentences are held in a set, the image description. The new type of description is a symbolic representation: we are going to replace the image or its transform by a set of statements about the image. For most images this set will be very large. An important feature of sets is that they can be any size and they can be increased or reduced in size at will. Another important aspect of sets is that the elements that belong to the set are all independent of each other and so are all equal in status. This means that the elements are not assigned to the set in a particular order. The left hand part of an image will not take precedence over the right hand part.

Let's start with an example. We could have the symbol

$$\mathbf{LINE}(\text{length}(L); \text{orientation } (\theta); \text{position } (x, y))$$

which is defined as meaning:

for a distance $\pm L/2$, in a direction θ, about the point (x, y) there is a line in the image which marks a consistent luminance difference.

The labels for position, orientation and length are parameters of the symbol. Each such symbol can be used to describe a part of an image by supplying real values for all the parameters. Thus we could have the descriptive sentence:

$$\mathbf{LINE}(\text{length}(33); \text{orientation}(49); \text{position }(5, 8))$$

The set of all such descriptive sentences, each corresponding to one image pattern, is then a symbolic representation of the image.

In practice symbols are most useful if they correspond to something significant in a scene. It is extremely likely that a symbol will be specified in terms of the general trends in luminance variation rather than actual luminance values. This would then allow the symbol to describe the same physical cause of a particular event in the image under a variety of different lighting arrangements. A symbol of this type might specify a number of critical points within a given distance of each other and their relative luminances, perhaps just as a list of the order, darkest to lightest.

The last point to make about the creation of a set of descriptive sentences to represent an image is perhaps, in practical terms, the most important. Images are always subject to small random fluctuations in luminance. This is noise and just as noise can interfere with an auditory signal, it presents some difficulties in vision. It means that symbols have to be specified with an appropriate level of tolerance. The symbol must allow for both missing data and for unexpected data.

2.4 Image Descriptions ⇒ Visual Descriptions

The creation of a set of descriptive sentences is really only a starting point. There are several ways in which sets and members of sets can be used. Let's start with the rather simplistic example of several non-overlapping wire-frame cubes.

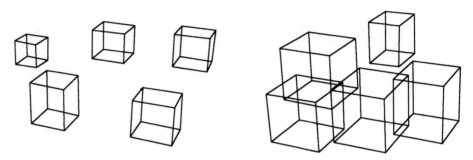

Figure 1.

Let's suppose that appropriate image processing leads to an initial description of the lines and line intersections in the image. It makes explicit the number of lines in the image, where they each are and how long they are. Suppose that we added a set of sentences that described which lines were connected to which. We could pick up any line at random, find out which lines it was connected to, pick those up, find out which they were connected to, and so on, stopping when there was no further line left connected to the ones we had picked up. We would have pulled out all the lines from one wire-frame cube but no others.

This is a rather simple and crude way of partitioning our description into separate descriptions of each cube. It only works because the images of each cube do not overlap each other as they do in the figure beside. We can achieve the same result for this image by ignoring places where lines cross each other as in X, and only collecting lines that meet at their ends, as in a V. The chances of this failing are slight, but do exist.

We could take another approach and define an area defined by three or more connected corners. In this case the areas that we will find are formed from four, six or eight connected corners. Look at those formed from just four connected corners; each corresponds to one face of the cube. How could we select such subsets? There are many ways that will work for our example: work one out for yourself; ask how it might fail.

The image of a cube will normally have nine connected lines forming three two-way intersections and three three-way intersections. If symbols for lines and intersections are available, then a description of the scene will include these particular ones in the set. Finding the cube is then a question of searching the set for likely candidates, bearing in mind that part of the cube may be hidden from view, occluded. Notice that the process knows quite a lot about the environment. This knowledge is resident in the definitions of the symbols and in the representation of the cube.

There is an important point here. We can specify the description of the appearance of a cube as a set of lines and their intersections. We can therefore create a symbol CUBE, which is defined, not in terms of image attributes, but as a specific combination of other symbols, such as edges and corners. There is no limit to the complexity of sentences that can be achieved in this way. With suitable symbols we could construct a sentence that described the image of someone's face.

When we are dealing with sentences of this complexity, it is sensible to have a general philosophy of how to operate. There are many different possible ways in which complex images can be described, how should we choose which? What are the desirable properties of these descriptions? A person's face is always changing shape as they breathe, speak, smile, blink and so on. The image of the face also depends on the angle from which it is viewed. We should devise a description of the image that is not radically altered by any of these changes. If we could accomplish this, then we would have a description that captured the essential, stable properties of the face. As such it would be very suitable for deciding whether or not the face belonged to someone we had met before. How could we decide this? We would have, stored away in some memory structure, a description of the face of the person we had previously met. The question of whether the present face was the same as this previous one could be answered by looking at the two descriptions. The more similar they were, the more likely it would be that they belonged to the same person.

Similarity of descriptions is a concept that will need some clarification. For the present it will suffice to note that two sets of sentences, each a description, are similar if a high proportion of their elements are common to both.

2.5 Visual Interpretation

There is a fundamental weakness in the types of operation described so far. Descriptive sentences can be derived from an image; they can be combined to make more powerful sentences and symbols, and in so doing describe the three-dimensional structure of many things in the image. The descriptions can be compared to stored sentences to allow recognition of some aspects of the image or the scene. However, there is no way in which the sentences can be used to constrain or modify each other. The sentences are essentially independent members of a large set.

We know from everyday experience that it is impossible for two things to be at the same place; that it is impossible for one solid body to move through another; that it is impossible for things to suddenly stop falling unless they hit something else; and so on. There are many other instances of this type of general constraint and they are all obviously useful items of information about the world. The weakness in the behaviour of visual sets is that they cannot implement constraints of these types.

We need to introduce a new type of representation, a model. The word model has two different usages which are both appropriate. In colloquial language a model is a device for illustrating the important features of something. A child's model car is smaller than the thing it stands for, but it has the same shape, many of the details, and behaves rather similarly. It is not just the next best thing, so far as its owner is concerned, it is actually very much better. It is more useful because of its scale; there is none of the oil and grease of the real thing; it doesn't damage as easily; and it does not need to be taxed and insured! The model exists for a purpose and encapsulates all that is necessary for that purpose, without any of the unnecessary aspects of what is being modelled. To a mathematician or a physicist, the term model also has a technical meaning. A model of a process is an alternative process that achieves the same end result. A model for the process of multiplication is to take logarithms, add and then antilogarithms. Models are used as ways of specifying certain regularities in nature, the laws of nature.

The type of model that I am interested in here has both meanings of the word. On the one hand it is a way of using the laws of nature, space and time, but on the other it brings them to play on representations of things in the scene.

The model is constructed by forms of reasoning. If A is moving in that direction and if B is in its path, then C, which is beyond B, will not be hit by A. The model is needed when the geometry of the scene is important, as when I have to plan a route to the door of my office, past and through a range of expensive and rather dangerous electrical equipment. I can try out the route on my current visual model of the office space to see how to do it and where the most caution is needed.

There are a number of spatial consequences of the optical projection from a three-dimensional world to a two-dimensional image. For example, the size of the two-dimensional image of a three-dimensional body depends on the distance of each from the lens of the camera or eye. Clearly the most useful symbols will be those that are not fixed at a particular size, and therefore allow size invariance. There are other effects of the optical projection. Think how the corner of a cube projects into an image. Assuming that each edge or crease on the box is distinctive, then the corner projects as two or three intersecting straight lines or nearly straight lines. The number of lines, two or three, and the angles between them in the image depend entirely on the way in which the box is rotated with respect to the observer. Now think about a body that is geometrically less regular, such as a face.

Let's start with a simple example. Imagine a potter making a clay bust of the head of someone who is sitting nearby. The real head is a solid which has a characteristic three-dimensional shape. Because of this shape it forms a characteristic two-dimensional image. The light strikes the cheek bones which give rise to two bright blobs in the image. Further down the cheeks and round towards the ears, the lighting is less direct and the brightness of the image falls off. There is a shadow on one side of the nose which also has its counterpart in the image. The hair is darker than the skin, and so on. We can describe each of these patterns in the image and in doing so are catching a great deal about the three-dimensional nature of the subject.

With this description, the potter knows what and who the subject is. From the two-dimensional shapes in the image it is quite possible to make a description of the surfaces on the head and their shapes. From this representation of surfaces, the potter can then construct a description of the solid volume of the head and its shape. This can all be done with sets of descriptive sentences.

Now we come to the difficulty. The potter also has a lump of clay to be shaped into a fair likeness to the subject's head. The shape of the clay can be represented by sentences, but the potter needs to know how to alter the shape of the clay. The two descriptions of the head and the clay can be compared to find out what is missing in the clay head. Perhaps it has no nose. To you and I, the solution is simple: pinch some of the clay out between but just below the eyes. We know what effect this will have, not just for the nascent nose but also for the other structures around about. We are using general knowledge about space and the behaviour of clay in space. We need a model.

How is a model constructed? A model is a representation of the dependencies between descriptive sentences, so we must take some or all of them and explore how they interact. Visualize the model as an old-fashioned iron bedstead. We start with a frame, made from cast iron and therefore rigidly fixed in shape and size. Next we have a set of springs, each of which is at rest and has its own characteristic size and shape. The springs correspond to a set of descriptive sentences, and there are latent relationships between them defining how the springs of the bedstead should be connected to each other. Now we have to fit the resting springs to the frame and this will require stretching some of the springs and deforming them a little. Very quickly the system will reach a new equilibrium where all of the springs are stretched a minimum amount. The general constraint imposed by the frame is distributed through the springs.

The model is made by examining the initial discrepancy between the frame which is the set of geometric rules and the resting springs which are the descriptive sentences, and then propagating this error through a network of relations so that each sentence is deformed in a predefined manner until the mismatch has disappeared. The bedspring analogy is too unstructured to be of much further use. If one of the springs is removed or changed, all the other springs feel the effect. In practice it would make a lot of sense to use a graded series of springs: some very strong, large springs and lots of smaller and more deformable springs. The model should be hierarchically structured so that minor changes do not propagate changes throughout the system to any significant extent.

Once constructed and maintained a model can be used for several different types of behaviour. Navigation is an obvious case where a model would be immensely useful. Each point in the optical image corresponds to a specific direction away from the observer out into space. If the observer is free to move in any direction, left or right, up or down, without hindrance then navigation towards some specific thing in the scene is easy. I can usually move my arm freely like this; but I cannot usually move myself so freely. Gravity forces me to follow certain surfaces. As a result, I need to use some geometry in order to reach my goal.

2.6 Recapitulation

In this chapter, I have described three different types of visual system. The three employ three different types of data, of processes and produce different outputs. They each embody certain distinctive understandings of the environment, its structure and how that relates to certain types of action. Together they become a powerful tool for any machine that must think and act in the three-dimensional world that we all appear to inhabit.

Visual algebra is used in the most basic visual system. We are going to discuss it in more detail in Chapters 4 and 5. The input data is an optical image, which we can specify by an array of luminance values. The processes available are all the simple algebraic operations like addition, multiplication, differentiation and convolution (more about these later), which take one or more images and treat or combine them in some fashion to produce a new image. Notice that each operation leaves as an end result a new, transformed image which is guaranteed to be in the right format for more operations. The operations that we shall examine in more detail later are always going to be selected for their ability to highlight or exaggerate useful aspects of the optical image that derive from important events in the scene.

In order to drive behaviour, there is a set of linking processes which convert the final image array of numbers into a movement response. This linking process could be very simple, like finding the position in the array that is its centre of gravity, or even just deciding whether the average value of numbers in the array is increasing or decreasing. This linking process takes an image as input and creates a single vector as output (a vector in this context has a direction and a strength). The vector specifies the direction and strength of a particular action.

Visual sets of descriptive sentences offer a more sophisticated system. We are going to discuss these in more detail in Chapters 5 and 6. We shall discuss the concept of symbolic representation, a set of statements or sentences about a data base, such as an image. The input data are created from an image. The processes available are what we will call description operations. Examples of these are comparing sentences for similarity, and combining sentences to create new sentences of higher complexity. The result of any description operation is a sentence that is guaranteed to be in the right format for any more description operations that might be desired.

In order to use visual descriptions we need a set of linking processes that can take an algebraic image and convert it into some primitive sentences. Curiously, these are going to be very similar in specification to the linking processes between visual algebra and possible actions. The difference is that instead of creating a single vector from each image, we shall now be creating many, each of which is expressible as a sentence, each corresponding to a part of the image. Many of these will be created by examining only small localized patches of the image, as distinct from the whole image. There must also be linking processes between the sets of sentences and potential behaviour. These linking processes are much simpler than those for visual algebra, because the information is in a more suitable format already.

Visual models are the basic structure of the most sophisticated visual system that I am going to discuss. When we talk about them in Chapter 7, we shall be using the language of geometry, particularly solid geometry. This is interesting: geometry is a model of the world, and so that is actually what we shall be talking about. Visual models are made and maintained by a particular set of operations on symbolic sentences. The most conspicuous feature of the operations in visual models concerns the knowledge that is implicit. This is knowledge of how matter and space interact. Two solid bodies cannot occupy the same place; the exact position of one body with respect to another in a scene is always the same irrespective of where the observer is and of the route chosen between them.

Why do we need to introduce the concept of a model, rather than just a symbolic description? The answer to this question is that the set of sentences that are the model are not independent entities. They are not even just mutually referential entities. They are a coherent set of statements about the scene. Each statement has consequences for the truth or accuracy of each other one. This means that we have to introduce the concept of a model as a means of co-ordinating the set of sentences.

2.7 Coda

The central argument in this chapter is based on three points which are central to an understanding of vision.

Vision is purposeful. In order to do something successfully you need a specification of what it is that is to be done. This then allows you to design a method for achieving your purpose. Vision is a part of the method that provides the specific information about the environment.

Vision is cognitive. Once the purpose is specified and the available information has been decided it is necessary to examine how to obtain and deliver the information in the required format. I have identified three general formats: images, sets of descriptive sentences and models. The categorization is based on the logical properties of the types of data representation and the types of operation that each implies.

Vision is opportunistic. We cannot really consider a visual system with infinite capacity for new operations and formats. When a new requirement arises it is necessary to examine available competences to see how they can be organized to achieve the new goal.

3

What are Images Like?

Imagine a room filled with countless photons all moving at the speed of light, but each one in its own direction. Their movements form a pattern which reflects the structure of the scene. As you enter, your eyes capture a very small proportion of these photons. The task of a visual system is to read the pattern in this tiny sample in order to discover the structure of the scene. The eye focuses the captured photons into a two-dimensional image in which the location of each photon corresponds to the direction that it came from.

Photons start from a source, such as the sun or an electric light bulb, and move through the scene in straight lines. When they meet matter they are either absorbed or reflected. The amount of light that is reflected at the surface of matter depends on how much light is arriving at the surface and at what angle, and how reflective the surface is. The light photons can continue bouncing around until eventually they are absorbed. The pattern of light that is focused into an image has a structure that depends on where the sources of light are, how matter is distributed through the scene, and how reflective the various surfaces are. However, each photon can only "tell" a visual system what direction it has been travelling in since its last reflection. How far it has travelled since then, where it originated from, and the rest of its past history is lost. In the image, there are photons from all directions, and all the information lies in variations in their density. The image has an intensity pattern.

To discover what patterns of intensity are common in images, we need to make some generalizations about the types of light sources, the range of physical bodies and their shapes and how their surfaces reflect light. The number of light sources will usually be small; they are nearly always high up; matter clumps into quasi-rigid bodies with large clear spaces between; surfaces are usually fairly matt, not highly glossy. In the sections that follow, I shall consider such general statements, seeking to understand what we are likely to find in ordinary images. There is a brief appendix at the end of this chapter which explains the basic terminology of photometry (the measurement of light).

3.1 Surface Shapes

The shapes of surfaces are important in determining the pattern of an image. In order to be able to reason about the images of things and of scenes, we must have a way of describing the shapes of surfaces. It is decidedly difficult to describe a three-dimensional shape: imagine picking up a rock and then trying to describe its exact shape. The problem is that there is so much of it. Its shape could be given by the spatial position of each point on its surface with respect to some arbitrary co-ordinate system. This would be quite adequate, or we could use the spatial relationships between all the points on its surface. There are infinitely many such points, and infinitely many relationships that would need to be described. The science of geometry has been very much concerned with finding ways of treating quantities of data of this enormous magnitude by treating the shape with a number of regular patterns of spatial relationship. So, for example, the term planar surface refers to a surface where all the points lie in one plane, their relationships are all constrained to only two dimensions and conform to a pattern that is easily defined for all of them. The principles of describing the shape of a line in two dimensions are the same as for a three-dimensional surface, but they are easier to understand and so I start with lines.

A *line* is a set of *points*, and we could encapsulate all the information about the shape of the line by an exhaustive set containing the spatial position co-ordinates of every point. Obviously all the points cannot have the same spatial position, and so all the co-ordinates have to be given. The line is also a set of connected points, which means that each point has a neighbour on each side. Neighbouring points are only infinitesimally separated, and so the distance between any two neighbouring points can be treated as being always the same. For the moment, we will only consider the neighbour on one side of each point. We could describe the position of each point as a displacement from its neighbour. Since the distance in this displacement is always the same, the only factor that we need to consider is the direction of one point from its neighbours. If we now consider that each point on a curve has two neighbours, one on each side, then we can see that the curve at each point has two potential orientations. In fact, with the exception of singularities such as sharp corners, these two orientations will always be equal and opposite. It might happen that every point along the line had the same direction from its neighbour, in which case the line would be straight. We would then have a pattern: the one direction can be used to simultaneously describe all the points. The direction of one point from the next on a line is known as the *orientation* of the tangent to the line. This orientation may itself change from point to point. If the change in orientation was the same everywhere on the line, as it would be along a circular arc, then this single parameter, the *line curvature*, can be used to describe the shape of the line.

In these two cases of a straight line and a circular arc, we have found single spatial relationships that are the same everywhere on the line, and can thus be used to represent the line. The two relationships that I have discussed, the line orientation and the line curvature, have analogues,

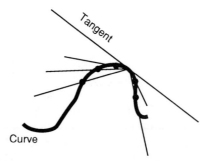

Figure 1.   Line orientation. A curve is shown, and a point on the curve is marked. Two lines are drawn from the point in opposite directions. These two lines connect with two adjacent points on the curve. As the neighbouring points are taken nearer to the original point, the two lines tend to become one. This line is known as the tangent, and its orientation is the angle that it makes with some external reference such as the horizontal.

surface orientation and surface curvature, although the extra dimension makes them more complicated. There is also an analogue of the corner singularity, a crease in a surface.

(i) Surface Orientation

All points except those at the ends of a line have two neighbours and at every point a line could have two orientations and curvatures. Except at singular points like a sharp corner on the line, the two orientations and the two curvatures will have the same value. For a point on a surface there is an infinity of neighbours, and so there could be an infinity of orientations and curvatures, and it is not the case that they will all have the same value. The tangent to a line just grazes it at one point, and except at singularities, there is only one tangent at any one point on a curve. For a surface there is only one plane that just grazes the surface at each point, except for singularities such as creases. This plane can be used analogously to the tangent to a two-dimensional curve.

Imagine taking a small part of a surface. We could stand a match on end at the centre of this surface patch so that it was pointing out from the surface. If the angle between the match and the surface was 90° in all directions, then the match would be aligned along the *surface normal*. Every point on a surface has such a normal. Of course the distance away from the match over which the angle remains 90° may only be infinitesimal. In the case of a planar surface it will be at 90° for a considerable distance, but for any curved surface it changes immediately away from the match. The suface normal is a way of defining the orientation of the surface in 3-space. Suppose that we take vertical as the standard direction from which surface orientation is expressed. Any surface normal will be aligned at some angle from the vertical and this angle is called the *slant* of the surface. If we then look down on to the surface from vertically above, then the surface normal will

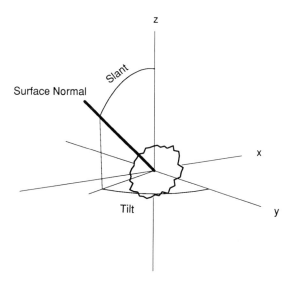

Figure 2. The slant and tilt of a surface. A small patch of surface is shown, and the surface normal is drawn pointing away from it. The angle that this makes with the vertical is called the slant of the surface. The direction of the normal, with respect to some arbitrary co-ordinate frame in the xy plane is called its tilt.

also be pointing in some direction round the clock, and this direction is called the *tilt* of the surface. These two parts to the orientation of a surface are quite independent so that for any given tilt, the surface can have the full range of slants and vice versa.

(ii) Surface Curvature

Imagine cutting through a surface. If we did this with a sphere, then the cut would reveal a circular outline; if we did this with a cube, then depending on how the cut was made, we would reveal an outline that was a polygon with three to six sides. If the cut was along the line of the surface normal, then the circle would always have the same radius as the sphere, and the polygon would be bound to be a rectangle with two of its sides of the same length as the edges of the cube. In these two cases, the cut would be in the plane of the surface normal at every point along its outline where it intersected the surface. This need not be the case, and would never be true for a pyramid, for example. If we concentrate on one point on a surface, then a cut along the surface normal at that point could lie in any direction around the clock and we could obtain many different lines, all running through the same point. At this point of the surface normal, each line has a particular curvature in its own plane. We could cut through the surface in any direction through the surface normal and there is a value of curvature for each direction. For example, at a point on the surface of a sphere, the curvature in all directions is the same; at a point on the surface of a cylinder the curvature varies, being zero when the direction of the plane is along the

Figure 3. Cross-section curvatures of a cylinder. Several different cross-sections through a cylinder are shown. Two of these, drawn along the axis of the cylinder and at right angles to its axis, are the principal curvatures.

axis of the cylinder, and reaching a maximum at right angles to the axis. The curvatures are known as normal curvatures.

We can draw a graph of normal curvature as a function of the direction around the clock. For all such functions there will be one maximum, the

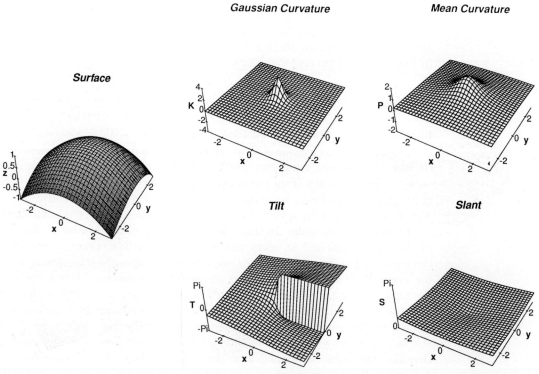

Figure 4. Positive Gaussian curvature. A surface with positive Gaussian curvature is shown on the left. Also shown are plots of its Gaussian and mean curvatures. Beneath these are shown plots of the slant and tilt angles across the surface.

greatest value, and one minimum, the least value, and it is a standard theorem that the directions of these two are always at right angles to each other. The product of these two *principal curvatures*, as they are known, is called the *Gaussian curvature* of the surface. The Gaussian curvature at a point on a surface is a measure of the surface curvature in two dimensions: that direction with the largest curvature and that direction with the least (or most negative). Since it is the product of these two principal curvatures, if either is zero, than the Gaussian curvature is also zero. This happens on a straight cylinder. If both have the same sign, then the Gaussian curvature is positive, as on a sphere. A saddle-point has a negative Gaussian curvature because the two principal curvatures have different signs.

Another measure of the curvature of a surface is the *mean curvature*. This is defined as one half of the sum of the two principal curvatures. The simplest surface is planar: an absolutely flat surface with zero Gaussian curvature and zero mean curvature. We can have surfaces that have a zero Gaussian curvature, but a non-zero mean curvature, such as a cylinder. Thirdly there are surfaces that have non-zero Gaussian curvature, such as the surface of a sphere. if they have non-zero Gaussian curvature then they will normally have non-zero mean curvature. The only exception is if the surface has negative Gaussian curvature, with the two principal curvatures equal and opposite.

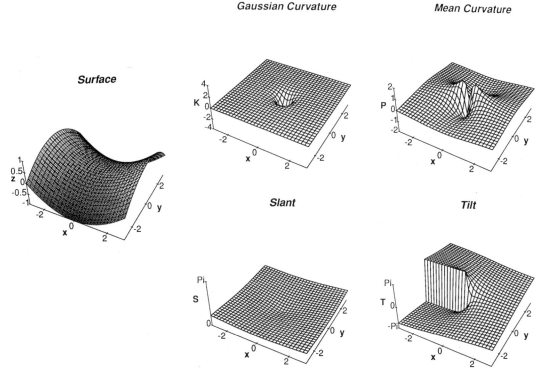

Figure 5. Negative Gaussian curvature. A surface with negative Gaussian curvature is shown on the left. Also shown are plots of its Gaussian and mean curvatures. Beneath these are shown plots of the slant and tilt angles across the surface.

(iii) Surface Creases

Surfaces may also have creases which are sudden changes in orientation. A truly sharp crease is discontinuous in surface orientation at the crease and hence one of its principal curvatures is infinite (positive or negative). This means that both its Gaussian curvature and its mean curvature are both infinite or indeterminate.

(iv) Surface Texture

Most natural surfaces are not so easily dealt with. The surface that is a lawn looks planar from afar, but is very different when seen close to. The bark of a tree is quite cylindrical from afar, but quite corrugated on close inspection. Natural surfaces tend to have *texture*. Look at a tree. How could you describe its shape? The image of a tree will not contain many of the types of pattern that I have described so far. There are not many planar or smoothly curved surfaces. The trunk of the tree is roughly cylindrical but is misshapen and has cracks in it. For the moment we are interested in the type of image that a tree might form and so it is quite important to be precise. Nature tends to build very richly carved and textured surfaces. Let us consider how two types of texture are created, in order to understand how to describe the pattern.

In natural textures there is a combination of fixed and random processes involved. Take the texture of a layer of fallen leaves beneath a tree: the pattern can be described in terms of a typical leaf and its variations (in colour, size, curling and shape), plus the layout of the leaves in terms of their positions and orientations. These positions are determined by a fixed process, the leaf position on the tree, and a random process of air currents during its fall. The fixed process ensures that the carpet of fallen leaves has a certain extent and density, and the random process distributes the individual leaves within this overall pattern. There are many other instances of the same arrangement in nature, such as the pebbles on a beach, the trees in a forest, or the spots on a leopard. Notice that in many cases the elements of the pattern are forced to take up a quasi-regular spatial arrangement. Gravity ensures that the pebbles on a beach are not piled high in a narrow tower, but are spread out flat. This means that the pebbles tend to pack together in a way which is determined by their size, and is far from random but which is not exactly regular either. This type of texture can be described by giving the form of a typical or general element, the range of variations in the form of the element as it is repeated over the surface, and the statistics of the distribution of the repetitions of the element over the surface. Of course for a texture like the scribbling of a child on a sheet of paper, such a description is a little contrived.

Sometimes a texture is created by a pattern of events that repeat themselves many times. The bark of some trees is formed by this type of pattern. The young sapling has a thin trunk with a cork bark stretched all around. When the trunk swells, the bark also grows, but not enough and so has to split once or twice and a new section of bark grows in the notch.

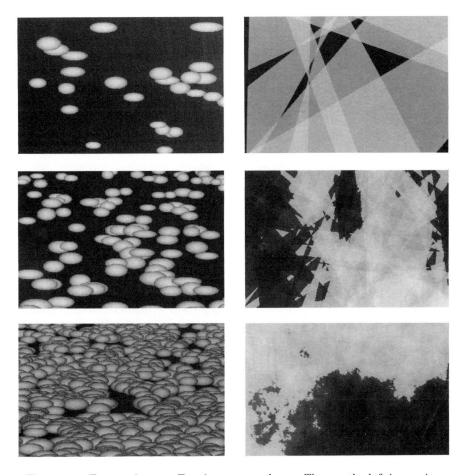

Figure 6. Texture images. Two images are shown. That on the left is a series of synthetic pictures of pebbles on a beach. That on the right is a synthetic fractal texture image shown at various stages in its creation. It is made by repeatedly cutting the image along random lines.

This new section grows along with the tree as does the old bark until another split occurs. Eventually the bark is patterned by cracks of varying ages and depths; sometimes there are cracks in cracks and so on. It is a characteristic of this type of pattern that it is self-similar. This means that at whatever magnification we choose to examine it, the texture statistics that we will see are always nearly the same. This type of pattern is called a *fractal*. Some fractals are very jagged, like the pattern of the bark of a Scots pine tree, and others are relatively smooth, like the bark of a Douglas fir tree. The degree of roughness is expressed by the *fractal dimension* of a pattern.

(v) Occluding Contour

There is one other important aspect of the shape of surfaces from the point of view of vision. When I look at a sphere it has an edge beyond which I see other things. This edge is called the *occluding contour*. It does not really exist except with respect to a particular line of sight: you could not pick the sphere up and examine it for its occluding contour. The occluding contour of a body is what we would loosely call its outline or silhouette. It is where the *line of sight* just grazes the body before passing onwards. Technically the occluding contour is the locus of all points on the surface where the angle between the line of sight and the surface normal is a right angle.

Start at the near point on the surface of a sphere and move around the surface. At the near point, the surface normal and line of sight coincide and the angle between them is zero. Moving around, the angle between slowly opens out until at the occluding contour the angle is 90°. Moving further, the angle is greater than 90°, and these parts of the surface are invisible or in the shade. Now start at the apex of a cube which is nearest and move over one of the planar facets. All the surface normals have the same direction and the angle between these and the line of sight only changes very gradually. When you reach a crease the angle between the surface normal and the line of sight changes suddenly because of the sudden change in the direction of the surface normal. It may change to an angle greater than 90°, in which case the crease is also an occluding contour.

Lastly if the surface patch is planar then an occluding contour cannot cross it, although the patch can be co-planar with a line of sight in which case the occluding contour runs over the near boundary of the planar region of the surface.

3.2 Light Sources

When someone turns the lights off, we cannot see. Clearly vision depends on light. Abu'Ali Al hasen ibn Al Haytham was a Persian physicist who lived around the year AD 1000. He was probably the first person to realize that the light is out there already, and part of the world that we live in, rather than being something that our eyes emit.

Light source is a term usually reserved for bodies, such as light bulbs, that emit light independently of any illumination they may receive. When there is light in the environment, most surfaces give off light by reflection, and we can usefully extend the term to include all the sources of illumination, both by emission and reflection.

The illuminance of a surface is the measure of how much light is landing on a surface. There are two laws of physics that can be used to calculate the illuminance of a surface from a point source of light.

(i) The Inverse Square Law

The further away from a surface a light source is, the less light it casts on the surface. The reason for this is that the light moves away from the source equally in all directions. This means that a fixed amount of light is filling

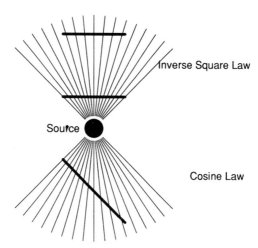

Figure 7. The laws of illumination. A point source is shown at the centre of the figure. Light leaves it in all directions with equal density. Two surfaces are shown intercepting the light. Notice how the density of the light reaching them depends on their distance from the source and their angle to it.

larger and larger spheres of space and so becomes increasingly less dense. This is expressed by the inverse square law, which states that

The illuminance, i, of a surface is inversely proportion to the square of the distance, d, between the surface and a point source of light

$$i \propto 1/d^2$$

(ii) The Cosine Law

The more a surface is facing the direction that the light is coming from, the greater is its illuminance. Imagine a narrow beam of light illuminating a surface. As the surface is tilted away, the light illuminates a larger area of the surface, and is therefore spread more thinly. This is expressed by the cosine law

The illuminance, i, of a surface is proportional to the cosine of the angle, θ, of light incidence

$$i \propto \cos \theta$$

These two laws are the two principle determinants of the illuminance of a surface. They can be combined to give an expression relating the illuminance, i, to the intensity of the light source, I, its distance, d, and its angle of incidence, θ.

$$i \propto \frac{I \cos \theta}{d^2}$$

(iii) Large Sources

An important factor in determining the effect of a light source is its surface area. The light from a point source gives illumination which falls off very rapidly with distance; a surface acts as a large number of point sources and illumination is much less affected by distance. The illumination provided by a point source reaches things at a specific angle, it is locally directional; the illumination provided by a surface is much more diffuse.

For example, consider a disc source of light, with a radius r. We can start with one arbitrary point on the disc at a place (r', θ) in polar coordinates about the disc centre. The illuminance from this place on the disc, $i(r', \theta)$, that is measured at a point with a distance d from the centre of the disc is given by the inverse square law:

$$i(r', \theta) \propto \frac{1}{d^2 + r'^2}$$

We can get the total illuminance from the whole disc by integrating the illuminance measured from all such points. This is done in two stages. First we integrate around an infinitesimally thin annulus through this point, using the dummy variable s to represent distance around the circle. We have

$$i(r') \propto \int_0^{2\pi r'} \left(\frac{1}{d^2 + r'^2} \right) ds \propto \left(\frac{2\pi r'}{d^2 + r'^2} \right)$$

Then we integrate all such annuli for $r' = 0$ to $r' = r$ and we have

$$i \propto \int_0^r \left(\frac{2\pi r'}{d^2 + r'^2} \right) dr \propto 2\pi \ln\left(1 + \frac{d^2}{r^2} \right)$$

Note that when r is very large, then illuminance is a very weak function of distance.

(iv) Real Sources

There are three qualitatively different types of lighting which are illustrated by full sunshine, a cloudy sky, and a single electric light bulb. On a cloudless day, some of the illumination is primary illumination direct from the sun, and deep shadows are cast. The sun is so far away that the differences in distance of different surfaces from it are a very small proportion of the total distance. Because of this, inverse square law has a negligible effect on illuminance variations within the scene. The cosine law applies and the illuminances of all surfaces depend on their angle with respect to the sun. There is also diffuse illumination caused by light reflected off surfaces and from the sky. The atmosphere scatters some sunlight, particularly short wavelengths, both because of interaction with the gas molecules themselves in the far reaches of the atmosphere (which is why the sky looks blue and bright, even away from the sun) and also because of dust within the lower atmosphere (which is one reason why sunsets are orange-red). The overall effect on the scene is a mix therefore of strongly directional illumination from the sun and diffuse secondary illumination.

On a cloudy day, the illumination is lower because the clouds reflect light back towards the sun and only transmit some. Cumulo-nimbus clouds (the cause of electrical storms) can reduce the illuminance by a factor of 10^3. Clouds also change the illumination type to predominantly diffuse illumination because of internal reflection and refraction of light in the clouds. As a result shadows are much less deep on cloudy days and the illuminance of a surface does not markedly depend on its orientation. Fog and mist are only variants on cloud, and they affect the illumination level in very much the same manner. Within fog, the illumination is almost exclusively diffuse, but the complication is that reflection and refraction within the droplets of water make each a secondary source, and light only travels a very short distance, on average, before being diverted. As a result the light entering the eye has only travelled from near surfaces, and we cannot see very far in fog.

A single electric light bulb provides locally directional primary illumination plus some secondary diffuse illumination. In considering its effects it is necessary to apply both the inverse square law and the cosine law. The range of indoor illuminances is lower than that provided by the sun, usually by a factor of between 10 and 100. Lighting indoors is normally placed near the ceiling, so that the ceiling acts as a secondary and diffuse source.

Within any one scene there will be a range of different illumination, depending on the various surface orientations and distances from the light sources. If it is assumed that the layout of bodies in a scene is irregular, then their orientations are in effect randomly scattered with respect to the various directional, primary sources of light. This means in converse, that the positions of the sources are not particularly important in determining the distribution of illuminances even though they will determine the illuminance of individual surfaces. Diffuse illumination can be treated as providing fairly general, uniform illuminance of all the surfaces in a scene and is therefore not an important factor in illuminance variations across the scene. Illuminance variations arise because of remote point sources like the sun and near point sources like electric light bulbs.

3.3 Illumination Variations over Surfaces

The next step is to examine how the physical laws of illumination determine the manner in which illuminance varies over the different shapes of surfaces. The purpose here is to gain an impression of the range of visual stimuli that are to be encountered in the images of ordinary scenes.

(i) Planar Surface

Under remote illumination neither the angle of incidence of the light nor its path length vary appreciably across a planar surface and so the illumination of the surface is uniform. For a near source of light the

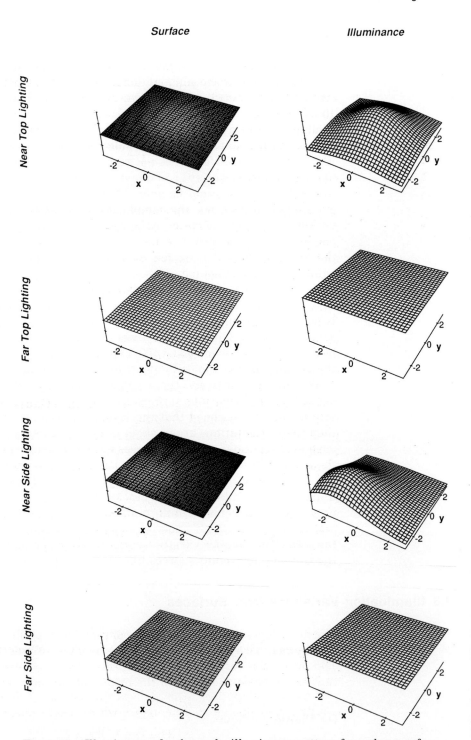

Figure 8. Illuminance of a plane: the illuminance pattern for a plane surface illuminated from a point source of light is shown. On the left, the surface is shown illuminated; on the right a graph of illuminance across the surface is shown.

illuminance of the surface will vary because the two factors, angle of incidence and length of light path, both change across the surface. As we move across the surface away from the point nearest to the source, both the angle of incidence and the length of the light path from the source increase. The cosine law and the inverse square law both result in a reduced illumination as the distance away from the source increases. The change in illuminance of the surface is not linear with radial distance from the source, but it is continuous and gradual.

(ii) Curved Surfaces

The surface of a sphere is a simple form of smoothly curved surface with a positive Gaussian curvature. Near and remote sources of light have very similar consequences for a sphere. Light from a remote source is parallel and will illuminate a complete hemisphere. In the case of a near source rather less than a complete hemisphere is illuminated (think how much of the earth is illuminated by a lighthouse).

In each case the part of the sphere nearest to the source also happens to have the smallest angle of incidence with respect to the source and consequently will have the highest illuminance. The illuminance of the surface will be reduced away from this point, although more so in the case of the near source because of the distance inverse square law effect.

A saddle surface has negative Gaussian curvature. Its illuminance is not very different to that for a surface with positive Gaussian curvature. If the light is directly overhead, then the angle of incidence of light at the saddle point is zero, and illuminance is maximum. If we take a circle around the saddle point, and a little distance out from it, then the angle of tilt with respect to the direction of the light source varies around the clock, ranging either side of zero, but the angle of slant need not change. Since the angle of incidence of light depends on the slant in this case, the illuminance will be maximum at the saddle point, and will fall off in all directions around.

In general, smoothly curved surfaces give rise to smoothly varying illuminance where the variations are determined by the slant of the surface and its distance from the source.

(iii) Creases

A crease in a surface is a discontinuity (an abrupt change) in surface orientation. This means that there is a similarly abrupt change in surface slant with respect to the direction of the source of light. There is therefore an abrupt change in the surface illumination at the crease.

If the two slants on either side of the crease are I_1 and I_2, then there results a step change in illuminance whose magnitude, dI, is given by:

$$dI = \cos I_1 - \cos I_2$$

Since

$$\cos I = \cos(-I)$$

then

$$dI = 0 \quad \text{if and only if } I_1 = -I_2$$

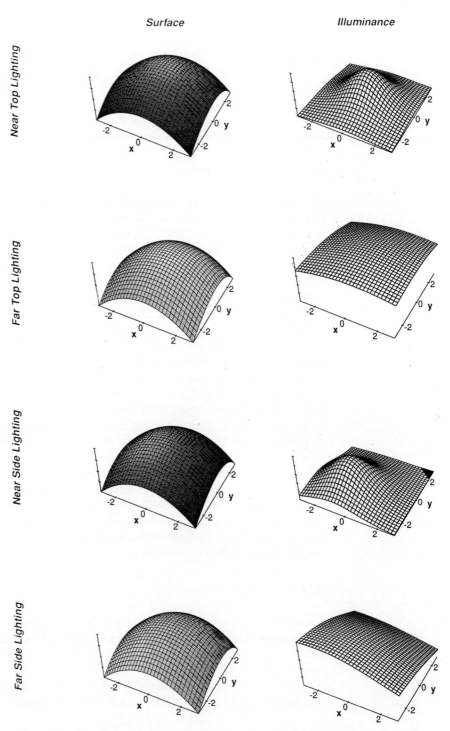

Figure 9. The illuminance pattern for a surgace with positive Gaussian curvature illuminated from a point source of light. The surface is shown illuminated on the left; a graph of illuminance across the surface is shown on the right.

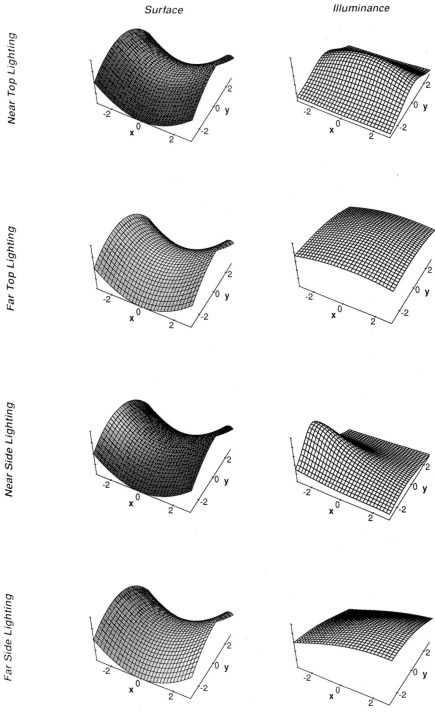

Figure 10. The illuminance pattern for a surface with negative Gaussian curvature illuminated from a point source of light. The surface is shown illuminated on the left; a graph of illuminance across the surface is shown on the right.

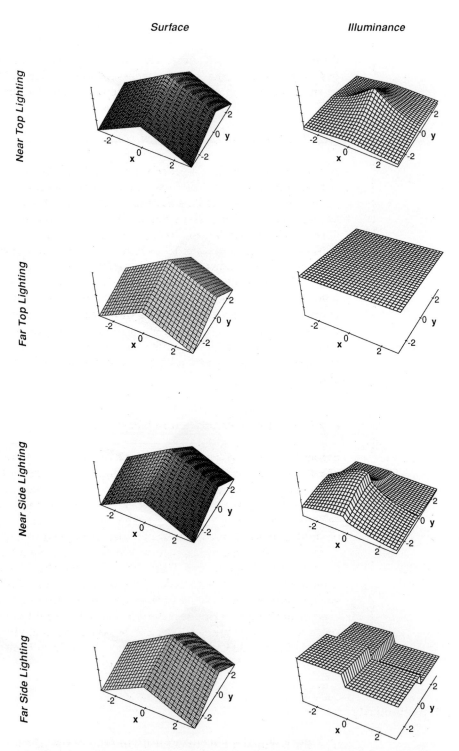

Figure 11. The illuminance pattern for a crease illuminated from a point source of light. The surface is shown illuminated on the left. On the right a graph of illuminance across the surface is shown.

Notice that the difference is determined by both the change in surface orientation, which is independent of where the light source is, and also the direction of the light source. The crease is a very localized feature, and so even for a near source it is not necessary to consider, at the crease, changes in the distance of the source or in the direction of illumination.

(iv) Textured Surfaces

A textured surface has a lot of creases, folds, bumps and so on. The result is that the surface will be a mosaic of parts that are fully illuminated and parts that are shaded. This mosaic is closely related to the structure of the surface, so that if a surface has a lot of sharp creases then there will be a corresponding number of sharp illuminance transitions.

When a texture pattern is made up of a collection of randomly scattered elements, like pebbles on a beach or leaves under a tree, the illuminance conditions for each will be broadly similar, although at different absolute levels depending on where they are and how they are oriented with respect to the light source. These factors of location and orientation with respect to the light source obey the laws of illumination, and so the illuminance of such a textured surface is thus a compound of a local regular pattern due to the surface texture plus a longer range variation due to the overall surface shape.

(v) Occluding Contours and Shadows

Smooth surface patches and creases are aspects of surfaces that do not change as the body is moved in three-dimensional space. There is one aspect of the surface of a body which does change with free motion in 3-space. This is its *occluding contour* with respect to a given viewpoint. Although the term viewpoint implies a light path between the surface and the eye, a line of sight, the occluding contour can also be applied to a line of illumination.

In a two-dimensional image of the scene, the occluding contour of one surface with respect to a light source marks the boundary between the illumination of the two surfaces. The two surfaces are likely to have different surface slants with respect to the direction of illumination, and also in the case of near light sources, different distances from the source. As a result there is an illuminance difference between the occluding surface and the occluded surface. The occluded surface is likely to have a shadow.

3.4 Reflectivity

The third major factor in determining the image of a scene is the extent to which and manner in which the various surfaces reflect their illumination. The amount of light that the surface reflects, its luminance L, depends on the surface illuminance, i, and also on its reflectance, R:

$$L = iR = \frac{IR \cos \theta}{d^2}$$

There are two basic parameters that describe the reflectivity of a surface. Its reflectance is a measure of the total proportion of light that is reflected, and its specularity is measure of how widely diffused the light is on reflection.

(i) Reflectance

The reflectance of a surface can vary from 0.0, for an absolutely black surface that reflects no light, to 1.0, for a brilliant white surface that reflects all light. Most surfaces are somewhere in between these two extremes. The proportion of light that is reflected also varies with the wavelength of the light. A red surface will usually be found to reflect more red light than blue light.

Natural surfaces are either geological or biological. Most biological surfaces are designed with the joint need to absorb some heat and light energy and also to protect from excessive amounts of these energies. As a result, plant material such as leaves and flowers reflect some but not all light. Animal skins are usually designed to be camouflaged to some degree against naturally occurring foliage and thus have similar general reflectivity to plant and geological material.

It is likely that different surfaces in a scene will have different reflectances, unless they are different surfaces on the same thing, like leaves on a tree. These will usually cause the surfaces to have different luminances since the chances of an equal but opposite difference in illumination are obviously low. It is also the case that reflectance can vary over one surface, like the stripes on a zebra. Such changes in reflectance can be sudden and large or they can be quite gradual like the pattern in the petals of some flowers.

Reflectance changes often take similar patterns to those that texture can take, and usually for similar reasons. The grain in a piece of wood is determined by growth processes. Texture, such as the bark of a tree, often has associated reflectance changes. These reflectance patterns give rise to similar image patterns to those of texture. In practice it is convenient to treat both types of pattern as visual texture, especially where the detailed three-dimensional structure is not important. Texture may itself vary across a surface and between different surfaces.

(ii) Specularity

Most surfaces are both diffuse and specular reflectors, and so most surfaces show a directional component of reflection which is determined by the direction of primary illumination. We see a glossy highlight under these circumstances.

An environment filled with only specularly reflecting surfaces would present enormous problems for vision. Imagine what you would see in a room made from and furnished with bodies made entirely from mirrors. This is roughly the case for hearing: most surfaces in the environment are smooth at the scale of the wavelength of sound and so reflect the sound specularly. It is possible to navigate with sound: bats use echo-location and some blind people have a form of spatial perception. But in these cases the observer is also the source, a rather special case.

Specular reflection is directional with most light reflected along a path whose angle to the surface normal is equal and opposite to the angle of incidence. An observer sited along that path will see a highlight in surface luminance at the point of reflection. As the observer moves, so does the point on the surface at which the two angles of incidence and reflection are equal, and the position of the highlight thus moves on the surface. Highlights will be most likely and stable (move least as the observer moves) on patches of surfaces with very high curvature such as slightly smooth creases. With the wider range of surface orientations on a small area of surface at these places, there is a greater probability of meeting the requirement for observing a highlight.

3.5 Images of Surfaces

The intensity of light in the image of a surface depends on the luminance of the surface and how it is being imaged. The surface behaves like a light source when it reflects light. If it has a low specularity then the light is reflected equally in all directions and so it is not usually very important what direction it is being viewed from. Since the surface is unlikely to be a point, then it is like a large source, and the effect of viewing distance is also not very great.

As the light passes through the optics of the viewing system, some of it is absorbed because no material perfectly transmits light. This means that the intensities of the light arriving from the different surfaces in the image will be lower than the luminance of those surfaces, but by a constant factor.

The lens system focuses the light into the image, although not perfectly. The image will always contain some degree of defocus, and for several different reasons. First, the lens can only focus the images of surfaces at one distance from itself. Those surfaces at other distances will have unfocused images. Second, the lens system will always have a few imperfections, such as spherical abberations, so that different parts of the image will be in slightly different focus planes. Third, the lens system is also limited by the process of diffraction, which means that the image of a point or a sharp edge will always be slightly blurred, even if the lens has no spherical abberation. The degree of blurring by diffraction depends on the diameter of the entrance aperture of the lens system, being greater the smaller this is.

3.6 Changing Images

Images change for a variety of reasons. The commonest causes are changes in illumination, movement of the observer and the motion of bodies in the scene. Simple changes in illumination do not change the structure of the scene and so they do not change the image structure except by altering the disposition of shadows. Changes in illumination are also usually of no visual significance.

Movement of the observer can have a number of different consequences, but in each case the whole image is changed. With the exception of the very fast saccadic eye movements, all movements of the observer can be treated as smooth and continuous. Therefore they usually result in smooth continuous changes of the image. The simple case is when the structure of the scene does not change, and all the changes in the image are due to changes in the position and viewing direction of the eye or camera.

The third common cause of image change is the independent movement of things in the scene. These movements are generally highly constrained by the laws of physics. Things can move, deform or grow; they cannot suddenly materialize from nowhere. If they appear in an image, then they are likely to have moved into view from behind something else. Things in the world cannot experience infinite acceleration, and so they move in predictable time and space paths, constrained by their inertial mass and the impelling forces involved. Image changes due to the movement of things in the scene are thus generally continuous and smooth.

(i) Movement of Self

Simple changes in viewing direction cause the image to slip across the retina without any change in its structure. The image moves through an angle that is equal and opposite to the angle of the rotation. Such a simple change in viewing direction can only occur when the optical device is rotated about a point at the centre of its lens although this rotation may be side to side, up and down, or a twist about the optical axis. A rotation about any other point will cause changes in the structure and layout of the image as we shall see. In fact, it is also strictly necessary that the image be formed on a spherical surface whose centre is also at the centre of rotation. In short, the frequency of occurence of simple changes in viewing direction is vanishingly low.

It is useful to be able to treat any movement of the observer as a displacement plus a simple change in viewing direction. The change in viewing direction can be considered as an image wide transformation, with the whole image moving intact, as I have just described, but the displacement has to be treated point by point in the image.

Let us start with one point, marked in Fig. 12 by an A. The observer is at O, looking in the direction of the double-headed arrow, so that the angular bearing of A is θ. Note that I am making a two-dimensional analysis for simplicity: strictly θ should be a pair of angles. Now let the observer move to O$'$, but remaining looking in the same direction. To achieve this the observer moves through a distance of d at angle α. This results in A having a new angular bearing of θ'.

Some straightforward trigonometry leads to the relationship that:

$$\frac{r}{\cos(\theta' + \alpha)} = \frac{d}{\sin(\theta' - \theta)}$$

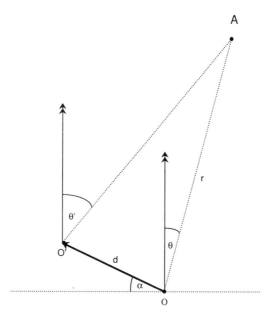

Figure 12. The effects of self-motion. As the observer moves from O to O′, the angular bearing of A changes from θ to θ'.

where r is the distance that O was from A. It can be seen that the value of θ' which is the new place of A in the image depends on the movement (d, α) and also on r, its range. This means that each point in an image moves through an angle that is potentially unique since its own values of r and θ are likely to be unique. Points in an image can change their order, passing behind or in front of each other.

If we take α to be at right angles to the line of sight, like sitting looking out of the window of a train, then the rate of change in visual angle for any point in the image is inversely proportional to the range r of the corresponding point in the scene. It also depends on the visual angle θ and the rate of observer motion d. If we could transform an image under these circumstances so that the values were the rate of movement of the points at each place in the image, this new image could be translated into a map of the range r of each point in the scene, provided that d was known. If d is not known then it is still possible to obtain a range map by noting how the change in visual angle continues to proceed. This, of course, has led us to a situation where d, the self-motion of the observer, can be measured from the image. The significance of this can hardly be underestimated. Similar arguments apply where α, the direction of movement, is for example along the line of sight.

(ii) Movement of Other Things

The scenes that we tend to find have many moveable things in them. We can have a situation where the eye or camera is still, most of the scene doesn't move, but one thing does. What happens to the image? Obviously a part of it, at and around the movement, is changed. There are three distinct effects involved.

At the occluding edges of the moving thing, some parts of the scene are revealed and some are concealed depending on which way the edge is moving locally. You can imagine a uniform grey card moving across a scene: at its leading edge parts of the image change to grey from whatever they were before; at its trailing edge grey values in the image are changed to new

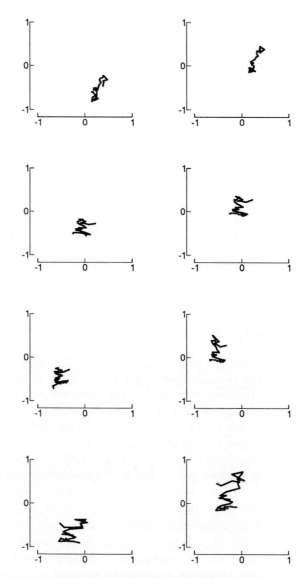

Figure 13. The effects of object motion. This figure shows the image trajectories that are projected from the eight corners of a cube that is executing a random walk in three dimensions.

values that depend on what is behind the card. The luminance values at different places along either trailing or leading edge can be increased or decreased. If the card has a visible shadow this will also move in some related fashion. The movement of a shadow means that the illuminance of parts of a scene are changing. Since luminance is a product of illuminance and reflectance, the effect is for the image luminance values to be multiplied by a common factor.

The second factor concerns what happens to the image within the occluding edges of the thing that is moving. In the case of a uniform grey card, nothing in the image changes. If the card had a line drawn on it, then this would move with the card and its image would be displaced. If the direction of the movement was at right angles to the line, then the image would be changing all along the line. If the line lay along the direction of movement, then the image would only change at the line ends. The luminance within an occluding contour is most likely to have some variations and so these will move with the surface. This means that luminance values within the occluding contour are changed, but in a way that is determined by the distribution of luminance variations themselves.

The third consequence of the independent movement of something is that its projected image may change shape. Physical bodies are free to rotate and translate in three dimensions. What happens to the image then depends on the shape of the body. Start by thinking about a sphere; if it just rotates then its outline in the image is unaltered. If it translates, its outline remains a sphere, but shifts and changes in size. Now think about a cube. As it rotates its outline changes size and shape; when the cube is translated its outline changes size and position. Now think about a tree blowing in the wind.

3.7 Summary: What are Images Like?

Without light sources we don't see and without reflective surfaces we don't see. Light is emitted from sources, bounces off reflective surfaces, enters the eye and forms an image, with the help of which we do see. So far I have discussed the factors which govern how the illumination of surfaces varies and how the reflectivity of surfaces varies. These two factors determine the *luminance* of a surface.

The type of illumination is an important variable. Most scene illumination is a mixture of one or more point sources plus diffuse secondary illumination caused by reflection of the light from the sources at surfaces including the sky. The directions of the point sources are a factor that determine how luminance varies across the surfaces in a scene and hence across an image.

Surface shape is another factor which determines how luminance varies. Surfaces may be creased or smoothly curved, but in any case will present an occluding contour. Luminance varies smoothly over smoothly curved surfaces, but may change abruptly at a crease. At an occlusion, there may be a local minimum in grey level.

The reflectance of surfaces is the final factor which determines the luminance of the surface. This will typically vary from surface to surface, and thus vary across the site of an occluding contour in an image. It also may vary over a single surface, particularly as a texture or pattern of markings or engravings in the surface.

Texture can sometimes be treated as a quasi-regular layout on the surface of a small pattern element. The important aspect of this is the size of the element and its density or spacing on the surface. The manner in which these vary over the surface can provide useful information about the shape of the surface. It may alternatively be fractal, in which case we expect to find similar types of detail at all magnifications of the pattern.

When reflecting light a surface becomes a source of light that illuminates the scene. A part of this reflected light illuminates the image according to the inverse square law and cosine law, because the image is also a surface just like any other. If a particular surface has an illuminance pattern, then a similar illuminance pattern will also be found in the corresponding part of the image. It is convenient although only approximately correct to treat the illuminance pattern of the image as a faithful copy of the luminance of the visible surfaces in the scene.

An optical image is a picture of a scene from a particular viewpoint. It illustrates whatever is nearest in each direction away from the viewpoint. The nature of matter ensures that the scene is filled with things that have continuity and a definite surface. Each thing has a definite volume and shape, so that it occupies a particular part of space. It will fill a small but continuous range of directions from the viewpoint. This means that the image is made up of a patchwork of interlocking segments each one corresponding to the set of continuous directions occupied by one thing in the scene.

Different things have different illumination, shape, texture and reflectivity and so different segments will have different luminances and visual texture.

Across each thing in the scene illumination varies as we have seen because of the shape of the surface or shadows and other variations in illumination. Reflectivity also varies across things, and if there is specularity then highlights are found. All of these mean that the illuminance will vary within each image segment. If the thing is angled away from the direction in which it is being viewed then the farther parts of it are seen at a smaller magnification than the nearer parts because of perspective and consequently there will be equivalent variations in the pattern of visual texture.

APPENDIX: LIGHT, PHOTOMETRY, AND OPTICS

This appendix is intended to provide a simple guide to the physical properties of light that are important for vision. The treatment is only mildly algebraic and therefore far from rigorous: the reader who wishes to learn more should read the book by Longhurst (1973).

3.A1 The Emission and Propagation of Light

(i) Radiation energy, such as light, is noisy. Photon noise is proportional to the square root of the radiation intensity.
(ii) Photons travel in straight lines until they meet a surface.

When elelctric current passes through the coiled filament in a light bulb, the filament is heated up. The electrons in each atom are excited, they move up in frequency. This leaves gaps in the spectrum of permissible frequencies, and any electrons with frequencies above the gaps can lose energy by emitting a light wave and move down into the gaps. Striking a match has much the same effect and result.

We can assume that the exact moment at which an electron changes down in frequency is the business of that electron alone. This means that the emission of light is a Poisson random process. All the individual photons, or light waves add up to a steady mean rate of radiation, but the radiation is also subject to variability called *photon noise*. For the light that we are interested in, the photon noise, v, is proportional to the square root of the radiation intensity, R:

$$v = R^{1/2}$$

The process of light emission can be triggered by a photon which is the same as the photon emitted. This results in two identical photons appearing at the same instant. If each in turn triggers more photon emission, then the photons are no longer emitted randomly in time. The result is the very energetic laser.

The illuminance, E, of a surface by a point source of luminous flux, I, at a distance r from the surface and at an angle of θ to the surface normal, is given by

$$E = \left(\frac{I \cos \theta}{r^2} \right)$$

This expression combines the *inverse square law* and the *cosine law* of illumination.

Units

Units for describing the characteristics of light are quite complex and belong to a field known as photometry. The following are generally useful.

(i) *Luminous flux* is the total light flow across a surface per unit time. It is expressed as lumens.
(ii) *Luminous intensity* is the luminous flux per unit solid angle (in a particular direction) of an emission source. It is expressed as candelas.
(iii) *Luminance* is defined as the luminous intensity of light emitted per unit projected area of the surface for any particular direction. It is expressed in candelas per square metre, cd m^{-2}.

(iv) *Illuminance* is the luminous flux per unit area on an illuminated surface. It is the standard measure of light strength arriving at a surface. It is expressed in lm m^{-2} (lux).

Notice that illuminance is defined as the luminous flux per unit area; luminance as the luminous intensity per unit area. Luminance is directional: it could depend on where you observe the surface from. Illuminance is not: it doesn't matter, once it's there, where the light came from.

3.A2 The Reflection and Scattering of Light

(i) Reflected light at surfaces may be specular and directional, particularly at highly polished surfaces like mirrors. The spatial pattern of the light is preserved in the reflection.

(ii) Reflected light at surfaces may be diffuse and not directional, particularly at matt surfaces. The pattern of light is lost in the scattered reflection.

Light is reflected when it meets an obstacle. There are two types of reflection. One is easier to understand in the terms of the wave nature of light; the other is easier understood as interactions between photons and electrons.

The waves of light propagate through different media, such as air, water or a vacuum, with different velocities depending on how many electrons there are in the medium that are free to interact with the photons and slow them down. Wherever there is a boundary between different media, the light has to change velocity, but not frequency, and as a consequence part of the light wave is returned away from the second medium. The wave nature of light means that at a perfectly smooth boundary between two dielectric media, the reflected light travels back in a particular direction with respect to the direction it was travelling in and the orientation of the dielectric boundary. This type of reflection is *specular*. Specular reflection is a characteristic of highly polished surfaces such as a mirror, and the reflected light keeps its spatial pattern.

The reflection of light can also be considered as due to collisions between photons and the electrons of the second medium. If there is a match between the energy level available in the photon and the energy needed to promote the electron into a permissible higher energy state then the energy can be absorbed by the electron as heat, causing the annihilation of the photon. The electron may loose the energy again, perhaps to release a new photon. If this photon proceeds further into the medium it has a second chance to become heat. If it returns in the reverse direction then it may well escape back into the first medium: it has then been reflected. When a photon is re-emitted by surface in this manner, its direction has no clear relationship to the direction from which its precursor arrived. The reflected light is scattered at random and the reflection is *diffuse*. Diffuse reflection is found at matt surfaces such as blotting paper.

The electrons in media have one of two types of relationship with the medium: they may be free to move or bound to individual atoms. Electrons that are bound require specific energies to be promoted to a higher level, whereas a population of free electrons is much less selective. Glass has many bound electrons and is transparent to visible light because such light does not contain the specific energies necessary to excite these electrons. The atomic structure of metals leaves a large number of free electrons (free to move that is). The incident photons readily excite these electrons, but the excited electrons are unlikely to collide with atoms to be lost as heat and so the light may penetrate the metal by up to 0.1 mm before being returned as reflected light.

Units

Reflectance is defined as the ratio of the luminance of the reflected light to the illuminance of the incident light. Reflectance is usually different for different energies of light, that is for different wavelengths of light. Reflectance is often expressed as a percentage, and often all visible light is taken together.

3.A3 The Refraction and Diffraction of Light

(i)   If light strikes a boundary between two media obliquely, it is refracted by an amount that depends on the angle of incidence and the refractive indices of the two media.

(ii) A special case of this is what happens when light meets a spherical lens surface. The light is *focused* into an *image*.

(iii) When light passes through a small aperture it is scattered a little in space. This is called *diffraction*.

When a wave of light meets a boundary between two different media, part of the wave is reflected, but part is also transmitted across the boundary. If the wave strikes the boundary obliquely then different parts of the wave front will reach the boundary and change their velocity at different times, with the result that the direction of wave propagation is changed. This is called *refraction*.

If the incident wave meets a plane surface at an angle of I from the surface normal, and the refracted wave leaves the plane surface at an angle of I', and if the velocity of light in the two media is v and v', respectively, then Snell's law states that:

$$\left(\frac{\sin I}{\sin I'}\right) = \left(\frac{v}{v'}\right)$$

The media are usually characterized by their *refractive indices*, n and n', in which case Snell's law states that

$$\left(\frac{\sin I}{\sin I'}\right) = \left(\frac{n'}{n}\right)$$

The particular case of interest to vision is what happens when a wave front meets a spherical boundary between two different media, such as a lens or the cornea of the eye. In this case the angle of incidence varies along the wave front and the shape of the transmitted wave is altered. A planar wavefront meeting a convex spherical lens becomes bent so that its middle is delayed behind the edges. This is the principle of image formation.

A lens is physically specified by the refractive index of its material, n, and the radii of its two spherical surfaces, r_1 and r_2. For an ordinary positive (convex) lens, r_1 is positive in value and r_2 is negative in value, and usually:

$$r_1 = -r_2 = r$$

Snell's law can be used to calculate the spatial distribution of light that has passed through the lens. A special case is for a point of light on the optical axis of the lens in a medium of refractive index.

Light is emitted in all directions, and some passes through the lens. Within certain limits there is a point on the optical axis beyond the lens where all the light is *focused* back into a point. If the source is d distant from the lens, and the focused *image* is d' distant from the lens on the other side, then from Snell's law it is found that:

for $n' = 1$ (i.e. a lens in air)

$$\left(\frac{1}{d'} - \frac{1}{d}\right) = (n-1)\left(\frac{1}{r_1} - \frac{1}{r_2}\right)$$

When d is infinite, we have

$$\frac{1}{d'} = \frac{1}{f'} = (n-1)\left(\frac{1}{r_1} - \frac{1}{r_2}\right)$$

where f' is the *focal length* of the lens. It can be seen that the focal length is smaller if either n is larger or r is smaller.

The position of the focused image depends on r and n, as well as d. When d is not infinity we have

$$\frac{1}{d'} = (n-1)\left(\frac{1}{r_1} - \frac{1}{r_2}\right) + \frac{1}{d}$$

In order to keep d' constant so that the image is always focused in the same place, either n or r must vary as d changes. In the eye, r varies with the distance of whichever body in the scene is being examined, although the eye has a fixed spherical surface, the cornea, as well as its lens. The process of adjusting r is called *accommodation*.

All of this argument has assumed that the source or object lies on the optical axis of the lens. If it is off axis then d' is not accurately given by these equations, and a planar image field will be slightly out of focus. This is known as *spherical aberration*.

A second phenomenon which is a result of the wave nature of light is *diffraction*. When a wave front meets an obstruction with a small hole or *aperture* in it, only part of the wave front passes through. This aperture

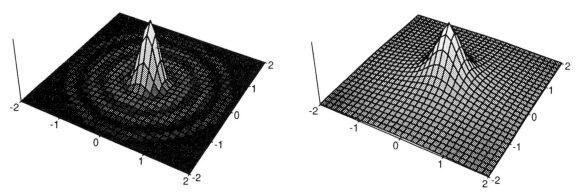

Figure A1. Diffraction and point spread functions for the human eye. The idealized point spread function for the human eye, were it only diffraction limited, and the actual point spread function measured by Campbell and Gubisch (1966).

becomes, in effect, a point source of light, and the transmitted wave spreads out in all directions.

This is based on Huygen's principle which supposes that every point on a light wavefront acts as a point source of so-called secondary wavelets. The principle is modified to assume that these secondary wavelets have their greatest effect on the forward-moving wave front. The same principle explains why shadows are fuzzy.

Diffraction is important in vision because the eye has a small aperture, the *pupil*, through which the light enters the eye. Diffraction in an image-forming system results in a slightly blurred pattern, the degree of blurring increasing as the aperture decreases. As the aperture decreases, the light is increasingly confined to the optical axis, and spherical aberration is reduced.

Light from a point source that has a wavelength λ passing through a narrow aperture of radius a is spread out in a circular pattern, expressed as a function of angular deviation, u in radians, from the centre of the image:

$$I(u) = \left[\frac{2J_1(2\pi a/\lambda \sin u)}{2\pi a/\lambda \sin u} \right]^2$$

where J_1 is the first order Bessel function. Most of the light is concentrated in a circle of radius z, where

$$\sin z = \frac{1.22}{2\pi a/\lambda}$$

but there are several faint rings around this.

Units

Refractive index n' of a medium is the ratio of the velocity of light in air to the velocity of light in that medium:

$$n' = v_{\text{air}}/v'$$

Lens power F is the reciprocal of the focal length f'

$$F = 1/f'$$

In air

$$F = (n' - 1)/r$$

The power of a lens, expressed in dioptres, D, is the reciprocal of the focal length in metres. A convex lens has positive power; a concave lens has negative power.

For an eye which is accommodated at infinity, i.e. relaxed, an object 1 m away is brought into focus by placing a $+1$ D lens in front of the eye; an object 0.5 m away requires $+2$ D, etc.

3.A4 Spatial Frequency Analysis of Optical Devices

There are many ways in which the quality of an optical image can be specified. For what follows, an analysis in terms of the transmission of sinusoidally varying luminance patterns is appropriate. Such a pattern of parallel light and dark stripes in which luminance varies across the stripes in a sine wave is called a *sine-wave grating*. A sine-wave grating can be specified by just four parameters: its *mean luminance* L_0, its *amplitude* of luminance modulation a, its *spatial frequency* f, and its *phase* or position p. The amplitude is the difference in luminance between a peak and a trough on the waveform. The spatial frequency is the number of cycles of the sine-wave per unit distance, which is the same as the reciprocal of the distance between adjacent peaks, the *period*. The phase of a sine-wave grating is the position of the pattern with respect to a fixed origin of coordinates. Phase is usually described as an angle: 2π radians (360°) corresponds to a complete cycle. A special case is when the phase is equal to $\pi/2$ radians (90°): this is called a *cosine wave*.

Since luminance only varies in one direction, the pattern is completely specified by giving just an equation for this variation in one dimension (variation in x)

$$L(x) = L_0 + \tfrac{1}{2}a \cos(2\pi f x + p)$$

It is more usual to describe the strength of the luminance modulation by its Michelson contrast, m, which is defined as:

$$m = \left(\frac{L_{\max} - L_{\min}}{L_{\max} + L_{\min}} \right) = \frac{a}{2L_0}$$

The grating may then be written as:

$$L(x) = L_0(1 + m \cos(2\pi f x + P))$$

The image of a sine-wave grating object pattern is also a sine-wave grating pattern with the same spatial frequency. The image contrast is determined by the quality of the optical device and is always less than the object luminance contrast. The grating is *attenuated* by the optical device.

The performance of an optical system can be described by giving the attenuation characteristics of the system as a function of spatial frequency. This function, which gives attenuation as a function of spatial frequency, is called a *modulation transfer function* (MTF). The MTF for the human eye is shown in Fig. A2. Notice that the MTF is at one for zero cycles per degree and declines with increasing spatial frequency until the *cut-off* spatial frequency is reached, beyond which no modulation is found in the image.

The attenuation, MTF(f) of a grating of given spatial frequency, f, by a given optical system is a number, less than one, which gives the ratio of the image contrast, C', to the object contrast, C:

$$\text{MTF}(f) = \frac{C'(f)}{C(f)}$$

Rearranging this we have:

$$C'(f) = \text{MTF}(f)C(f)$$

which shows that if we know the MTF of an optical system, then we can predict the image contrast for a grating pattern by multiplying together the attenuation and the object contrast.

The MTF of an optical device is a way of specifying its performance in general, not just for sine-wave gratings. This is because any pattern can be specified as the sum of a range of sine-wave gratings. For example if we were to add together every sine wave with a frequency between 0 and infinity, each set to the same amplitude, then the result would be one infinitesimally narrow impulse. If the amplitude of each sine wave was inversely proportional

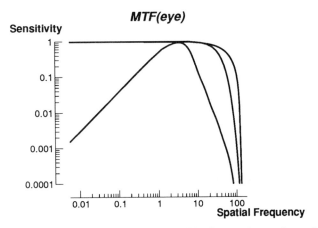

Figure A2. The MTF of the human eye. This figure shows three functions. The uppermost function is the MTF for an ideal optical device with an entrance aperture of 2 mm and light of wavelength 550 nm. The function immediately beneath this is the MTF for the actual optics of the human eye. The third and lowermost function is the contrast sensitivity function for human vision, which plots the variation in amplitude of cosine waves necessary for detection. This would correspond to the MTF for human vision if equal sensitivity to two different spatial frequencies implied equal cosinusoidal response (see Chapter 9).

to its frequency and they all had a phase of $\pi/2$, then the result would be one step change.

The *Fourier transform* of a pattern converts the pattern into a function relating phase and amplitude to spatial frequency. It is an alternative way of specifying the pattern.

If we take the Fourier transform of a pattern of light, and multiply this by the MTF of an optical device, we have then the Fourier transform of the image of that pattern. More information can be found in Bracewell (1978).

References

Brodatz P. (1966) "Texture: A Photographic Album for Artists and Designers". Dover, New York.
Bracewell R.N. (1978) "The Fourier Transform and its Applications", 2nd edn. McGraw-Hill, London.
Campbell F.W. and Gubisch R.W. (1966) Optical quality of the human eye. *J. Physiol.* **186**, 558–578.
Ditchburn R.W. (1976) "Light", 3rd edn. Academic Press, London.
Goetz A. (1970) "Introduction to Differential Geometry". Addison Wesley, Reading MA.
Gubisch R.W. (1967) Optical performance of the human eye. *J. Opt. Soc. Am.* **57**, 407–415.
Longhurst R.S. (1973) "Geometrical and Physical Optics", 3rd edn. Longman, London.
Mandelbrot B.B. (1977) "Fractals: Form Chance and Dimension". W.H. Freeman, San Francisco.
Mandelbrot B.B. (1982) "The Fractal Geometry of Nature". W.H. Freeman, San Francisco.
Stevens P.A. (1974) "Patterns in Nature". Little, Brown, Boston.
Thorpe J.A. (1979) "Elementary Topics in Differential Geometry". Springer Verlag, New York.
Westheimer G. (1977) Spatial frequency and light spread descriptions of visual acuity and hyperacuity. *J. Opt. Soc. Am.* **67**, 207–212.

Exercises

1. What are the basic shapes that things take? What rules have you used in trying to answer this question?
2. What might be a suitable definition of the term "texture"? For what purposes would it be suitable?
3. What is the luminance distribution on the surface of a sphere from a single remote source, from a single near source, from a single remote source plus diffuse lighting?
4. Now repeat this but with more exotic surfaces, such as the so-called "monkey saddle":

$$z = x^3 + 3xy^2$$

4

Image Algebra

The optical image formed by a lens is a two-dimensional function. It can be thought of as a relief map of a landscape: the brighter a place in the image is, the higher is its altitude. We can take this analogy further and show the image as a surface, just like a landscape. The essential point here is that for any map location there is a numerical value of the intensity of the image. Numbers are good for representing a simple physical quantity like light intensity; maps are good for representing how quantities vary over an area. There are many useful things to be done to an image that retain this format of a two-dimensional function. In this chapter I will describe a few varieties to give an idea of the scope of what can be achieved in this way.

There are three important and fundamentally distinct types of image algebra process. Each type produces an output image from one or more input images. If an operation only requires one input, then it is an *unary operation*; if it requires two input images then it is a *binary operation*. Members of the first type, *point operations*, are only concerned with taking the values at individual points in the image, applying the same operation to each of these independently of all the others, and placing the result in one place in the output. In the second type of process, *neighbourhood operations*, a set of values from nearby points surrounding each point in the input, a neighbourhood, is involved in producing the output. The third type of process are *global operations*, where the output at any point involves all of the points in the input image. There are, of course, many possibilities and examples of each of these categories, and in this chapter I describe several examples of each that are both representative and also particularly useful. The main body of the chapter describes the examples themselves. At the end of the chapter, there is a section which develops a formal system for understanding image algebra, and in so doing recapitulates some of the examples. The essential algebra is introduced in this summary section of the chapter for readers who would like reassurance that it is simple to understand and use.

The outcome of any image algebra operation is a new image, in the sense of a numerically valued two-dimensional function of a connected spatial domain. Such an output is not itself suitable for controlling actions, but is to be taken as a part of a sequence of operations that lead to action or decision. This means that in considering image algebra, the main goal is to find a sequence of transformations that will place distinctive numerical

Figure 1. A landscape illustration of an image. This figure shows an image in two alternative forms. On the left is the normal pictorial form. On the right is a two-dimensional graph of the intensity function of the image. The vertical axis represents intensity so that the higher a point is the brighter the corresponding point in the image will be.

values at places in the image that have significant information and not elsewhere. In practice, distinctive values are those which are least common in the image. The distribution of values in the image is normally unimodal (i.e. has only one main peak), in which case the distinctive values are the extremes, those furthest from the mean value. The most significant point or region in an image, plus how significant it actually is, can be used to decide what appropriate actions need to be taken.

What is significant in an image? Scenes are filled with matter. The matter is not homogeneous, but is instead organized into relatively large clumps. The clumps vary in size and are themselves distributed unevenly. The distribution of clumps gives rise to certain *scene properties*. For example the distribution of matter in a forest causes the scene to have some areas that are deeply shaded and other areas that are light glades. Matter is bounded by surfaces. Some of the properties of these surfaces depend only on the surface itself and not on how it is observed. These are the *intrinsic surface properties*. For example, the reflectance of a surface and its texture are qualities of the surface that move with the surface and don't change if it is viewed from other places in the scene. Surfaces also have properties that do depend on how it is illuminated and viewed. These *extrinsic surface properties* include its size and its luminance. Some of these properties of scenes and surfaces can be discovered and assessed by the techniques of image algebra.

4.1 Two Practical Considerations

Before describing the various image algebraic processes that are useful, there are two practical considerations that need to be borne in mind right from the start. Images, as intensity patterns in a light wave front, are continuous. Images in all recorded forms, photographic, video, or in the eye, are represented by an array of samples of the intensity at discrete locations. Secondly, all images are subject to noise.

(i) Sampling Images

An image is a continuously varying function of two spatial dimensions. For practical purposes it is convenient to be able to take a set of sample values of the image at discrete points in the image in place of the continuous image itself. In principle, this can be done without any loss of information, provided the samples are taken densely enough over the image.

How dense should the samples be? The top row of Fig. 2 shows a set of samples obtained from a one-dimensional image. Notice how their amplitude is slowly modulated across the page. Along with the samples is shown the actual image before sampling, which is very different from what you might have expected because the samples were not taken close enough together. This behaviour is called *aliasing*, where one pattern in a signal appears to be another when that signal is sampled too coarsely. In order to avoid this aliasing problem, we need to have more than two samples per cycle of the highest frequency component of the image. The manner in which images are formed, through an aperture and a lens of finite size, ensures that they have a limited extent of spatial frequencies. If there are no frequencies above some maximum $F_{\max}$, then the pattern is adequately sampled when the interval between samples is less than $1/(2F_{\max})$. This condition, which avoids aliasing, is known as the Nyquist limit.

(ii) Noise

Noise is an important consideration in any visual system. The light arriving in the optical image is fluctuating in intensity from instant to instant and

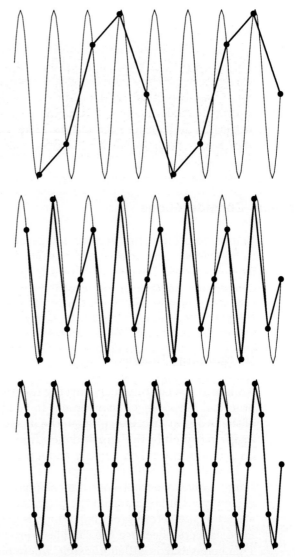

Figure 2.   Image sampling and aliasing. This figure shows a one-dimensional slice through an image and three sets of samples from it. The first set of samples are taken at too large an interval, and consequently give a misleading impression of the contents of the slice. The second set are taken at an intermediate interval and just fail to correctly represent the image. The third set are taken at a sufficiently fine interval to correctly represent the image.

each stage in the process thereafter adds its own random component to whatever signal is present. Noise can be treated as an image function in which the value at every point is random. If the value at each point is not dependent on the value of any other point, the random values are said to be uncorrelated. If the values are uncorrelated in space and in time then the noise is said to be white noise.

 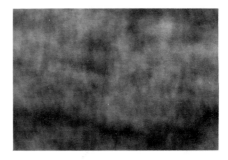

Figure 3. White noise. This figure shows white noise on the left and noise with a power spectrum that is the same as that encountered in ordinary images on the right.

The distribution of values of noise is an important characteristic. The typical random number generators available as software in computer systems have a uniform distribution of pseudo-random values. Any value between $+1$ and -1 is equally likely. The type of noise found in electical components typically has a Gaussian distribution of values, so that small values are more likely than large values. The amplitude of noise in a system has to be specified, and since it is a rapidly fluctuating signal, some sort of average measure has to be employed. If the values are drawn from a known distribution, such as the Gaussian, then the amplitude of the noise can be expressed as the standard deviation of the values. The standard deviation of the values is also called the "root mean square" or RMS.

The RMS is obtained by squaring every random value, thereby making them all positive, calculating the mean of the squared values, and then taking the square root of the result. If we have n random values, e_i, then

$$\text{RMS} = (\text{mean } (e_i^2))^{1/2}$$

It is normal practice to remove any DC level in the noise before such calculations. The DC component is the mean value of the noise. Noise with a uniform distribution of values between 0 and 1 has a DC level of 0.5.

Noise can be additive, in that its amplitude is a fixed quantity, not dependent on the signal at all. Noise can also be multiplicative, where its amplitude is a function of the signal amplitude.

4.2 Point Operations: Grey Levels in Images

Point operations are those where there is no interaction between the different values at different places in the input. The value at any one place in the output image is obtained from just one place in the input. Usually they are the same place, but this is not necessary. We will be able to write all unary point operations by a simple formula of the general form:

$$L'(x, y) = \text{function } (L(x, y))$$

which says that the new value, L', at the point (x, y) is given by applying some *function* to the old value, L. Examples of unary point operations are grey-level transformations, and examples of binary point operations are the addition and subtraction of images.

(i) Grey-level Transformations

The intensities in an optical image range, potentially, from zero upwards without limit. The range of values depends very strongly on the illumination of the scene, and much less on what is in the scene. The reflectances in a scene, on the other hand, are a fairly fixed property of the scene. Physically, they range from 0 to 1 (from absorbing all light to reflecting all incident light), which means that they are bounded. It is a conjecture, but a likely one, that the range of reflectances in any scene are distributed according to some statistically stable pattern. Moderate reflectances seem to be more common than extremes, irrespective of what actual scene is being considered, and this is a constraint on the nature of images. I shall show in this section how this constraint can be used to transform images in the general direction of mapping intrinsic scene properties.

Consider an image containing a step function, with luminance values L_1 and L_2 either side of the step, so that the difference in luminance is $(L_2 - L_1)$. Let us suppose that the two luminances arise because of an equal illuminance, I, and two different reflectances R_1 and R_2:

$$L_1 = IR_1$$
$$L_2 = IR_2$$

The difference in luminance can now be written as:

$$(L_2 - L_1) = I(R_2 - R_1)$$

This depends on both the reflectance difference, which is of particular interest, and the illuminance which is less interesting. There are some transformations that can be applied to the image before examining the difference across the step that will serve to remove the influence of illumination on the response. Two such transformations are the log transform and the H transform.

The Log Transform
Suppose that each value in the image is replaced by its logarithm: the image is subjected to a *log transform*:

$$L'(x, y) = \log(L(x, y))$$

since

$$L(x, y) = IR(x, y)$$

therefore

$$L'(x, y) = \log(IR(x, y)) = \log I + \log R(x, y)$$

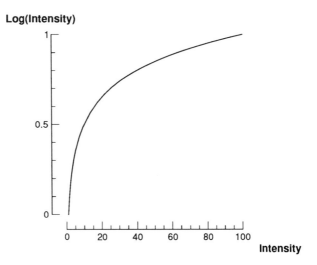

Figure 4. The log transform. The x axis gives the input image intensity value, and the y axis gives the output value. Note that the log transform compresses high values, devoting a high proportion of its dynamic range for smaller values.

The difference in response across the step edge of the log-transformed image is given by

$$((\log I + \log R_2) - (\log I + \log R_1)) = (\log R_2 - \log R_1) = \log(R_2/R_1)$$

This is independent of the illuminance and as a result, the response to a given reflectance change will always be the same (photon noise apart), irrespective of illumination conditions.

The H Transform
There is another transformation which achieves a similar result. This is called the *H transform*, and each luminance value in the image is replaced by:

$$L'(x, y) = \frac{L(x, y)}{H + kL(x, y)}$$

where H is some large constant and k is some small constant. If, as before, we replace L by IR, then:

$$L'(x, y) = \frac{IR(x, y)}{H + kIR(x, y)}$$

The difference in response across the step reflectance change is given by:

$$\frac{IR_2(x, y)}{H + kIR_2(x, y)} - \frac{IR_1(x, y)}{H + kIR_1(x, y)}$$

If the value of H could be set to equal the luminance of a surface with a reflectance of 1.0, it would then equal I, and would be the largest possible luminance in the image. This cannot be directly obtained from the image, but if H was set to the largest actual luminance in the image it would tend to be a stable fraction of I. We can write:

$$H = IR_{max}$$

The amplitude of the response is now given by:

$$\frac{IR_2(x, y)}{IR_{max} + kIR_2(x, y)} - \frac{IR_1(x, y)}{IR_{max} + kIR_1(x, y)}$$

This expression can be divided throughout by I, leaving:

$$\frac{R_2(x, y)}{R_{max} + kR_2(x, y)} - \frac{R_1(x, y)}{R_{max} + kR_1(x, y)}$$

which is independent of I.

For this transform to be useful there are several important conditions that have to be met. H has to be set to some value which is a stable factor of the illuminance of the reflectances in question. Suppose H was simply set to the largest value in the image. This largest value would be a stable factor of the illuminance if it was derived from a surface with high reflectance and that was illuminated by the same source as the two surfaces we are considering. Thus success would only be guaranteed if all scenes had roughly the same distribution of surface reflectances, and had fairly uniform illumination.

An alternative approach would be to set H to some factor of the mean luminance of the scene. This is more likely to be a stable factor of I. Even better would be to weight the values of luminance so that those far away in space from the reflectances in question had little influence. A special case is where H is set to twice the mean luminance and k is set to zero. We then have for the amplitude of the response:

$$\frac{L_2}{L_1 + L_2} - \frac{L_1}{L_1 + L_2} = \frac{L_2 - L_1}{L_1 + L_2}$$

$$= \frac{R_2 - R_1}{R_2 + R_1}$$

This is known as the *Michelson contrast*.

The Density Transform and Self-calibration

The two previous examples had specific properties when applied to luminance images. Since there are many forms of image in which the values are not luminances, their general use is less profitable. I shall now describe a rather different way of transforming the values which has the useful property of being self-correcting. If, as is possible in a real machine, the values are apt to change from day to day, then it is not easy to place any great significance on them at any one time. Imagine a thermometer which drifted in its reading by a degree each day. After a few days the reading of

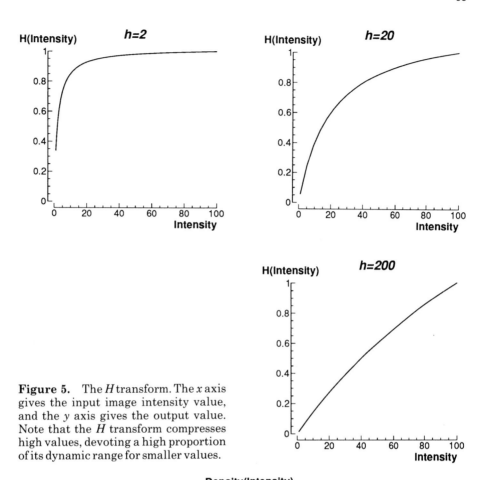

Figure 5. The *H* transform. The *x* axis gives the input image intensity value, and the *y* axis gives the output value. Note that the *H* transform compresses high values, devoting a high proportion of its dynamic range for smaller values.

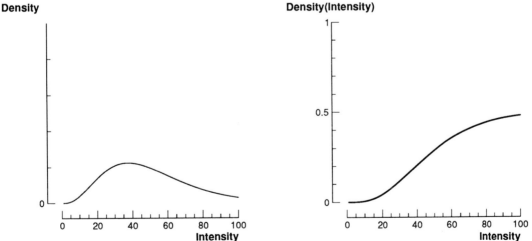

Figure 6. A typical density transform. The left-hand graph shows an imaginary but realistic density of grey-levels in an image. The right-hand graph shows the density transform. The *x* axis gives the input image intensity value, and the *y* axis gives the output value. Note that the density transform compresses both low and high values, devoting a high proportion of its dynamic range for middling values that are the most common.

$0°C$ would not necessarily apply to the freezing point of water, and the instrument would need recalibration.

Compare this with a mechanism that reported whether the temperature was warmer or colder than the recent average. Each measurement of temperature that it made was compared with the mean of its readings over the last 24-h period. It its readings were to drift, so would their mean and such a thermometer would be more reliable. It is self-calibrating.

We can treat the values in an image in this same way. For any one image we can replace each value by its distance in standard deviations from the mean value in the image. A good property of this transform is that we can add any constant value to each point in the image and/or multiply each value by a constant, and then, applying the transform, obtain always the same result.

(ii) Addition and Subtraction of Images

Binary operations involve taking two images and combining them to get a third. The simplest cases are where the third image is obtained point by point from the other two so that its value at any place is obtained by applying an operation to the values of the two input images at the same place. So for example, we can find the difference between two images by subtracting corresponding points in the two to produce the third image.

Subtracting images to find the difference rarely makes sense. The difference between an image of a face and an image of a rural scene is not really expressed by the numerical difference between the two images. There is a general type of instance where it does make sense, however. If the two images are of basically the same scene, and the difference between them is slight, then the effect of subtracting one from the other is to highlight the difference between them. For example, if the two images were obtained of the same scene, but at different moments, then there would be two major sources of difference between the image. The first is the image noise that each will have. This will be different in the two images, and the result of subtracting one from the other will be just the noise. From this result, it would be possible to estimate the level of noise in the two images. This might be useful in order to decide whether particular variations in the image are significant or whether they are most likely to be just the effects of noise. Another application of image subtraction is if something in the scene has moved a short distance between the taking of the two images. This will be made clear in the result of subtracting one from the other.

Two images can be added together in the same fashion that one can be subtracted from the other. Just as with subtraction, this is useful when considering the effects of noise, because adding two images with different samples of noise will double the amplitude of the signal in the image but will only increase the amplitude of the noise by $\sqrt{2}$. In this case the signal/noise ratio has increased by $2/\sqrt{2}(=\sqrt{2})$. This can be repeated many times to give more improvements in the signal/noise ratio: for n samples added together the improvement in signal/noise ratio is equal to $\sqrt{n}$.

Figure 7. The result of subtracting images. Four different cases are shown. At the top are two wholly unrelated images, and their numerical difference. In the second row are shown two images differing in the position of two of the things in the scene. In the third row are shown two images of the view from my laboratory windows but taken a few seconds apart in time. At the bottom are two images differing only in the noise.

4.3 Neighbourhood Operations

Neighbourhood operations are those where there is interaction between the different values at different places of the input. The value at any one place in the output image is obtained from several places in the input. Usually they are contiguous regions around the location of the output, but this is not necessary: the neighbourhood could be non-contiguous and could be shifted with respect to the output point. The first example of a neighbourhood operation is one in which the neighbourhood is set to be infinitesimally small, and so does not need to be specified. In the second example, the neighbourhood is a finite region that must be specified. This makes the operation a kind of binary operation, although the two inputs are not both images: one of them is a specification of the region.

(i) Differentiation

Variations in image values yield information that is more useful than the values are themselves. The important information in optical images is how intensity varies, both across space and in time, rather than the actual values at any one point or points in the image. For this reason, it is necessary to consider operations that assess the variations.

The mathematical technique for analysing variations in the value of functions is called *differentiation*. To differentiate a function is to replace that function by a new one which records how much the value is changing in the original function at each point. This new function is called the *derivative* of the original function. We can differentiate a derivative to produce a function recording how rapidly the derivative is changing. This is called the *second derivative*. The operation of differentiation is a unary operation: the input to the operation is only one image and the output from the operation is only one image. However, unlike the unary point operations that were considered above, where the output at any one point depended only on the input at that point, the output from differentiation depends on more than one point.

The basic technique is to find, at each point, how much the value of the image differs a small distance away, and to divide this difference by the extent of the distance itself. Starting at the point (x, y), if we write a small distance as ∂s, and the change in value as $\partial I(x, y)$, then we can calculate:

$$\frac{\partial I(x, y)}{\partial s}$$

The derivative is found by evaluating this as ∂s tends to zero, and is written:

$$\frac{dI(x, y)}{ds} \equiv \lim_{\partial s \to 0} \left(\frac{\partial I(x, y)}{\partial s} \right)$$

Of course, if ∂s is simply set to zero, then the derivative is infinite in value, and so we let ∂s approach zero gradually and watch to see how the derivative levels off at a particular value. The technique of differentiation is detailed in the summary section to this chapter.

As we shall see below, second derivatives are most important in vision. We can write a second derivative as:

$$\frac{d}{ds} \frac{dI(x, y)}{ds}$$

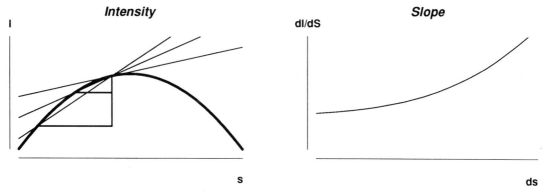

Figure 8. Differentiation by letting ∂s tend to zero. This figure shows how the value of the derivative, the ratio of the change in value, ∂I, to the change in position, ∂s, tends to some stable value as the change in position is gradually reduced to zero.

It is more convenient to write:

$$\frac{\mathrm{d}^2 I(x,y)}{\mathrm{d}s^2}$$

Two Dimensions
The derivative is found in a particular direction. In one-dimensional signals, there are two different possible directions (forwards or backwards in time for example). The derivative in these opposite directions has opposite signs, but is otherwise equal in value and so it does not matter particularly which direction is chosen. For two-dimensional signals, such as images, there is a continuum of different possible directions. The derivative in different directions is not equal in magnitude and it makes a great deal of difference which direction is chosen. This poses a fundamental problem for image algebra: it is not simple to construct an isotropic first derivative operator. There is rarely any advance indication or expectation that a derivative in one particular direction will be of greatest interest, and so it is necessary to consider derivatives in different directions. This is not a problem when we consider second derivative operators in two dimensions. There are directional second derivative operators, such as $\mathrm{d}^2 I/\mathrm{d}x^2$ and $\mathrm{d}^2 I/\mathrm{d}y^2$ which measure the second derivatives in the x and the y directions, respectively. However, there is also an isotropic second derivative operator, the Laplacian operator:

$$\nabla^2 I \equiv \frac{\mathrm{d}^2 I}{\mathrm{d}x^2} + \frac{\mathrm{d}^2 I}{\mathrm{d}y^2}$$

which measures the mean second derivative in all directions. The symbol ∇^2 is pronounced "del squared".

Other Derivative Operators
The standard derivative approach treats the image as a function and seeks the rate of change in its values as small changes are made in position within

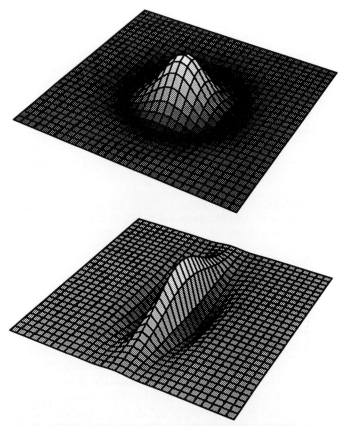

Figure 9. Second derivatives: directional and isotropic. The two panels show the second derivatives for a two-dimensional Gaussian intensity profile. The bottom panel shows a directional second derivative, and the top panel shows the Laplacian.

the coordinate space of the image (i.e. x and y). It is also possible to treat the image as a surface and to calculate the surface orientation and changes in the surface orientation as small changes are made to position on the surface. The image surface has surface normals, one at each point on the surface, and these are constrained to lie within a hemisphere. Each surface normal has a slant and a tilt, which are measures of the steepness of the surface and the direction in which it is rising, respectively. At each point on the surface, there are two principal curvatures, from which a mean curvature and a Gaussian curvature can be calculated. Because the image surface is constrained so that all surface normals must not point downwards, these surface curvature terms can be calculated from the derivatives with respect to x and y. For example, the Gaussian curvature of a point on an image surface is given by:

$$\frac{\dfrac{\mathrm{d}^2 I}{\mathrm{d}x^2}\dfrac{\mathrm{d}^2 I}{\mathrm{d}y^2} + \dfrac{\mathrm{d}^2 I}{\mathrm{d}x\,\mathrm{d}y}}{\left(1 + \left(\dfrac{\mathrm{d}I}{\mathrm{d}x}\right)^2 + \left(\dfrac{\mathrm{d}I}{\mathrm{d}y}\right)^2\right)^2}$$

The symmetry of this expression, so that x and y are completely inter-changeable, indicates that it is isotropic, as would be expected.

The Consequences of Differentiating Images

The first and most striking change caused by differentiating an image is a change in the range of values of the function. An optical image may have any values from zero upwards. The actual range of values in an image is not a very useful statistical description of the image. The range will depend on the type of illumination: direct sun, shaded sunlight, dark cloud, and so on. The range and distribution of luminance values in a real image are more

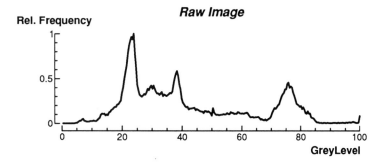

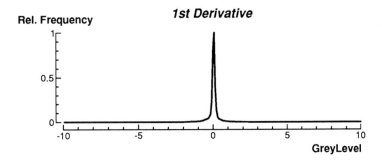

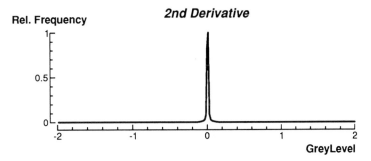

Figure 10. Grey-level histograms for an image and its derivatives. Typical histograms for an image, and its first and second derivatives are shown.

or less unconstrained from zero upwards. The second derivative of an image has a much more constrained range of values. These will on average be zero, and will also be distributed symmetrically about zero. Small values are more likely than large values.

Since larger values are less common, statistically, than small values, it follows that the magnitude of a value is a measure of the interest manifest in a particular place in the image. If a value is at or near to zero, then it is likely that nothing interesting is to be found at the corresponding point in the scene. If a value is not zero, then something useful has probably been identified. The reason for this result is that only smooth homogeneous surfaces can give rise to smooth luminance patterns and, of course, smooth surfaces are not usually interesting, except at their edges where luminance changes. Second derivatives do not give large values for smoothly varying functions.

The mean value of a second derivative is nearly zero, but the standard deviation of the values will depend on how much luminance change there is in the image. A smooth part of an image such as the sky will have a low standard deviation of values, whereas a region that is rich in detail such as a tree will have a high standard deviation. In this way we can have a measure of the richness or complexity of an image area.

The top row of Fig. 11 shows two one-dimensional functions. On the left is a function which only has two values: left of centre it has the value of zero; right of centre it has the value one. This is called a step function, and it could represent a sudden change in luminance, for example. On the right is another function which only has two values: it is everywhere zero, except for just one point in the centre where it is one in value. This is called an impulse function.

What happens when these two functions are differentiated? The second row of the figure shows the results. The step function becomes an impulse function and the impulse function becomes a function with two impulses, side by side, but with opposite signs. The third row of the figure shows the second derivative in each case. Notice that the second derivative of the step function is the same as the first derivative of the impulse function. Let us write the step function as

$$I_1(x)$$

and the impulse function as

$$I_0(x)$$

We have seen that

$$\frac{\mathrm{d}I_{-1}(x)}{\mathrm{d}x} = I_0(x)$$

Let us use the subscript in these expressions as a count of the number of differentiations, so that

$$I_{i+1}(x) \Leftrightarrow \frac{\mathrm{d}I_i(x)}{\mathrm{d}x} \qquad \text{for any } i$$

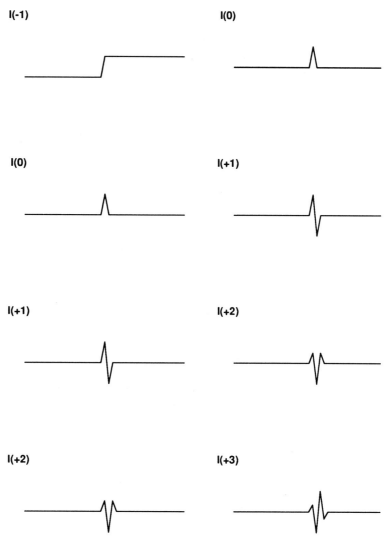

Figure 11. Symmetry and differentiation. A symmetric and an antisymmetric function, and several of their derivatives. Notice how the symmetry changes sense with each differentiation.

Look at all the functions with an odd subscript on the figure. These are all said to have odd symmetry: they can be made symmetric about their centres if the left side is turned upside down. This can be achieved algebraically by changing the sign of all the values on the left, and the odd symmetry can be expressed by

$$f(x) = -f(-x)$$

This expression says that the value of the function at position $+x$, which is right of centre, is equal to the value at position $-x$, which is the same distance left of centre, when that value is multiplied by -1. All the functions on the figure with even subscripts are even-symmetric, which is expressed by the relationship

$$f(x) = f(-x)$$

The value of a point at distance x away from the centre is the same as the value of the point at the same distance but in the opposite direction.

Each time we differentiate the functions in Fig. 11, we change the symmetry from odd to even or back again. This means that if we take the second derivative of a symmetric function, we do not change its symmetry.

Luminance Change and Surface Shape

In Chapter 3 we saw how some types of luminance pattern are more likely than others because they arise under general illumination of surfaces of certain types. What is the effect of differentiation on these prototypical luminance changes?

We can start by thinking in just one dimension and take four common types of luminance profile. These are shown in Fig. 12, and they are: (i) an abrupt change or discontinuity in luminance, such as might be found at a crease; (ii) a smooth change in luminance, such as might be found across a shadow; (iii) a sharp luminance valley, such as is often found where a surface becomes tangential to a line of sight and illumination (the occluding contour on a smoothly curved surface); and (iv) a luminance ridge, as at a specular highlight. Beside these on the figure are shown the first and then the second derivatives of each.

Notice how the second derivatives tend to be near zero over most of the extent in each case. The abrupt change in luminance causes a very narrow peak in the first derivative, and a narrow peak plus a narrow trough in the second derivative. The more gradual change in luminance behaves in the same fashion, but the peaks and troughs are broader and lower. Both the luminance trough and luminance peak become changes of level in the first derivative and a single peak or trough in the second derivative. Because these various derivatives are qualitatively different for the different types of luminance change, it is possible to examine an image and its derivatives to discover what types of luminance change it contains. If we take an image and search its second derivative for places where it is significantly different from zero, then we will find most of the occluding contours, creases, shadows, etc.

The Laplacian in two dimensions provides a useful extension to the peaks/troughs result. Take the case of a luminance step change. In one dimension across this step change the second derivative has a peak and a trough. In two dimensions, the Laplacian produces a continuous ridge and a continuous valley which follow along either side of the occluding contour. The height of the ridge and the depth of the valley depend on the luminance difference, and also on the curvature of the occluding contour. In particular, if there is a sharp turn or corner on the occluding contour, the ridge will rise to a discrete summit, and the valley will fall to a discrete pit. The same is true where two or more contours meet, that is at contour intersections and also at the end of a contour.

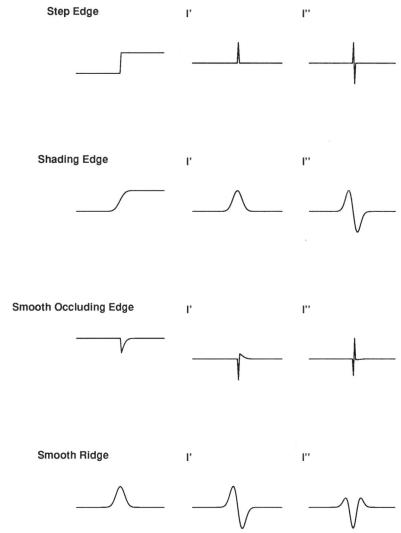

Figure 12. Four basic luminance profiles. The left column shows the basic luminance profiles. To the right of each are its first and then its second derivative.

(ii) Local Statistics

Recall the standard luminance waveforms in Fig. 12. These are abstractions. Except in carefully prepared environments images will not be found to be so regular. It is only man-made surfaces that are untextured or are covered with, for example, precisely parallel and equally spaced lines. More surfaces in the environment exhibit local variations in surface reflectance (markings) and in surface orientation (engravings). Most surfaces have a characteristic texture, so that different surfaces in a scene will tend to have different textures. The statistical structure of such surface texture does not itself usually vary rapidly over a surface, and the consequence is an image that

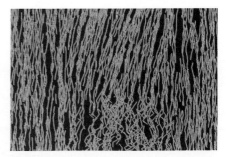

Figure 13. Images with texture. Two different types of texture are shown: a simple random noise image and an image made from oriented lines. In each case there are two different regions: one with a different mean from the background and one with a different variance.

is usually irregular but in a stable manner. Textured surfaces result in an image with locally varying grey levels superimposed on underlying trends that correspond to the idealized waveforms and we need a technique for revealing these stable local statistics in the intensity patterns and their trends.

Local Means

Let us start with a relatively common and simple case of two adjacent patches of a surface, each textured. The two have different mean luminances, but have ranges of luminance values that overlap. The value of the derivative at the junction may be smaller than at many places within each patch. Since the two mean luminances are defined to be different we just need to replace the luminance at each point in the image by the local mean luminance and then look for the places where this is changing fairly rapidly.

A mean of a set of n samples is defined by the formula:

$$\frac{1}{n} \sum_{i=1}^{n} (I_i) \equiv I_1 + I_2 + \cdots + I_i + \cdots + I_n$$

The symbol $\sum$ means the sum of the values specified. Another way of writing this that will be more useful is to replace the $1/n$ by a summation of the constant 1 (one):

$$\frac{\sum_{i=1}^{n} (I_i)}{\sum_{i=1}^{n} (1)}$$

The local mean of an image is similarly defined, except that we have to use a different way to specify the domain, the part of the image, over which the summation should occur. To do this we use integral signs rather than summation signs, because we are discussing areas rather than sets of samples. Let us start at a place in the image, (x, y). The neighbourhood of this point is specified by a function, $n(x, y, \sigma)$, which has as parameters the location of the point itself, and a scaling term, σ, which is used to set the

Signal

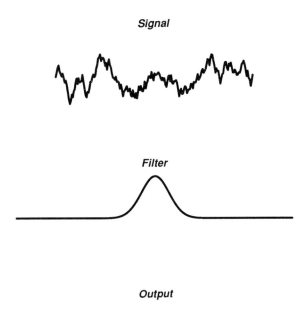

Filter

Output

Figure 14. The calculation of a local mean. This figure shows a typical slice through an image. Beneath this is a neighbourhood for calculating the local mean. The value of the local mean is placed in the output function, as can be seen.

size of the neighbourhood. Then we integrate for all values of (x, y) that lie within the neighbourhood:

$$\frac{\int^{n(x,y,\sigma)} I(x,y)\mathrm{d}(x,y)}{\int^{n(x,y,\sigma)} 1\,\mathrm{d}(x,y)}$$

The top part of this says that the function $I(x,y)$ is to be integrated $\int$ over all values of (x,y) that lie in the neighbourhood $n(x,y,\sigma)$.

Local Variances
Another possible difference between two adjacent textures could be in the variability of the values rather than in their local mean luminances. Under these circumstances, smoothing by taking local averages will not reveal the border between the two textures, although it may suppress both textures. An obvious alternative, once again by definition, is to assess the local variability. This is in many respects quite analogous to using the local mean. If I_i is one of a set of n values, then the variance of the set is given by

$$\frac{1}{n}\left[\sum_{i=1}^{n} (I_i)^2 - \frac{1}{n}\left(\sum_{i=1}^{n} I_i\right)^2\right] \equiv \frac{1}{n}\sum_{i=1}^{n} (I_{\mathrm{mean}} - I_i)^2$$

Notice that the two terms in this expression have the same ingredients, but in a different order. For the first term, the individual values are squared and then summed. For the second term, the values are summed and then squared. We can write the equivalent integration for an image as before:

$$\frac{\int^{n(x,y,\sigma)} (I(x,y))^2 \, d(x,y) - \dfrac{\left(\int^{n(x,y,\sigma)} I(x,y) \, d(x,y)\right)^2}{\int^{n(x,y,\sigma)} 1 \, d(x,y)}}{\int^{n(x,y,\sigma)} 1 \, d(x,y)}$$

Other Local Statistics

The mean and variance that I have described are representatives of a particular class of statistics. The mean, for example, is the value that causes the expression

$$\frac{1}{n} \sum_{i=1}^{n} (I_{\text{mean}} - I_i)^2$$

to be at its minimum value. In other words, the mean is the value which minimizes the sum of the squared deviations about itself. There is a more basic relative of this, the median, which only assumes that the order of the samples can be relied on, not their actual values. This is found by finding that value which has equal numbers of values greater and less than itself.

The mean and the median are estimates of the most typical single value for the whole population. This assumes that the population is stationary over the neighbourhood, that there are no trends in the values. It is equally possible to assume that the statistics are continuously changing according to some formula, and then to find a version of the formula that minimizes the sum of squared deviations from itself. For example, it is possible to find a flat surface that best fits the values in a neighbourhood. Whereas the mean has only one parameter, the value itself, a flat surface will have several parameters to define how high above zero it lies and what its orientation is.

Spatial Scale and Precision

The expressions for local mean and variance both have a spatial scaling term, σ. This important parameter can be thought of as a scale that is applied to all distances, shrinking them or expanding them, thereby changing the extent of the neighbourhood. Changing the scale has two consequences: it changes the number of samples that are used to calculate the local statistic, and it changes the area from which they are drawn.

When we apply a formula for calculating a local statisic, we are effectively forming an estimate of its most likely value from a set of samples of the population. The precision with which a local statistic is estimated is always likely to be some positive function of the number of samples. Therefore, the greater the scaling term, the greater the number of samples and the more precise the estimate. However, increasing the size of the neighbourhood also increases the number of places in the image where it will encompass two or more different populations, thereby blurring the distinction between different regions in the image. These two opposing effects of the scale factor are always a problem, and it is necessary to achieve a balance.

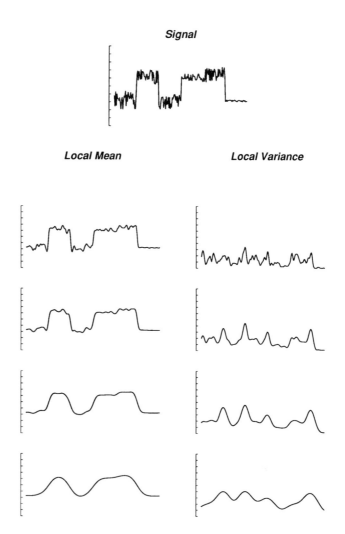

Figure 15. The effects of scale. A slice through an image is shown which contains several different regions all of different means and variances. Beneath is shown the effects of different scales on the outputs of a local mean operator and a local variance operator.

Weighted Neighbourhoods

In general, the greater the distance between two points in an image, the less likely it is that they derive from the same physical cause. This means that the further apart two points are, the lower the degree of correlation between their values. In computing local statistics, this means in turn that the further a point is from the centre of a neighbourhood, the less likely it is to belong to the same distribution of grey levels. In order to take this into account, it is usual to employ a *weighting function* which gives greater weight to central points than to the peripheral points in a neighbourhood. If we write the weighting function as $w(x, y, \sigma)$, a function of the point (x, y)

that we are considering and a scaling term, σ, then the local mean becomes

$$\frac{\int^{n(x, y, \sigma)} (I(x, y) \times w(x, y, \sigma))\, \mathrm{d}(x, y)}{\int^{n(x, y, \sigma)} w(x, y, \sigma)\, \mathrm{d}(x, y)}$$

The form of the weighting function has a strong effect on the manner in which texture is transformed. This is illustrated in Fig. 16 which shows the effect of several different weighting functions on a simple luminance pattern with three points of light. The functions are a rectangle, a triangle, a semicircle and a Gaussian, and each is shown at three different scales (or degrees of dispersion). Notice that all three fill in the gaps between the bars even at fairly modest scales. However, what happens at larger scales is quite different in the three cases. The Gaussian smooths out the pattern until all that is left of the structure is a function that looks rather like another Gaussian. The rectangle always has ten abrupt changes in value (except when they coincidentally align), irrespective of the scale. The semicircle has ten abrupt changes in the slope of the resultant function, also irrespective of the degree of dispersion. Each weighting function represents a form of local averaging of the image. The result in each case has a *structure* which is different in its layout and complexity. The Gaussian has the property of smoothing the image, whereas the other three do not. This is because the Gaussian is the only one of the examples which is itself smooth.

Spikes

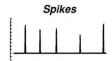

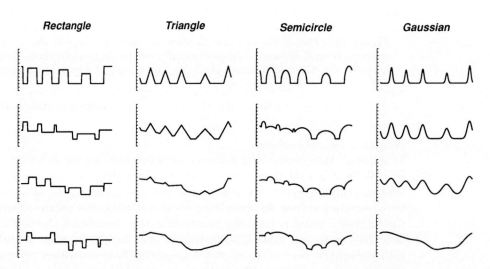

Figure 16. Different weighting functions at different scales have different effects on the resultant local mean image.

(iii) Smoothing

Under what conditions will the calculation of a local statistic obliterate a texture? We have already seen that a smooth weighting function like a Gaussian is a necessary condition. We have also seen that the size of the Gaussian must be greater than some particular value that is determined by the distance between texture elements. Notice that the important factor here is the mean distance between the centres of adjacent texture elements. This is because of the requirement of luminance symmetry in the situation. The texture is simultaneously a set of dark markings on a light ground and a set of light markings on a dark ground. Since the smoothed image can be considered to have been obtained by smoothing either light or dark elements, the necessary distance of smoothing must be the same in each case and therefore must be related to the spacing of the elements. This spacing may not be the same in all directions, and so the smoothing can be different in different directions: it can be *anisotropic*. An anisotropic pattern can also result when a texture has elements that at not oriented randomly. A plank of wood has a grain that is not oriented randomly and will require dispersion over different distances in different directions.

The scale, or distance of spatial extent of dispersion, is an important parameter. No matter what form the dispersion function takes, its spatial scale can be expressed by its spatial standard deviation. This is convenient because the standard deviation is a linear measure of size, so that if we stretch a function out to twice its original size, its standard deviation also doubles.

The Consequences of Smoothing Images

The smoothing of an image reveals the underlying trends in the values that may otherwise remain obscured by local fluctuations. Consequently one effect of smoothing an image is to restrict the range of values that it contains. Another closely related effect is to reduce the range of gradients in an image. In other words, the range of values in the derivative of an image is also reduced by smoothing.

The effect on texture patterns is of a considerable attenuation in amplitude. It is normal for the elements of a texture pattern to be smaller than the surface that they adorn and as a consequence it is often feasible both to attenuate the texture fluctuations and to reveal borders between different textures.

4.4 Convolution and Filtering

The two processes of differentiation and smoothing can both be performed by an operation known as convolution. Convolution is a process that takes two functions, such as images, and creates from them a third. Suppose that we identify one of the images as a *filter*, and treat the other as the input to the filter. We can take any one place in the input image and put a version of the filter function into the output image, centred at this place and scaled

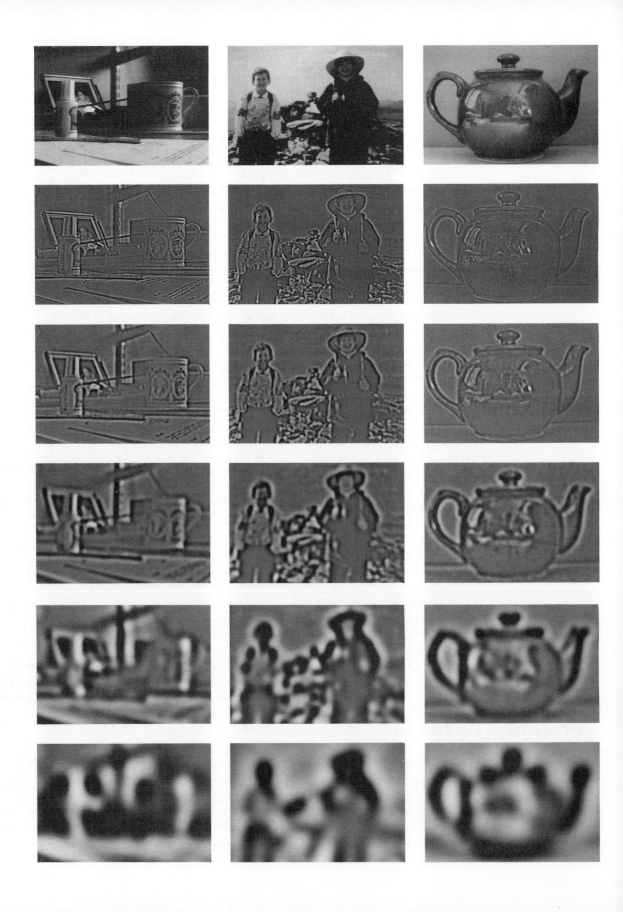

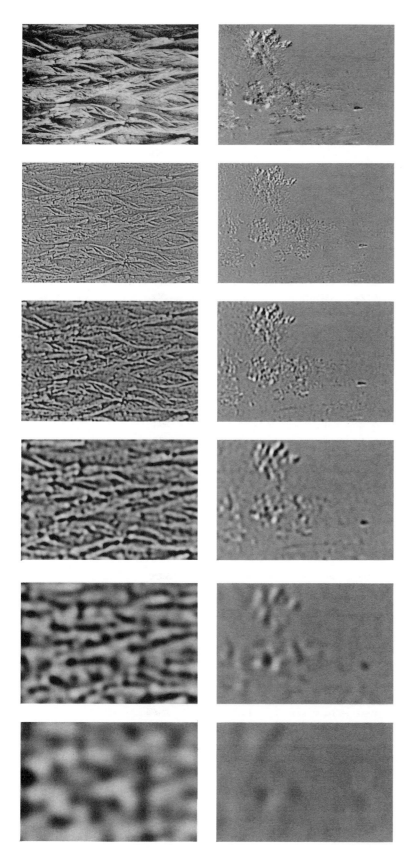

Figure 17. Filtered images. This figure shows a variety of different images and the result of applying Laplacian of Gaussian filters of various different spatial scales (in steps of factors of 2).

in amplitude to the value of the input at this point. If we do this for all points in the input image, then the result is a number of overlapping copies of the filter function. These are simply added together to create the output image.

The value at any one point in the output is obtained from a number of superimposed copies of the filter function. In fact the value at any point in the output has a contribution from every point in the filter function. The result is exactly the same as if we were to take a point in the input image, shift the filter function to be centred at this point, flip it over the x and the y directions, then multiply it by the input image and finally sum the result. The operation is exactly the same as calculating a weighted local mean, where the weighting function is provided by the filter function.

Convolution is symmetric in the sense that it does not matter which of the two inputs we call the filter, the result is the same. Convolution behaves just like many other arithmetic operators, so if we are convolving an input image with a filter function to do differentiation and then with a filter function to do smoothing, it is possible to combine them together in one single step and concolve the image with a filter that is the second derivative of the smoothing function.

In principle, any filter function can be used; in practice there are only a few different general types that have any real utility.

Types of Filters
The introduction of differentiation and of smoothing leads naturally to the *Laplacian of a Gaussian* (LoG, $\nabla^2 G$—pronounced del squared G) filter. There are others commonly in use in vision, and I now give a brief description of the most common.

The *difference of Gaussians* (DoG) filter is a filter that is made by combining two Gaussian functions, one positive and the other negative. Generally they are centred at the same place but have different spatial spreads or standard deviations. If the area of each Gaussian is the same (volume for two-dimensional filters) so that the narrower filter is larger in amplitude, then the filter is balanced. This filter can also be considered to be the second derivative of a function that looks rather like a Gaussian.

The *difference of boxes* (DoB) filter is constructed along the same lines as the DoG filter, but with two regular functions. Its use in vision is limited.

The *Canny operator*, named after its inventor, is a first derivative spatial filter that was designed to meet a particular optimum balance between sensitivity to weak edges and precision in localizing the edges. It is a first derivative because it has odd symmetry.

Gabor filters are a class of filter which may be either odd- or even-symmetric. They may have one, two, three, four, and larger numbers of modes (peaks and troughs). Gabor filters are obtained by multiplying generally either a sine wave (odd symmetry; even number of modes) or a cosine wave (even symmetry; odd number of modes) with a Gaussian function. They are named after Gabor, who showed that they represent a compromise between being restricted in spatial extent and restricted in spatial frequency extent. For coding signals such a compromise is sometimes useful.

The Consequences of Filtering

Filtering with a filter that has no fine detail, that is coarse in its spatial scale, will result in an image that also lacks in fine detail. If we take a range of filters that are all similar except for their spatial scale, then we can obtain a set of related images, all derived from one original but differing in their spatial scale. The structure and information that is present in these has relationships that are due to the changing spatial scale. Fine detail can be seen to be superimposed on, or nested inside the coarser structure.

4.5 Global Operations

Convolution can be a global operation or it can be a local operation, depending on the extent of the filter function. I shall now turn to describe three types of global function. These are all related to the operation of convolution. The global operations rarely have any real use on an image that contains more than one thing because they are global, effectively mixing up all the different parts of an image. They are generally used when an image is thought to be formed from just one surface or simple shape. They do not warrant a great deal of description.

(i) Auto-correlation

A mirror symmetric image is one that is identical to a version of itself that has been reflected about some axis. A rotationally symmetric image is identical to a rotated version of itself. Suppose that we have an image that is all either at the value of 1 or at -1 and in which each value is equally frequent. How can we assess if it is mirror symmetric about a particular axis? We can take the image, create a reflected version, and compare the two. A simple and effective way of comparing the two is to multiply them together, point by point. If two corresponding points have a product that is positive, then they are the same. The degree of symmetry can then be measured by summing all the values of the product image. For perfect symmetry, it should have a positive value equal to the number of points in the image: it should have a mean value of 1. If the image is not mirror symmetric about the axis in question, then the product will have a mean value around 0. If the image is mirror antisymmetric, so that all the values are inverted on one side of the axis, then the product will have a mean value of -1. The results of multiplying two images together, summing all the values, and dividing by the number of values is called a correlation product. The values that it takes depend on the range of values in the image. For general images with many different grey levels, the correlation product will have a value that ranges from minus the mean value of the squared image (for perfect antisymmetry) through the square of the mean value (for no symmetry) to the mean value of the squared image (for perfect symmetry).

There are many different axes for mirror symmetry through an image. Each is a straight line and so has two parameters. We can take these two parameters as being the x and y points at which it crosses, respectively, the $(y = 0)$ line and the $(x = 0)$ line in the image. Thus for each (x, y) pair of parameters we can calculate the correlation product, and in this way build up a new two-dimensional function, a new image. In producing this new image we have evaluated the correlation product from an image and a particular transformation, reflection about an axis, for all possible variants of the transformation. There are many different transformations that can be applied to an image, such as rotation and translation. For each of these we could also produce an image that records the correlation product, as a function of the parameters of the transformation. This process is known as generalized auto-correlation. Simple auto-correlation is the case where the transformation is translation.

(ii) Cross-correlation

Closely related to auto-correlation is cross-correlation. The difference is that a transformed version of an image is compared, not with itself, but with some other image. Cross-correlation assesses the extent to which two images are the same, subject to an arbitrary value of some transformation.

The process of shifting an image, multiplying it with another and then summing the results is very similar to the steps in convolving two images, the only difference being that in the latter case, the image is also reflected.

(iii) Fourier Transform

It is a standard result of mathematics that any one-dimensional periodic signal or function can be constructed from a set of cosine waves of varying amplitudes and phases. There is a simple extension to two dimensions, although the image or function must be periodic in two orthogonal directions, and then it can be constructed from a set of cosine waves of varying frequencies, amplitudes, phases and orientations. In practice, it is often possible to take an image and suppose that it is one cell of a checkerboard arrangement of identical cells, thereby being part of a periodic two-dimensional function. The result can be constructed from a set of cosine waves of particular frequencies, amplitudes, phases and orientations, which means that it can be transformed into such a set. This is done by the Fourier transform.

Consider an image, in which the position of every point corresponds to the frequency and orientation of a different cosine wave and the value at every point corresponds to the amplitude and phase. The position of each point can be described by a distance from the origin (corresponding to the frequency) and a direction from the origin (corresponding to the orientation). This new image will contain a complete set of frequency and orientation combinations. At each point a two-dimensional value is needed to record the amplitude and the phase. These two values can be obtained by cross-correlation with a cosine and a sine wave.

4.6 Summary: A Formalism of Image Algebra

This section sounds and looks a bit tougher than the preceding sections. It repays some attention however, because it shows how one goes about defining in logical structures the types of process that we have been discussing.

We start with a few elemental definitions from which we can build more complex statements. I shall be using a number of typographical conventions that are listed below:

an *Image* is written with an initial capital

a *single* value is written in lower case.

Images and values may be scalars or vectors with more than one component:

a ***vector*** is printed in bold typeface

a *scalar* is printed in ordinary typeface.

The components of a vector are written as a list of (usually) scalars, separated by commas. We can define some standard images:

Zero: an image which is zero everywhere

Unit: an image which has the value of unity everywhere

Position: an image which has at each point the value of **location**$(\mathbf{x}, \mathbf{y})$.

Now we define the following standard functions:

Constant(k) an image where every point has the value k

Point($\mathbf{x}, \mathbf{y}$; k) a Zero image except that at $\mathbf{x}, \mathbf{y}$ it has the value k.

Notice that these are variable images which depend on the parameter k (a scalar in this case).

Next we can define a function which returns a scalar value in place of an image:

value(*Image*; $\mathbf{x}, \mathbf{y}$) the scalar value of Image at **location**$(\mathbf{x}, \mathbf{y})$.

(i) Basic Algebra

A function is a mathematical operation that takes one or more input values and produces one output value. A function can be defined by a record that lists explicitly the output value to give in response to each or any expected input value or input values. In this sense, an image is a function. It is a record of the value (luminance for an optical image) to give in response to two input values which are an x coordinate and a y coordinate.

$$l = \text{image}(x, y)$$

We use a lower case initial letter here, because the output of the function is a single value.

We can define some basic algebraic functions on images, vectors and scalars. Taking a *logarithm* is a *unary function*; in scalar arithmetic it looks like:

$$x' = \log(x)$$

It takes one input value, x, and produces one output value, x'. There are vector and image equivalents:

$$\mathbf{a}' = \mathbf{log(a)}$$

$$\text{Image}' = \text{Log}(\text{Image})$$

This expression says that there is an image function *Image'* which can be obtained from the image function *Image*, by taking its output and using that as input to the function Log. If this is applied to every point in *Image*, then we will have a full specification of the image *Image'*.

Addition is a *binary function*, which takes two input values, x_1 and x_2, and adds them together to give one output value:

$$c = \text{add}(a; b)$$

Vector addition is similar:

$$\mathbf{c_x, c_y = add(a_x, a_y; b_x, b_y)}$$

where

$$c_x = \text{add}(a_x; b_x)$$

and

$$c_y = \text{add}(a_y; b_y)$$

Just as we can add two numbers to give a single output, so we can add a scalar k to every point in an image, *Data*, to obtain a new image as output:

$$\text{Result} = \text{Add}(\text{Data}; \text{Constant}(k))$$

We can add two images to give a single image as output. We take the value of each input image at a particular place, (x, y), and add the two values together to give the number for the output image at that place:

$$\text{Image}_c = \text{Add}(\text{Image}_a; \text{Image}_b)$$

When this has been done for all expected places then we have completely calculated the output image. The value at any point in Image$_c$ is the sum of the two values at the same point in Image$_a$ and Image$_b$. Similar operations for subtraction, multiplication and division can easily be written down. It is generally more convenient to adopt a relatively ambiguous shorthand and to write:

$$c = a + b$$

$$\mathbf{c = a + b}$$

$$\text{Result} = \text{Data} + 2$$

$$\text{Image}_c = \text{Image}_a + \text{Image}_b$$

This operator notation has the benefit of not looking strange; from a purist's point of view, it has the great disadvantage of not making explicit the sequence in which the functions should be carried out. Compare these two:

$$I' = \text{Image}_1 + \text{Image}_2 \times \text{Image}_3$$

$$I' = \text{Add}(\text{Image}_1, \text{Multiply}(\text{Image}_2, \text{Image}_3))$$

The latter makes the order of operations explicit; the former requires the conventions of operator precedence to make it clear that the intention is not:

$$I' = \text{Multiply}(\text{Add}(\text{Image}_1, \text{Image}_2), \text{Image}_3)$$

We need to build one more function on an image, to shift the image through a displacement vector. Recall that the value of an image at a point is given by *value* (*Image*; $\mathbf{x}, \mathbf{y}$). We can put this in another image, at a different point using:

$$\text{Point } (\mathbf{x} + \mathbf{dx}, \mathbf{y} + \mathbf{dy}; \text{value } (\text{Image}; \mathbf{x}, \mathbf{y}))$$

Then, to shift an image through a constant displacement $\mathbf{dx}, \mathbf{dy}$, we just repeat this for all values of $\mathbf{x}, \mathbf{y}$:

$$\text{Shift}(\text{Image}; \mathbf{dx}, \mathbf{dy}) \Leftrightarrow \sum_{\mathbf{x}, \mathbf{y}} \text{Point}(\mathbf{x} + \mathbf{dx}, \mathbf{y} + \mathbf{dy}; \text{value}(\text{Image}; \mathbf{x}, \mathbf{y}))$$

We can use summation because Point is zero everywhere except at its vector parameter. For two-dimensional images there is a similar rotate function.

(ii) Integration and Summation

We can define a very useful function which takes an image and adds up all the values in the image to give a scalar value. The integral of an image function takes the whole image as input and gives a single value as output:

$$\text{sum} = \text{integral}(\text{Image})$$

There is a special algebraic symbol for the integral function:

$$\int \text{Image} \Leftrightarrow \text{integral}(\text{Image})$$

Notice that we do not specify one place in *Image*; integral works on it all. There is a closely analogous function which is more appropriate when we are dealing with sampled images:

$$\text{sum}(\text{Image}) \Leftrightarrow \sum_{\mathbf{x}, \mathbf{y}} (\text{value}(\text{Image}; \mathbf{x}, \mathbf{y}))$$

This is cumbersome to write, and I shall adopt the typographical convention that an expression where the argument is missing is taken to be available over all possible values for that argument. We can then write:

$$\text{sum}(\text{Image}) \Leftrightarrow \sum (\text{value}(\text{Image}))$$

to mean the sum of all the values in the image. The symbol $\Leftrightarrow$ just means that each side implies the other.

The mean value of an image is given by the ratio of two sums:

$$\text{mean}(\text{Image}) \Leftrightarrow \frac{\text{sum}(\text{Image})}{\text{sum}(\text{Unit})}$$

Note that *sum(Unit)* is not 1; it is the size (area) of the images we are using. We can also write:

$$\text{mean}(\text{Image}) \Leftrightarrow \text{sum}\left(\frac{\text{Image}}{\text{sum}(\text{Unit})}\right)$$

where each point in Image is divided by sum(Unit), but on a computer this would mean many, many more divide operations.

The standard deviation of the values in an image is given by:

$$\text{sd}(\text{Image}) \Leftrightarrow \text{mean}((\text{Image} - \text{mean}(\text{Image}))^2)^{1/2}$$

A better, more general expression for the (weighted) mean value of an image is:

$$\text{mean}(\text{Image}; \text{Weight}) \Leftrightarrow \frac{\text{sum}(\text{Image} \times \text{Weight})}{\text{sum}(\text{Weight})}$$

(iv) Differentiation

The technique of differentiation is used to analyse how functions such as images change. Suppose that we start with a simple one-dimensional function, just a function that specifies a value of y, if you specify a value for x. Differentiation of this function is a technique for finding out how much the value of y is increased if x is increased by a very small amount. Suppose that the value of y at a particular point, x_1, is y_1, and that a point x_2 just a little greater than x_1, the value is y_2. Then differentiation is equivalent to measuring

$$\frac{y_2 - y_1}{x_2 - x_1}$$

When the difference between x_2 and x_1 is infinitesimally small, this is called the first derivative. It is a new function which specifies the amount of change in y at each point for a fixed small change in x. The two changes are written as $\mathrm{d}y$ and $\mathrm{d}x$, respectively, and the first derivative is then:

$$\frac{\mathrm{d}y}{\mathrm{d}x}$$

This function specifies the slope of the original function at every x value. We can differentiate this new function again to obtain the second derivative and so on. If we write a function D equivalent to the first derivative

$$D(y) \Leftrightarrow \frac{dy}{dx}$$

we can then write the derivative of D as

$$\frac{dD(y)}{dx}$$

which is the same as

$$\frac{d(dy)}{dx(dx)}$$

It is conventional to write this second derivative as

$$\frac{d^2y}{dx^2}$$

or as

$$D^2(y)$$

Differentiation of two-dimensional functions like images is very much the same, except that it is done separately in each dimension. So, for example the second derivative of an image, I, in the x direction is written as

$$\frac{d^2I}{dx^2}$$

and in the y direction as

$$\frac{d^2I}{dy^2}$$

It is convenient to add these two new functions together so that we have a new function which is the second derivative of the image in any direction, not just x or y. This operation is called the Laplacian of the image, and is given the special symbol ∇^2:

$$\nabla^2 I = \frac{d^2I}{dx^2} + \frac{d^2I}{dy^2}$$

This Laplacian or second derivative in two dimensions is a useful one for vision because it is not directional, it is said to be isotropic. It is not possible to create a simple, isotropic first derivative function.

A simple first derivative in the direction $\mathbf{dx}, \mathbf{dy}$ can be written down:

Differentiate(Image; $\mathbf{dx}, \mathbf{dy}$) $\Leftrightarrow$ Image $-$ Shift (Image; $\mathbf{dx}, \mathbf{dy}$)

The second derivative in that direction is then

Differentiate(Differentiate(Image; $\mathbf{dx}, \mathbf{dy}$); $\mathbf{dx}, \mathbf{dy}$)

or

Differentiate^2(Image; $\mathbf{dx}, \mathbf{dy}$)

Differentiation of Sampled Functions

Differentiation has been defined as an operation which acts on continuous functions. If we treat a sampled image function in this way, then each sample will be replaced by the derivative of a sample. This is not what we want: what we want is a set of samples of the derivative of the image function. The two operations of sampling and differentiating cannot be performed in any order. This means that if we have a sampled image function we cannot obtain its derivative in the normal way. We do better to treat the sampled function as an ordered set of values, and introduce the operation of discrete differentiation.

There are several ways in which this can be done. The simplest is to replace the value of point i by the difference between it and the value at point $i - 1$:

$$\frac{\mathrm{d}z_i}{\mathrm{d}i} = z_i - z_{i-1}$$

An improvement on this would be to divide the difference by the distance s_i between the two points:

$$\frac{\mathrm{d}z_i}{\mathrm{d}i} = \frac{z_i - z_{i-1}}{s_i}$$

Strictly speaking this is the derivative at a point midway between points i and $i - 1$. There is another similar derivative:

$$\frac{\mathrm{d}z_i}{\mathrm{d}i} = \frac{z_{i+1} - z_i}{s_{i+1}}$$

which is the derivate midway between points i and $i + 1$. A closer approximation to the derivative at i could then be obtained by taking the mean of these two:

$$\frac{\mathrm{d}z_i}{\mathrm{d}i} = \frac{1}{2}\left(\frac{z_i - z_{i-1}}{s_i} + \frac{z_{i+1} - z_i}{s_{i+1}}\right)$$

$$= \frac{z_{i+1} - z_{i-1}}{2s_i}$$

If we are interested in taking the second derivative a good estimate is obtained by:

$$\frac{\mathrm{d}^2 z_i}{\mathrm{d}i^2} = \frac{1}{2s_i}\left(\frac{\mathrm{d}z_{i+1}}{\mathrm{d}i} - \frac{\mathrm{d}z_{i-1}}{\mathrm{d}i}\right)$$

$$\frac{\mathrm{d}^2 z_i}{\mathrm{d}i^2} = \frac{1}{2}\left(\frac{z_{i+1} - z_i}{s_i} - \frac{z_i - z_{i-1}}{s_i}\right)$$

$$= \frac{1}{2}\left(\frac{z_{i+1} - 2z_i + z_{i-1}}{s_i}\right)$$

(v) Convolution and Smoothing

In differentiating an image function we take the value at a particular point and subtract from this the value a small distance away:

$$I' = \text{Image}_1(x) - \text{Image}_1(x + \partial x)$$

Another way of specifying this is to say that we obtain the derivative by taking the value at a particular point and multiplying it by $+1$; taking the value at a point a small distance away and multiplying it by -1; then we add the two together:

$$I' = \text{add}(\text{Image}_1(x) \times 1; \text{Image}_1(x + \partial x) \times (-1))$$

We can go one step further and say that we multiply all other values of the image by 0, and then instead of adding two values we integrate the whole image.

Let us define an image function *Mask*, which is set to zero everywhere except at position 0 where it is set to value 1, and at position $0 + \partial x$, where it is set to value -1. We can now find the derivative of any other image function at a point $\mathbf{x}, \mathbf{y}$ like this:

We first shift the *Mask* function by an amount $\mathbf{x}, \mathbf{y}$:

$$\text{Mask}' = \text{Shift}(\text{Mask}; \mathbf{x}, \mathbf{y})$$

This means that the value 1 in *Mask'* is aligned with the place in *Image* that we are interested in. Now we multiply *Image* by *Mask'*:

$$\text{Image}' = \text{Image} \times \text{Mask}'$$

Finally, we can integrate *Image'* to give us the derivative of *Image* at the point $\mathbf{x}, \mathbf{y}$:

$$\int \text{Image}'$$

To summarize:

$$\text{value}(\text{Differentiate}(\text{Image}); \mathbf{x}, \mathbf{y}) \Leftrightarrow \int \text{Image} \times \text{Shift}(\text{Mask}; \mathbf{x}, \mathbf{y})$$

So that

$$\text{Differentiate}(\text{Image}) \Leftrightarrow \sum_{(\mathbf{x}, \mathbf{y})} (\text{Point}(\mathbf{x}, \mathbf{y}; \int (\text{Image} \times \text{Shift}(\text{Mask}; \mathbf{x}, \mathbf{y}))))$$

This summary shows that we can obtain the entire derivative by repeating the process for all values of $\mathbf{x}, \mathbf{y}$. I will now write the summary as a new operation, convolve:

$$\text{Convolve}(\text{Image}, \text{Mask}) \Leftrightarrow \int \text{Image} \times \text{Shift}(\text{Mask}; \mathbf{x}, \mathbf{y}) \qquad \text{for all } \mathbf{x}, \mathbf{y}$$

where *Image* and *Mask* can, in principle, be any two image functions. This new operation, convolve, is extremely useful. We can also express the convolution operation for sampled images in an analogous way:

Convolve(Image; Mask) ⇔
$$\sum_{(\mathbf{x},\mathbf{y})} (\text{Point}(\mathbf{x},\mathbf{y}; \text{sum}(\text{Image} \times \text{Shift}(\text{Mask}; \mathbf{x},\mathbf{y}))))$$

It is a long-winded way of doing a differentiation, but consider this next example.

Suppose that the mask function was zero everywhere except within the range of places between $-d/2$ and $+d/2$, where it was set to the value $1/d$. The output value at any particular place will correspond to the average value within a distance of $d/2$ from the same place in the input image function. This allows us to replace each value in an image with its local average.

Convolution is usually denoted by the symbol "$*$". It is a linear operation, which means that if

$$I'(a + b) = I(a + b) * D.$$

and

$$I(a + b) = I(a) + I(b)$$

then

$$I'(a + b) = I'(a) + I'(b)$$

and

$$I'(a + b) * D = I(a) * D + I(b) * D$$

Notice the similarity to multiplication: if we wish to convolve the sum of two image functions, we can either add the images and then do the convolution on the sum or we can convolve each image separately with the mask function and then add together the two transformed images that result. In mathematics, this behaviour is termed associative. If there are several subsequent convolutions to be performed on an image, then it does not matter what order they are done in:

$$I(a) * D_1 * D_2 = I(a) * D_2 * D_1$$

This is termed commutative behaviour.

Variances add under convolution. If a third function, D_3, is obtained by the convolution of two others, D_1 and D_2 which have standard deviations of σ_2 and σ_1:

$$D_3 = D_2 * D_1$$

then

$$\sigma_3^2 = \sigma_2^2 + \sigma_1^2$$

A good text for more information about convolution is Bracewell (1978), see Chapter 3.

(vi) Sampling

How can we describe sampling algebraically? We can replace an image by a new function which has the same value as the original image at one point only, every other value being zero. This is done by multiplying the image by a sampling function which is zero everywhere except for at the position that we wish to sample, where the sampling is set to one. When this multiplication is carried out the result is zero everywhere except for the place that has been sampled, which has the sample value of the image (multiplied by 1). We can then take the integral of this result over the entire area of the image to obtain a single value which is the sample value of the image. This sampling is done repeatedly all over the image to generate a set of sample values of the image.

$$\{ \quad \mathbf{P}_1 \quad \mathbf{P}_2 \quad \dots \mathbf{P}_i \dots \quad \mathbf{P}_n \quad \} \qquad \text{: set of sampling points}$$
$$\{ \quad z_1 \quad z_2 \quad \dots z_i \dots \quad z_n \quad \} \qquad \text{: set of sample values}$$
$$I \qquad \qquad \text{: the image}$$
$$\mathrm{Imp}(\mathbf{P}_i) \qquad \qquad \text{: an impulse at } (x_i, y_i)$$
$$S_i \qquad \qquad \text{: a sampling function}$$
$$S_i = \mathrm{Imp}(\mathbf{P}_i) \qquad \text{at } (\mathbf{P}_i)$$
$$S_i = 0 \qquad \text{elsewhere}$$

then

$$z_i = \int I \times S_i$$

It is worth noting in passing that we can replace the impulse function by any other function without changing the mathematics. For example, if we used a disc function which was one within a certain radius of $(\mathbf{P}_i)$ and zero beyond, then we would have a similar set of samples, but each would now reflect the local average value in the image taken over the radius of the disc. The disc function is an example of a weighting function:

$$S_i = 0 + \mathrm{Weight}\,(x_i, y_i)$$

When we sample an image, it is not our intention to generate just one value or a set of values because this does not contain any spatial information. Instead, we use two ordered sets, one for a set of sampling positions, and the other for the sample at these positions:

$$< \quad \mathbf{P}_1 \quad \mathbf{P}_2 \quad \dots \mathbf{P}_i \dots \quad \mathbf{P}_n \quad > \qquad \text{: list of sampling points}$$
$$< \quad z_1 \quad z_2 \quad \dots z_i \dots \quad z_n \quad > \qquad \text{: list of sample values}$$

in which case an association by index between the two will provide the spatial information.

References

Suggested further reading

Burt P.J. and Adelson E.H. (1983) The Laplacian pyramid as a compact image code. *IEEE Trans. Commun.* **COM-31**, 4, 532–540.

Buxton B.F. and Buxton H. (1983) Monocular depth perception from optical flow by space-time signal processing. *Proc. Roy. Soc. Lond.* **B218**, 27–47.

Canny J.F. (1986) A computational approach to edge detection. *IEEE Trans. Pattern Anal. Machine Intelligence* 8, 679–698.

Kalman R.E. (1960) A new approach to linear filtering and prediction problems. *J. Basic Eng.* **83**, 95–108.

Koenderink, J.J. and van Doorn A.J. (1988) Representation of local geometry in the visual system. *Biol. Cybern.* **55**, 367–375.

Koenderink, J.J. and Richards, W.A. (1988) Two-dimensional curvature operators. *J. Opt. Soc. Am.* **A5**, 1136–1141.

Marr D.C. and Hildreth E.C. (1980) Theory of edge detection. *Proc. Roy. Soc. Lond.* **B207**, 187–217.

Nagel H.-H. (1983) Displacement vectors obtained from second order intensity variations in image sequences. *Computer Vision, Graphics Image Proc.* **21**, 85–117.

Watt R.J. and Morgan M.J. (1985) A theory of the primitive spatial code in human vision. *Vision Res.* **25**, 1661–1674.

Exercises

1. Consider the factors that lead to constraints on the distribution of grey levels in optical images and in differentiated or smoothed images. What types of constraint are there?

2. Design a system using only image algebra that will place large values in an image at places where there is a high likelihood that a part of the image moved in any direction and will place low values elsewhere. Note that the simple process of differentiating in time does not distinguish between movement and sudden change.

3. Design an image algebra operation that will place high values at places where there are short vertical lines in an image. Note that any simple feature of this type can be found by cross-correlation of the image with the feature itself. How much difference would it make if that system were designed to respond to lines of various lengths?

4. What other aspect of an image would a simple line detector of this type respond to? How could it be improved to weaken its response to undesirable features?

5. Make a list of useful things that can be achieved by the use of image algebra alone.

5

Image Description

The image format is itself not useful for controlling behaviour, but it can be transformed in several simple ways to provide exactly the right format for the information that is useful for actions. Many of the actions that are determined by visual information can be broken down into a sequence of effector movements. Each movement has a time by which it should be completed, a location to which it is directed, and the force to apply. In each case it is obviously desirable to be able to state the tolerance with which the movement is specified, or in other words how accurate the movement has to be. This means that we need to convert an image from its structure as a two-dimensional function into a list of parameters. These parameters can be thought of as a description of the action, and also as a description of some aspect of the image.

In this chapter, I start by considering a way of creating a description of the image that involves information from the whole image. The description that is created is called an *image summary*. This will suffice in some circumstances, but will generally not be very useful. If the scene in the image is at all complex, then it will usually be necessary to isolate a part or parts of the image to be described independently of any other information in the image. The result of splitting an image into parts and describing each part, I will call an *image description*. Ideally each part of the image will be rather less variable in its properties than is the whole image, and the description of the part should reflect this local consistency.

5.1 Image Summary

Suppose that we have executed a series of algebraic processes on an optical image so that the numerical values that we now have form an explicit representation of some information in the image for some specific behaviour pattern. The larger the value at any point in an image the more likely that its place in the image corresponds to the appropriate direction for the proposed action. The larger the values are overall, the more important the proposed action is. How can this new image function be converted into a format which will indicate a direction for the behaviour?

The intention is to find a small number of descriptors of the manipulated image that can be used universally. The image function has values that are distributed across a range of locations. Perhaps a suitable way of summarizing the image function would be to quote the statistics of the values it contains and the statistics of how they are distributed.

For example, imagine a ball flying towards a catching machine. The sequence of images is treated algebraically so that only the changing projection of the ball has a non-zero value, perhaps by temporal differentiation. We can produce a vector image which records the approach direction of the ball as a place or visual angle in the image and its estimated time of arrival as a scalar parameter at that point. All that is necessary is to obtain numerical values for the location and amplitude of the processed ball image and estimates of the measurement errors. This will tell us where the hand should be placed, when it should be closed and how wide it should be held (to allow for error).

(i) Value Statistics

We can start by just describing the range of intensity values in the image function. The mean or average value is easily calculated by summing all the values together and dividing by the number of values:

$$I_{\text{mean}} = \frac{1}{n} \sum (I(x, y))$$

For example, if I is the temporal derivative of the optical image, then the sign of I_{mean} tells us whether the image has got dimmer or brighter. Its magnitude tells how much the image has changed.

It is also useful to know how typical the mean value is. It could be that most values are very close to the mean and that it provides a very good indication of what is present almost anywhere. The mean of the numbers 7, 7, 8, 8 is 7.5, which is a close approximation to all four values. Or it could be much less typical in the sense that many of the values in the image were not close to the mean. The mean of the numbers 1, 3, 11, 15 is also 7.5, but this time it is not very representative.

We can calculate a further quantity, the standard deviation, which tells us how broadly spread the values are. The standard deviation I_{sd}, is given by the formula:

$$I_{\text{sd}}^2 = \frac{1}{n} \sum (I(x, y) - I_{\text{mean}})^2$$

The standard deviations of the two sets of numbers above are 0.5 and 5.7. The smaller the standard deviation, the smaller is the range of values and so the more typical is the mean.

These statistics are ways of describing what values have been found in the transformed image. What we are really doing is treating the values at each place in the image as samples of a distribution and we are then making a characterization of that underlying distribution. By thinking about the response values as samples from a frequency distribution, we can generate further statistics to improve the characterization. For example, it might be useful to know if the shape of the distribution was symmetric or not.

For any proposed action, the main point is that the mean value gives us a measure of how important an action is. The standard deviation tells us whether there is much to choose between different locations in the image plane. The smaller the standard deviation, the more uniform the values are, and the less important it is where we act towards. On the other hand a large standard deviation suggests that some places in the image function have very much larger values than others. Under this circumstance, the choice of location is more important.

(ii) Location Statistics

We want to decide the direction in which to act, and we have arranged things so that the value in our image function is greater when there is something appropriate in the image for our intended action. How should we select the best location?

Can we devise a mean location in the image by analogy with the mean response value? Obviously, if we take all the places in the image and calculate their mean, it will always be the centre of the image. We can, however, give weight to each place by the value of the response at that place so that the mean will be moved towards those places where the response is greatest. What we must do is to multiply each value of location $L(x, y)$ with its own value of response $I(x, y)$ and then find the mean of all these:

$$\frac{\sum I(x, y) \times L(x, y)}{\sum I(x, y)}$$

This is known as the *centroid* or centre of gravity of the image. Its accuracy is usually considerably better than that of the peak and is limited mostly by the level of noise and other variability in the image.

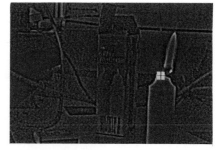

Figure 1. Centroid of whole image with one candle. This figure shows an image, with its centroid marked. A Laplacian of Gaussian filtered version of the image is also shown, with its centroid marked. Notice that the centroid of the filtered version is close to the candle. This is because the candle is the only high contrast part of the image. Without the filtering, the centroid tends towards the centre of the image by an extent that depends on the mean luminance of the image.

Just as the centroid is a mean measure of location, there is also a standard deviation of location which indicates how sharply defined the centroid is. A broad spread of response will have a large standard deviation of location; a sharp-peaked distribution of response will have a small standard deviation. In terms of any proposed action in the direction of the centroid, its standard deviation is an indication of how accurately the movement involved can be defined.

5.2 Image Segmentation

Consider the proverbial case of a moth faced with a choice of two lights of equal brightness. The moth needs to be able to make a choice unless it is to be caught midway between the two. In order to make a choice, the moth needs to know that there may be more than one light and to be able to evaluate each independently. The image will have two sharp peaks but one centroid between the two; the standard deviation of the centroid will be large. If the moth were to take the peak of highest value, it would have no problem. It is implicitly allowing for the existence of more than one light and will be guaranteed a choice in virtually all situations: one peak will usually be the greatest, although random fluctuations from moment to moment may cause some confusion. If the moth is using the centroid then it will not know that there are two sources of light and will get stuck midway. It is reasonable to consider the whole field as potentially the brightest, most familiar, etc. But sometimes the actions that are to be undertaken do not permit this image summary approach, and require that a region or regions of the image be isolated and treated differently.

The process that I now describe is called *segmentation*. The consequence of segmentation is a set of *segments*. Each segment comes from a compact *region* of the image.

There are two rather different aspects to this problem of how to proceed when image-wide statistics are not appropriate. The first case is where one small region of the image contains all the information necessary for some action or decision that is to be carried out. In this case, we shall need a

Figure 2. Centroid of whole image with two candles. When there are two high contrast areas in the image, the overall centroid is not useful. We need a way of breaking the image into parts before analysis.

way of isolating the relevant region from the rest of the image, so that its description can be created free from contamination by whatever else is present. The second case is more complex; it may often be the case that action must be taken which is based on different attributes of different regions of the image. In both cases, the general point is that we wish to operate as previously, but only on small regions of the image rather than on the entire image itself. For this to be possible, we must make ways of identifying where these putative regions are, how far they extend (i.e. where their boundaries are) and then determine which region or regions are relevant.

Recall the moth, seeking the point of greatest light in the scene and yet confronted by two candles some distance apart. The centroid of the light image lies midway between them, and for reasons of symmetry, so does the centroid of most simple processed versions of the image. Clearly, the moth has to choose one or other, but how, at a mechanistic level, can this choice be made and implemented? There are several pitfalls to avoid in discussing how to do this. For the operator of an image-processing system sitting watching a screen, it is easy to move a cursor around the screen to draw out the desired area. The operator's own vision is solving the problem. We are interested in systems that do not have visually intelligent operators, but that must do everything themselves. A trial-and-error approach sounds like another alternative, but here the main difficulty lies in evaluating the extent to which any particular trial is a success or an error. This cannot be decided unless all the possibilities are known.

(i) Fixed Segmentation

Let's start by considering the very simple technique of halving the image by a vertical division down through its centre. Each half could then itself be halved horizontally to give, in all, four quadrants. The process can obviously be repeated many times, if desired, producing ever smaller rectangles. Sometimes, as in the case of the moth between two lights, this will succeed, but a moment's thought will show that it cannot be guaranteed to work. What if the area of interest in the actual image is not of the same general proportions as the rectangles created by dividing the image?

There is a more serious problem to consider though. How can the moth know whether a particular subdivision has identified two lights or just two halves of a single light. The statistics in any subdivision could be rather similar where there is one or two lights. The basic problem with this simple technique is that it is not sensitive to the contents of the image.

(ii) Image-Sensitive Segmentation

We start with the image which has been transformed by a series of algebraic operations as desired. This has a mean value and a distribution of values that are obviously either less than or greater than the mean. In the example

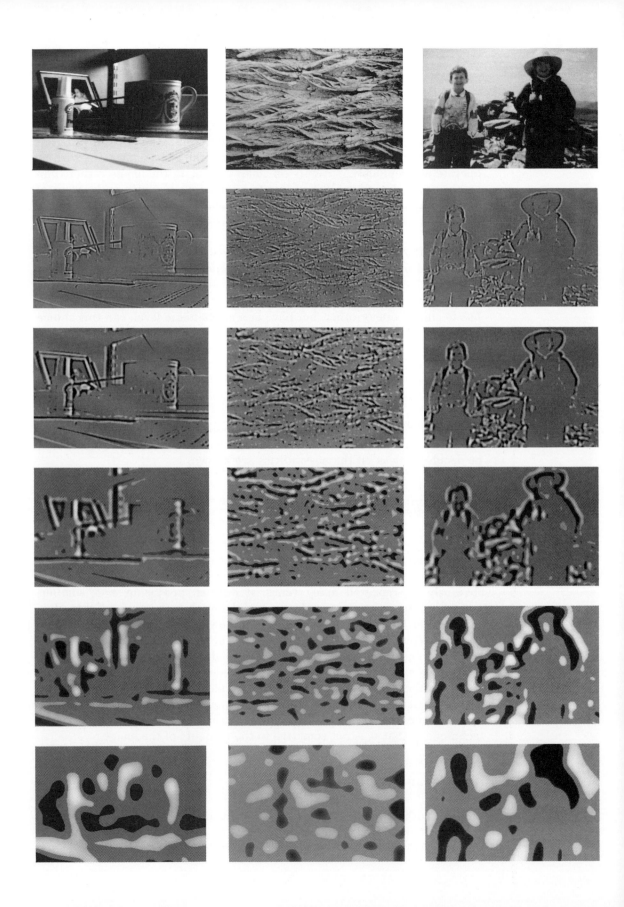

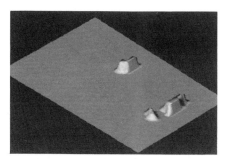

Figure 4. Seascape of whole image with two islands. If we set all the negative regions of the image to zero, we are left with a flat surface, a sea, with concavities, islands rising up. These islands can be treated separately.

of the moth, the values that we are interested in are all greater than the mean and so it follows that we can ignore all values that are less than the mean. If the optical image was originally subject to spatial constraints and, more particularly, positive spatial correlations, then the values above the mean will tend to be clumped together.

If we think of the mean as being a sea level, then there will be islands of high response values rising up out of the sea. The shape and size of these islands is determined by the contents of the image. Each island can be treated as a separate, independent segment of the image, with its own set of statistics. For present purposes, two of these are significant. Each island has its own *centroid* and associated standard deviation of location. We can create a list of the various centroids and then we simply have to select one of them as the direction for our proposed action. The second statistic will allow us to make that choice. Each island has a *mass*, which is just the sum of all the values that comprise it. The mass is obviously a near relative of the mean statistic, but it has the benefit of reflecting the area of island as well as its height. In order to make a selection we can just take the centroid of the most massive island.

5.3 Regions in an Image

There is another, more general way of thinking about the outcome of image algebra processes. Points that have values that are at or near to the mean value are likely to be the least interesting. Points that have values that are greater than the mean value are likely to have different physical causes from those that are less than the mean value. Contiguous parts of the image that have a consistent sign of response with respect to the mean are more likely to have a single physical cause than are those that have different signs.

◀
Figure 3. Some sample images and their response regions. This figure shows several different images. Each is shown filtered at a variety of spatial scales and with the different regions of like sign rendered.

(i) A Random Sequence

We can start with a simple image in which each point is set independently at random $+1$ or -1. Start by examining one line in the response, and start at a pixel at the centre of the line. The sign of the value at this pixel will be plus or minus with equal probability, as will the sign of the adjacent pixel. The probability that they will each be positive is

$$\left(\tfrac{1}{2}\right) \times \left(\tfrac{1}{2}\right)$$

The probability that the third will be positive is also $\tfrac{1}{2}$, and so the probability that all three will be positive is then

$$\left(\tfrac{1}{2}\right) \times \left(\tfrac{1}{2}\right) \times \left(\tfrac{1}{2}\right) = \left(\tfrac{1}{2}\right)^3$$

The probability of a run of *at least* n pixels all being positive is given by

$$\left(\tfrac{1}{2}\right)^n$$

The probability of the run of positive values being *exactly* n long, is given by the joint probability of the run being at least n long, and the probability that it is bounded at each end by a negative value

$$\left(\tfrac{1}{2}\right)^n \times \tfrac{1}{2} \times \tfrac{1}{2}$$

$$= \left(\tfrac{1}{2}\right)^{n+2}$$

The probability of a run of just n pixels all being positive or all being positive is then twice this:

$$\left(\tfrac{1}{2}\right)^{n+1}$$

This means that we can draw out a histogram of the probability of finding runs of different lengths (different values of n).

Sequence

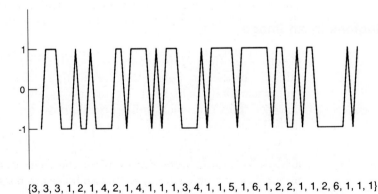

{3, 3, 3, 1, 2, 1, 4, 2, 1, 4, 1, 1, 1, 3, 4, 1, 1, 5, 1, 6, 1, 2, 2, 1, 1, 2, 6, 1, 1, 1}

Figure 5. A sequence of ± 1 and a run-length description. This figure shows a random sequence of the values $+1$ or -1. Beneath the sequence is a list of the lengths of the regions of same sign. This can be used to describe the original sequence completely, and is known as a run-length code.

Any one such run can be characterized completely by its length and where in the sequence it occurred. This means that a complete description of a line of random values can be created by recording, in their order of occurrence, the lengths of each run. Before moving on, we should just pause and consider why we have been making the sign of the values so significant. Our original sequence only had values of plus or minus one, and so the sign contains all the information. Moreover any one value was equally likely to be positive or negative. If we were to consider a random variable that could take any real value between -1 and $+1$, with equal probability, the sign would correspond to above or below the mean value, thereby preserving symmetry. If we choose a value that is not the mean, then symmetry does not hold. For example, taking a sequence of random values uniformly distributed between -1 and $+1$, if we chose to look for a sequence of length 3, all above 0.5 and terminated at each end by values less than 0.5, the probability would be:

$$(0.25)^3 \times 0.75 \times 0.75 = 0.0088$$

The converse case of three values less than 0.5 would have a probability of:

$$(0.75)^3 \times 0.25 \times 0.25 = 0.0264$$

(ii) A Random Image

We must now turn to consider how we can extend this to the more usual and useful two dimensions of images. Let us suppose that our image has been sampled by a hexagonal grid, so that each pixel has six neighbours. Straight away we can see that the probability of finding an isolated pixel with a positive sign is 2^{-7}, and that the probability of finding an isolated pixel of either sign is twice this, i.e. 2^{-6}. Two joining pixel have eight neighbours, and so the probability of finding an isolated part is then twice 2^{-10}, i.e. 2^{-9}. If we put a third pixel on the end, making a row of three all of the same sign surrounded entirely by pixels of the opposite sign then the probability falls to 2^{-12}. Each time we add another to the line, the probability drops by a factor of 2^{-3}, because we are restricting the values of another three pixels.

However three pixels can be arranged in a triangle as well as in a row on a hexagonal grid. The probability of finding a triangle of pixels like this is 2^{-11} because the three pixels have 9 neighbours. Four pixels can be arranged in six different layouts. The four elongated layouts all have 12 neighbours and thus probabilities of 2^{-14}; one other has a probability of 2^{-13}; and the blob of four packed together has a probability of 2^{-10}.

We can take this discussion further to shapes with larger areas, and always decreasing probabilities. When the area reaches 6, then the interesting possibility of a hole arises; at 10, two holes are possible; 13, three holes, etc.

There are several points to notice. For any particular size of area, the most probable configurations are the most compact ones: those with the smallest outline length. In fact the probability for any arbitrary shape is not just a simple function of its area and its outline length, but also depends

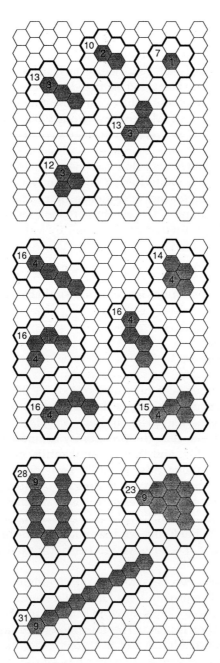

Figure 6. Some simple region shapes. This figure shows a hexagonal tessellation and several differently-shaped regions of like sign. The probabilities of finding the different shapes in a random image depend on the size but also on the shape of the region.

on the number of concavities and how close they are to each other. Consider the three layouts of nine pixels in the figure. The elongated line has an outline length of 22 and a probability of 2^{-30}; the compact blob has an outline length of 14 and a probability of 2^{-22}; the long shape folded back on itself has an outline length of 19 and a probability of 2^{-27}.

The structure of a random binary image is thus reflected in the distribution of regions within which the sign does not change. These regions are themselves fully described by their outlines (including any holes) and the entire image can then be described by a set of such outline descriptions plus a description of the spatial relationships between outlines. Note that if we have descriptions of all the positive valued regions, then by implication we also have a description of all the places in the image that are not positive, i.e. the negative regions.

When we turn to consider images that have random values between -1 and $+1$, then the outlines alone are no longer a very full description of the image, although we can obtain outlines at other values in addition to zero.

5.4 Analytical Descriptions

A great deal of the structure of an image can be seen by examining where it changes sign or changes which side of its mean value it is on. This section is concerned with how the regions that are delimited by these contours can be described. There are many different possible ways in which the regions can be described and it is helpful to have some criteria to guide our discussion. Recall that the purpose of creating descriptions is to link the visual image to potential actions and decisions. We saw above some simple ways in which this could be done image-wide. Obviously any descriptions that we discuss now should be similarly *useful*. This implies that they should be rather *compact* involving a small number of parameters, perhaps to very high accuracy. Obviously, the descriptions should be *stable*, so that minor perturbations of the input only produce minor perturbations of the description.

When we were dealing with image algebra, the mathematical objects that we used were the numerical values in images, and various algebraic operators and functions. Now, when we turn to consider descriptions of parts of images, we shall be concerned with *sentences*, each of which carries one piece of description. Don't be fooled by the linguistic sound to this: a sentence might just be a list of numbers. For example, here is a sentence of the sort that I have in mind:

$$\textbf{BLOB}(7.9; 24.1; (13, 12); 3.7; (9, 1, 1.2))$$

Notice that this sentence is itself a list of numbers, and the position of each number determines how it is to be understood. All the sentences arising from one image, one per region will be collected in a *set* or a *list*. The difference between a set and a list is one of organization. In a set all members have equivalent status and are only distinguishable by their value or content or meaning. In a list, the members are assigned an order of occurrence, which provides an alternative means of distinguishing between members. It makes sense to talk about "the element of a set that has the value 3.1" and "the third element of a list". It does not make sense to talk about "the third element of a set".

In the discussion that follows, I shall assume that the mean value of the image is zero, so that the values that are greater than the mean will be positive and those that are less than the mean will be negative. By subtracting the mean value from the image, this situation can always be arranged.

(i) Sequence Description

Recall the analysis of the structure of a random sequence of -1 and $+1$ from the previous section. Obviously we can represent all the information in such a sequence by a set (unordered) of the positions of each sign change, or by a list (ordered) of the distances between each sign change. These representations would allow us to reconstruct the sequence exactly and are only apparently more compact than the sequence itself because they use our decimal number system more efficiently.

Now consider the structure of a sequence of random values between -1 and $+1$. Here the positions of sign changes, or their separations offer a representation that does not permit a reconstruction of the sequence. The representation is truly compact because it contains less information. It would not be possible to reconstruct the sequence from this description. Nevertheless it may well be a useful representation. Suppose that we wished to know whether the sequence had been smoothed or not: the range and number of separations between sign changes would tell us. There are many ways in which a list of the intervals between zero crossings could be enhanced.

The mean of the entire sequence is zero, which was therefore the value that we chose to use in dividing the sequence into the various segments. Each segment now has its own mean value which in the case of a random sequence with a uniform distribution of probability will be $+0.5$ or -0.5. We can use this value to further examine each segment, and break the segment at each place where it crosses the new mean value. We could then record a list of the length of all the segments within each segment. This is moreover a process that can be repeated over and over again (each time using the latest mean), and you may have noticed a similarity to the bit patterns of the twos complement binary representation of integers. We have created a list hierarchy which in principle could exactly represent the original sequence, but we have structured it in such a way that the precision, which is related simply to the depth of the hierarchy, can be predetermined and matched to the task.

(ii) Outline Description

Two-dimensional images are not so simple. We can treat an image as having a structure that can be encapsulated by a set of interlocking regions. A description of this structure can then be created by describing the regions and their relationships. We have seen that size and shape are important factors even for binary images where the only values are $+1$ or -1. I am

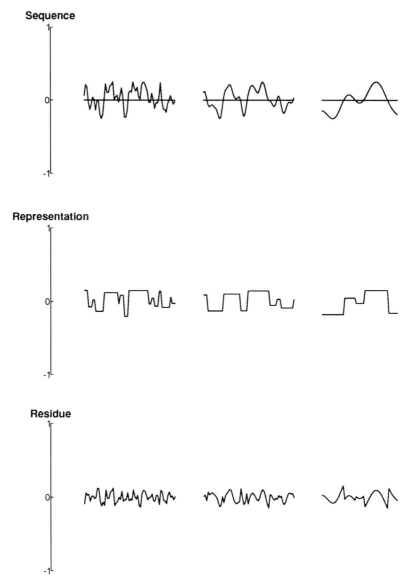

Figure 7. Run lengths for random and smoothed sequences. The sequences in this figure differ in the degree of smoothing that they have been subjected to. The number and range of regions distinguishes them.

now going to consider how the shape of the outline of such a region can be represented.

Suppose that we take a point as origin anywhere inside a particular region. The outline may then be described as a set of loci each a certain distance and direction from the origin. All these points are connected and so it is possible to describe the set as a list, each member being understood to be connected to the one before in the list. With this list of serial position

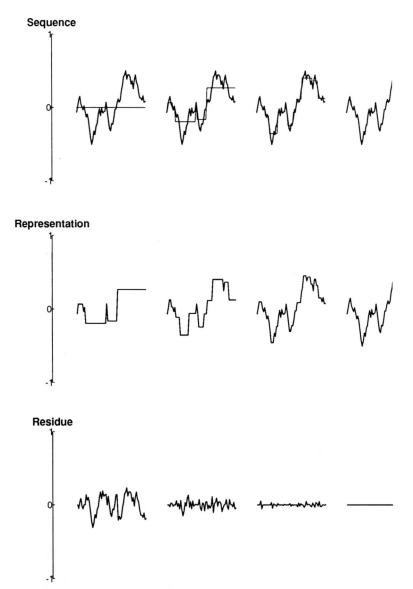

Figure 8. Hierarchical run-length code. A random sequence is shown with a hierarchical run-length code where each region is itself broken down into regions, and so on. The number of levels in the hierarchy determines the precision of the overall code.

round the contour it is possible to create functions that record distance or direction from the origin as a function of serial position along the contour. If the contour is not folded back on itself, that is if no two or more points share the same direction from the origin, then it is possible to use direction from the origin to make the list in place of serial position. The outline is then given as distance as a function of direction in the range 0–360°, and being a function, it can be manipulated algebraically. We can differentiate

Region Outline

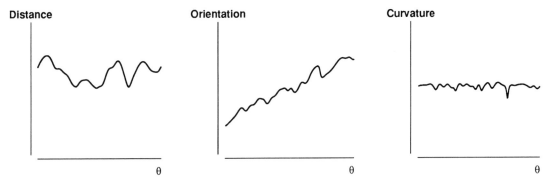

Distance   Orientation   Curvature

θ   θ   θ

Figure 9. Outline of a region. This figure shows the outline of a single region from an image. We can take any point as an origin, and then measure the distance of the outline from that point in each direction. This would give us a graph of distance as a function of direction, as is shown beneath the outline. We can also create graphs that show orientation or curvature as a function of distance along the line from some arbitrary starting point on the line.

the direction function to obtain a function which gives the slope of the tangent to the outline at each point. We can differentiate this function to obtain a line curvature function, and so on. These functions which relate serial position, distance, orientation, curvature and direction from an arbitrary, enclosed origin are ways of specifying the outline contour. How can they be described?

As soon as it is realized that these functions are just sequences, then we have already some ideas about how to describe them. It is worth noting that they are actually rather constrained sequences. For example, the orientation function has to end having turned through 360°. The curvature function has an analogous constraint. We can set about describing these sequences in terms of the sign of their values. Suppose that we take a curvature function that corresponds to a particular outline. Some parts of the outline will have sharp corners (high curvatures) and other parts will be smooth (low curvatures). It makes some sense to break the outline into smooth regions and this corresponds to breaking the outline at places where the curvature is high, i.e. where the derivative of curvature changes sign.

Curvature   *Region Outline*

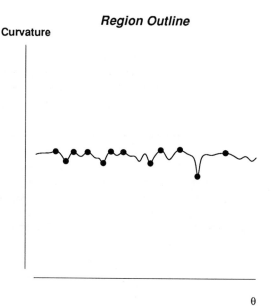

θ

Region Outline

Figure 10. Outline broken at points of high curvature. The outline can be snipped into short lengths at points of high curvature. Each short length can then be described. Each short length is a sequence that can be described using the techniques discussed above. A hierarchical description can be produced.

We can use the technique of creating a description that is based on the lengths of the sequence where the derivative of curvature remains on one or other side of zero.

The actual outline function that is used is clearly a choice that depends on the type of task that is being undertaken. In the example of derivative of curvature, the mean value for the whole sequence can be expected to be zero, just like in our random sequence. However we might prefer to use some other function which does not have a mean of zero: curvature, for example, has a mean of $2\pi/l$ where l is the length of the outline. Both a circle and an ellipse have curvature outline functions that never cross zero. The best approach here is to use mean crossings rather than zero crossings. We then produce a list of lengths where the function remains on the same side of the mean.

There are few constraints on the values that the sequence may take along each of these lengths. Consequently, the representation would be improved immensely by actually measuring and recording locally a new mean value for the part of the sequence between adjacent mean crossings. This is simply the sum of all the values divided by the number of samples. We now have a description of the outline which records (i) where its derivative of curvature (or some other measure) changes side with respect to the global mean and (ii) its local mean value between adjacent pairs of these places. We can make this description hierarchical in a way that is rather analogous to our approach in the case of the random sequence. There, we proceeded to analyse each segment further by breaking it wherever it changed sign with respect to its expected mean value. For the sequence that we are dealing with now, there is no a priori information that allows us to calculate an expected mean value, and so we have to use the actual mean value of the segment instead. We can then list the length and mean deviation value of each segment of the original segment. As before, this process can be iterated until the hierarchy that is being created has sufficient detail.

It is worth thinking a little bit more about the actual numbers that we might be recording in a hierarchical list of this type. Clearly all the lengths in any one list at any one level have to sum to be equal to or greater than the length of the corresponding segment at the next level up (i.e. the parent segment that was split into the various lengths). As we go down the hierarchy, lengths cannot increase in size, and the average length must reduce in size. The extent to which it reduces obviously depends on the average number of children that are produced from any parent segment. This in turn depends on the original outline, and is itself an interesting characteristic of the outline.

The mean deviation values also show a progression down through the hierarchy that is characteristic of the outline. There is a rather natural error correction aspect to the hierarchy. Suppose that our calculation of the mean deviation at any one level is inaccurate. Provided that we use this value for the breaking process at the next level, then we have not lost any information, although the description that is created is obviously altered somewhat.

The principle of this hierarchical process that I have been describing can be stated quite generally. I have given a rule for how to split a sequence into smaller sections each of which is statistically different from the parent sequence. We then characterize the child sequence by its length position and by the manner in which it is statistically different from the parent. Any such rule would suffice, as would any such statistical measure. The statistical measure is a sort of model or cartoon version of the actual sequence that it describes.

(iii) Axis Descriptions

The outline descriptions that I have just described are frequently useful, especially where the image that is being described is a transformed optical image so that zero crossings correspond to occluding edges. In this way a small but significant description can be created. In fact, a theorem due to Logan states that the zero crossings of a 1 octave band-pass signal (in one dimension) offer a complete representation. There are ways in which more of the structure of an image can be described, which take into account the values in the image.

Another type of description that really does little more than describe the outline in a different fashion is called the medial axis. We start by thinking of the image as being a series of islands rising above a sea level that is set by the mean value of the image. The outline of each segment then corresponds to the shoreline of the island. Imagine that the shoreline of the response islands was steadily and uniformly eroded by the sea so that the island area was being reduced. Eventually shorelines that were originally on opposite sides of the island will meet and then disappear. Each point where this happens lies on the medial axis. The medial axis is rather like the skeleton of the island.

Of course the contours produced at several different levels can be further characterized by their medial axes but there is another, more interesting modification to the medial axis method that will take some account of the segment structure. Suppose that the rate of erosion in the metaphor were to be made inversely proportional to the value of the segment at the point of erosion. The result will be a medial axis placed near to any high values. We can call this the centroid axis, because in any one-dimensional slide through the segment, it will mark a point approximately at the centroid (centre of gravity).

The medial axis is not very stable, being easily altered by small fluctuations in an outline.

5.5 Statistical Descriptions

An alternative approach is to regard a mean or zero-bounded segment as a small image and to use the summary statistics that were used earlier in the chapter. These statistics fall into several different categories depending on what is being summarized.

(i) Value Statistics

The first category is a set of statistics that simply describe the values of the image island, such as the mean value. The simplest quantity that we shall need to calculate is the mass of a segment. This is the three-dimensional volume filled by the segment if it is thought of as a surface above sea level. The information available to us concerning this surface is a set of samples of its height that are spaced some distance apart in a regular grid.

Clearly if we simply add up the values of all the samples, then the number that we obtain will depend on the spacing of the samples as much as on the actual mass of the island. Imagine spreading each sample out so that it filled a rectangular column that was in direct contact with all of its neighbouring columns. If the sampling grid was an equally spaced rectangular array, then the columns will have rectangular cross-sections. The volume of each column is given by the product of the area of its cross-section and its height. Its height is that of the sample and its cross-sectional area is the product of the sample spacing in the two dimensions. Thus an estimation of the volume of the segment can be obtained by summing the product of the volume of each sample, v_i, and the two sampling distances, Δx, Δy:

$$m = \sum_{i=1}^{n} (v_i \Delta x \, \Delta y)$$

(ii) Location Statistics

A second category of statistics concerns the values of an image island and where they are, such as the centroid of the island. Each point in a distribution such as a segment of an image has a position (x_i, y_i) and a value v_i. The product of these two quantities is called a first order moment. The centroid is the point in the distribution about which the sum of the first order moments is zero. You can think of a moment as being a lever, the force of which depends both on the push v and the distance from the fulcrum (x, y). This is the standard approach to understanding the centroid, and it explains why the centroid is sometimes called the centre of gravity.

An easier way to think of it is to imagine that the distribution was created from a number of samples each of which was an estimate of where the centroid lies. Where the value v_i, is say, 10, this means that 10 individual samples had the same position (x_i, y_i). The mean of this set of samples is then the best estimate of the centroid. The mean is obtained by summing the values of all the samples:

$$\sum_{i=1}^{n} (x_i, y_i) v_i$$

and dividing by the number of samples:

$$\sum_{i=1}^{n} v_i$$

The value of the centroid is given by:

$$(x_c, y_c) = \frac{\sum_{i=1}^{n} (x_i, y_i) v_i}{\sum_{i=1}^{n} v_i}$$

The distribution also has a width or spread. The standard deviations in the x and the y directions can be calculated in a fashion that is analogous to that employed for the x and y means (the centroid). It is tempting to suppose that the spread of the segment can be characterized by these values. However a long thin oblique segment will have values that are the same for these two standard deviations. This is because of the arbitrary nature of the directions of x and y.

Figure 11. Sample image with centroids marked. This figure shows a rendering of the regions in several images and their centroids. The images have been filtered with a Laplacian of Gaussian filter and three spatial scales are shown. For each the region is marked by displaying the original full image with a higher contrast than in areas where there is no region. The centroids are marked by a small square with a cross. The centroid is a measure of where in the image the region is, although for some regions, it does not actually lie within the boundary of the region.

These statistics are called the central moments of the distribution, and in principle if enough high order moments were to be used, then a complete characterization of a segment could be made. Moments are generally useful properties to measure because they take into account the segment values but are also relatively insensitive to any random noise errors. More specifically, if a substantial amount of the segment can be adequately characterized by just a few fairly low order moments, then a compact summary has been produced.

(iii) Principal Axis

The *principal axis* is a measure of the direction in which the segment is elongated. The direction can then be expressed as the angle whose tangent takes that value. Let us suppose that we have calculated the centroid of a segment. This means that each point can be written as:

$$(x_i', y_i') = (x_i, y_i) - (x_c, y_c)$$

We have mentioned in the previous section that we can compute the standard deviation of the segment in the x and the y directions. But we have noted that these may not be the same if the distribution is elongated. Of course, if the distribution is elongated along an oblique line then the two standard deviations will be nearly the same, so we cannot tell if the distribution is elongated or not. To do this, and then to measure the direction in which it is elongated, we need to introduce the idea of covariance.

Before that, we shall find it convenient to use the idea of polar coordinates. In the system of rectangular coordinates that I have been using so far, the location of a point is given by its distance across x and up y from the origin. In polar coordinates, we specify the same location by the direct distance, via the shortest path r' and the direction θ' of the location from the origin. These two formulae allow us to interchange coordinate systems:

$$x = r' \cos \theta' \qquad r' = (x^2 + y^2)^{0.5}$$

$$y = r' \sin \theta' \qquad \theta' = \tan^{-1}(y/x)$$

Now, we can start with some point (x_i, y_i) in the segment. This point has a certain deviation about the centroid in every direction. Let us call the direction that we are interested in θ. We need next to know how far, r_i, from the origin our point is, in this direction. This distance can be calculated to be

$$r_i = x_i \cos \theta + y_i \sin \theta$$

The standard deviation σ_θ of the entire distribution in the direction, θ, is given by the square root of:

$$\sigma_\theta^2 = \frac{\sum r_i^2 v_i}{\sum v_i}$$

$$= \frac{\sum v_i (x_i \cos \theta + y_i \sin \theta)^2}{\sum v_i}$$

What we want to know is the direction in which this standard deviation is greatest. There is a standard way of calculating this. We need to differentiate the above expression with respect to θ and then equate the result to zero.

It helps at this stage to introduce a little bit of extra convention. Most of the quantities that we are interested in have the general form

$$\sum v_i x_i^a y_i^b$$

where a, b are positive integer constants. So we will now write

$$m_{ab} = \sum v_i x_i^a y_i^b$$

Bearing in mind that

$$x^0 = 1$$

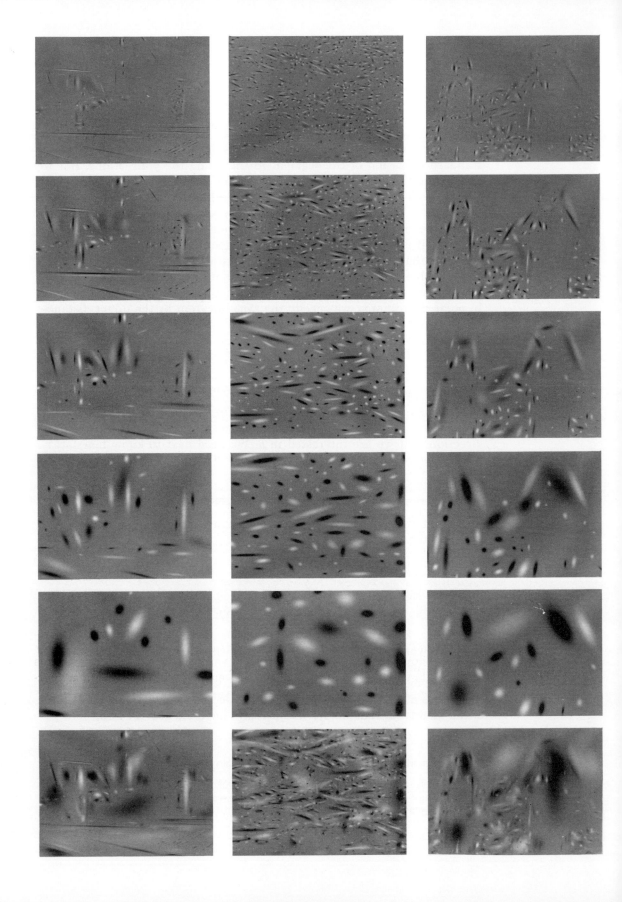

we have

$$m_{00} = \sum v_i$$
$$m_{10} = \sum v_i x_i$$
$$m_{02} = \sum v_i y_i^2$$
$$m_{11} = \sum v_i x_i y_i$$

This last example involves the product of x and y at every point and is some measure of whether a relationship exists between the two. It is a covariation term.

The slope of the principal axis, θ', is given by the expression:

$$\tan 2\theta' = \frac{2m_{11}}{m_{20} - m_{02}}$$

From this we can obtain a value for θ', the direction in which the segment is elongated. A little caution is necessary here because the equation has two solutions for θ; one will be the direction of elongation and the other will be at right angles. This is because

$$\tan 2\theta = \tan(2\theta + \pi)$$

The second solution will be the direction in which the standard deviation is least.

(iv) Second Order Statistics

The third category of statistic is a sort of hybrid of the earlier two. Any point in the image can be coupled with any other. Starting at any point in the island and looking around, we find that there is a set of combinations of distance and direction, a set of possible displacements. For each member of this set, we can define a pair of values: one for the point where we are starting from and one from the other point that is at the other end of the displacement. Thus for any given distance and direction of displacement we can obtain a distribution of pairs of values whose locations in the image island were separated by that distance and direction. For any given distance and direction displacement, we can draw up a two-dimensional frequency distribution with one dimension for each value of the pair. Of course, this can be done for each distance and for each direction, making a four-dimensional frequency distribution. This is then the complete set of *second order statistics*.

◄
Figure 12. Principal axis examples. This figure shows a representation of a description of the previous images. Each region is represented by an oriented and elongated Gaussian blob which uses centroids, principal axes, and standard deviations along and across the axis. The representation is not a particularly good pictorial substitute for the original: this is not its intention, it merely makes visible the information available in a description of the type being discussed.

Figure 13. Second order statistics. Several images are shown, each with different second order statistics. On the left is a collection of dark points that are placed completely at random. In the middle is a collection of points that have a preferred displacement distance, but not a preferred direction. On the right is a pattern in which there is a preferred displacement distance and direction. This latter is known as a Glass pattern.

We can create a seven-dimensional frequency distribution of third order statistics from three values and two two-dimensional vectors, and so on. However, these higher order statistics probably have little value. Suppose that for each of the seven dimensions we only had two values: 0 and 1 for the image; 1 and 2 for the distances; $0°$ and $90°$ for the directions. Even so there are 2^7 $(=128)$ different combinations.

Return to the second order statistics, whose frequency distribution for any one vector has two dimensions. What we really want to know is whether there is any interaction or interdependence between the two dimensions. Stated simply, what we are looking for is evidence that, given one of the pair of values, we have a better than chance probability of guessing what the other one was.

An example of this type of association between the two values can be found in an image that has been smoothed. For short distances in any direction, the two values are likely to be similar and are certainly not independent. In this case, the two-dimensional frequency distribution for a small separation is going to be a diagonal line which could be characterized by an expression of the sort

$$v_1 + \sigma_1 = v_2 + \sigma_2$$

which says that the first value, v_1, give or take some variability, σ_1, is the same as the second value, v_2, give or take some variability, σ_2.

5.6 Errors

If these descriptions are going to be used for some subsequent action or decision, it is obviously important to have an indication of how accurate they are. There are two aspects to this,

Obviously, given an image and a rule telling how to go about creating a description, then there is no variability in the process and, miscalculations excepted, no error of any sort. However, we should really be thinking of the image as one sample from a large number of images, all created in the same way but with different samples of noise in the process. What we want then is an estimate of both how reliable our segmentation is and how reliable the descriptions of each segment are.

(i) Mass

Let us see why the mass is both reliable and also sensitive. We start by supposing that each sample, v_i, that we have is in fact the "real" value, $\mathbf{v}$, plus a small random error, e_i

$$v_i = \mathbf{v} + e_i$$

The error term is a random variable of mean zero. That it has mean zero, means that

$$\sum_{i=1}^{\infty} e_i = 0$$

This means that our expression for the mass can be written as

$$m = \sum_{i=1}^{n} v_i + \sum_{i=1}^{n} e_i$$

The first of these two terms on the right hand side is the quantity that we are interested in; the second term tends to take the value zero.

If we repeat the calculation of the mass over and over again with a fresh sample of noise error each time, we will obtain a distribution of estimates of the mass. We are interested in knowing what the spread of this distribution might be. This is obviously related to the error term and the spread of values that it can take. Consider these two sets of random values

$$-1,\ 2,\ 1,\ -1,\ -2,\ 1$$

$$-2,\ 4,\ 2,\ -2,\ -4,\ 2$$

In each case the sum of the six values is zero. The sum of all the values, squared, is not zero because squaring ensures that all the quantities that we are summing will be positive. In the first case the sum of the squares is 12, whereas in the second case the sum of the squares is 48. We can compute the mean squares by dividing by the number of samples, 6 in this case. The values themselves all differ by a factor of 2, and the sum of their squares therefore differ by a factor of 2^2. If we take the square root of the mean squares, then we have a quantity that differs by the same factor as the samples themselves. This means that the root mean square (RMS) is proportional to the spread of values. When the values are the deviations from the mean (as they are, incidentally, in this case), the RMS is equivalent to the standard deviation. If σ_e is the RMS of the error term in our expression

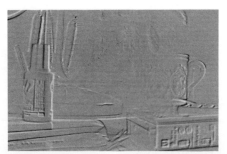

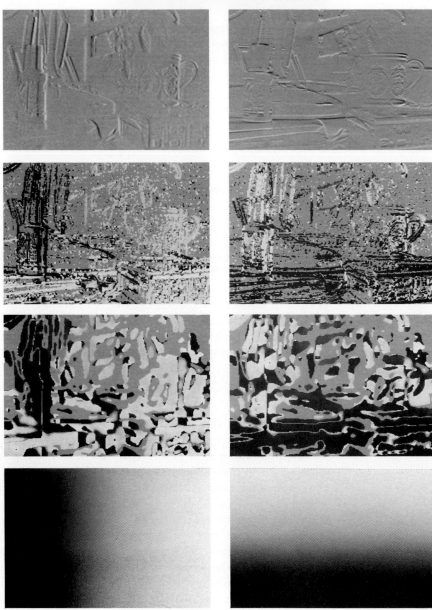

relating the "real" mass to our calculated one, then if we only had one sample to deal with, the standard deviation of estimates of the mass (from one value) would also be σ_e. This follows because, just as e_i was the deviation from the mean error (zero), so each e_i is the deviation from the mean mass.

Suppose that we had two values v_i with which to calculate the mass instead of just one. In this case the standard deviation of estimates of the mass is going to be equal to the standard deviation of this quantity:

$$\sum_{i=1}^{2} e_i$$

$$= e_1 + e_2$$

To calculate the standard deviation of this quantity, we square it

$$(e_1 + e_2)^2 = (e_1^2 + 2e_1 e_2 + e_2^2)$$

and calculate the mean of the squares for a lot of different samples:

$$\text{mean } (e_1 + e_2)^2 = \text{mean } (e_1^2) + \text{mean } (2e_1 e_2) + \text{mean } (e_2^2)$$

Now

$$\text{mean } (e_1) = \text{mean } (e_2) = 0$$

$$\text{mean } (e_1^2) = \text{mean } (e_2^2) = \sigma_e^2$$

therefore

$$\text{mean } (e_1 + e_2)^2 = 2\sigma_e^2$$

Finally we take the square root of this to obtain the standard deviation of estimates of the mass (from two values)

$$\sigma_m = \sigma_e \sqrt{2}$$

More generally, the standard deviation of estimates of the mass from n values is given by

$$\sigma_m = \sigma_e \sqrt{n}$$

This expression shows how the reliability of the mass depends on the level of noise and the number of samples.

◀

Figure 14. An example of image summary. This figure shows an example of using just the ideas of image algebra and image summary to compute the point of optic flow expansion in a sequence of images. At the top is shown the temporal derivative from a sequence of images obtained whilst the camera was moving forwards. Beneath this are computations of the x-component of the flow (left) and the y-component of the flow (right). The first pair show the respective spatial derivatives. Beneath these are shown, at two different spatial scales, the ratios of the temporal and spatial derivatives. At the bottom is shown an idealized version of each ratio giving the actual flow for movement towards a flat fronto-parallel surface. The point at which both x-component and y-component motions are at zero is the focus of flow expansion and can be found by a statistical technique of fitting an appropriately-oriented plane to each separately.

(ii) Centroid

When we turn to estimate the reliability of the centroid, we have to bear in mind that there are two sets of variability. One of them is the distribution of values of (x_i, y_i), the other is error in v_i.

We have to think of the distribution of values in a segment as being the dispersion, through error, of samples away from the centroid. Although we know that this is not strictly what happened, it is the correct way in which to assess the accuracy with which we can compute the centroid.

The squared deviation at each point is then

$$(x_i - x_c, y_i - y_c)^2$$

and at each point we have v_i of these, so that the total squared deviation is

$$\sum_{i=1}^{n} (x_i - x_c, y_i - y_c)^2 v_i$$

and the mean squared deviation is

$$\frac{\sum_{i=1}^{n} (x_i - x_c, y_i - y_c)^2 v_i}{\sum_{i=1}^{n} v_i}$$

The square root of this quantity is an estimate of how accurately the centroid can be known. Notice that there is no reason to expect that the accuracy will be the same in each of the x and y directions. If the segment is elongated these two may be very different.

(iii) Principal Axis

In estimating the principal axis, we calculate what the greatest and least standard deviations are, and thereby obtain some information about how elongated the segment is. The ratio of greatest and least standard deviations is a reasonable measure of how elongated the blob is. If we want to know the accuracy of the estimate of direction that we have obtained, then this ratio is a good indicator. Alternatively, we could look and see how the standard deviation peaks at its greatest value. If the peak is sharp, then our estimate is good; if it is shallow, then the estimate is less reliable.

An alternative is to estimate the actual error involved. We start with the expression

$$\tan 2\theta = \frac{2m_{11}}{m_{20} - m_{02}}$$

The error in this is equal to the combined errors in the three quantities involved:

$$\sigma^2(\tan 2\theta) = \frac{4\sigma^2(m_{11})}{m_{11}} + \frac{\sigma^2(m_{20}) + \sigma^2(m_{02})}{m_{20} - m_{02}}$$

From this we can calculate the error in θ to be:

$$\sigma^2(r) = \frac{\sigma^2(\tan 2\theta)}{2(1 + \tan^2 2\theta)}$$

Summary: A Formalism of Image Description

In this chapter, I have been considering two processes. The first one is the extraction from an image of all the points that belong to a segment and are relevant for the description of that segment. The second process is the actual description itself.

Recall the typographical conventions that I introduced in the previous chapter:

Images start with a capital

vectors are written in bold type

scalars are set in normal type

To these we now add:

SETS are written in capitals

A set can also be defined by its elements, which are enclosed in curly brackets:

$\{2, 3, 1, 4\} = \{1, 2, 3, 4\}$ The order is unimportant.

(LISTS) are written as sets enclosed in ordinary brackets.

Lists can also be defined by their elements:

$(2, 3, 1, 4) \neq (1, 2, 3, 4)$ The order is important.

Note that lists are similar to vectors. There are differences however. Lists can have non-numeric elements and different operations are defined on them. We have already encountered lists when specifying the arguments to functions.

The final typographical convention for this chapter is:

BOOLEAN are printed in small capitals and are underlined.

A boolean can have the values true or false. It is typically the outcome of applying a rule to some data, as we shall see. A set can be defined by a rule. Suppose that we have a rule:

x BETWEEN $(a; b)$

which was true if $(x > a)$ and $(x < b)$ then we can define a set:

$\{x$ BETWEEN $(0; 7)\}$

itive itself is defined at the level of the individual lexic

at several different levels of structural detail. When the

usual subject, the chances are high that certain longer

d particularly informative. The distribution of word le

e longer than normal words are preferentially inspecte

well become available, although at a coarser scale than

the appropriate sequence. Different words in a narrativ

ntents, depending on the extent to which syntax or sen

fore possible to select the degree of narrative detail tha

ding how many of the words to read and how much co

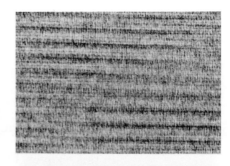

ve itself is defined at the level of the individual lexic

it several different levels of structural detail. When the

ual subject, the chances are high that certain longer

d particularly informative. The distribution of word le

e longer than normal words are preferentially inspecte

well become available, although at a coarser scale than

he appropriate sequence. Different words in a narrativ

tents, depending on the extent to which syntax or sen

re possible to select the degree of narrative detail that

ing how many of the words to read and how much co

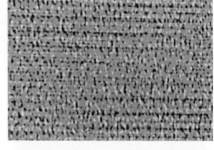

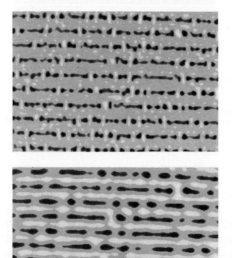

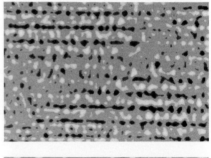

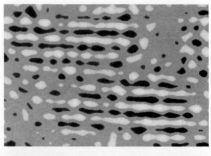

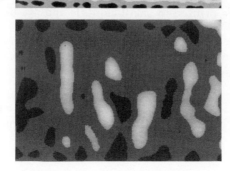

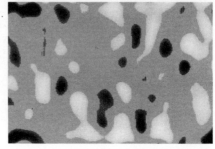

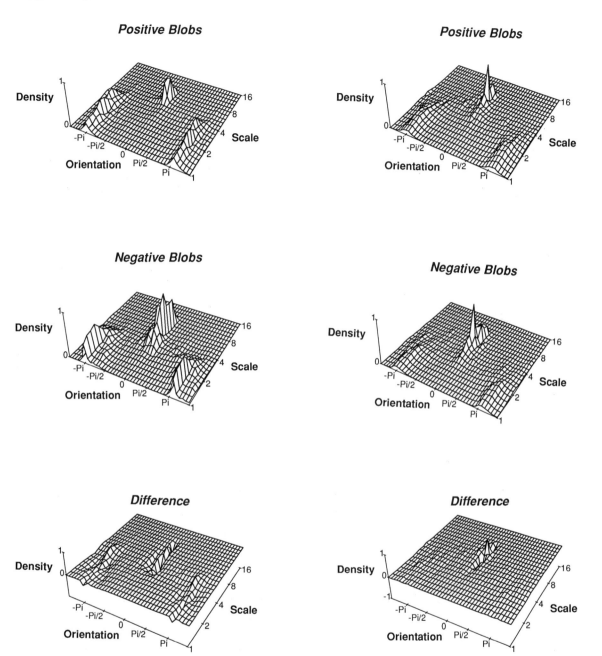

Figure 15. An example of image description. This figure shows two images. On the left is an ordinary page of text; on the right is a sample of noise that has the same power spectrum as the text image but is otherwise random. Beneath each is a series of images of the regions that are found at different spatial scales. The set of descriptions of these would constitute an image description. Finally, to the right, is shown a histogram plotting the distribution of principal axis orientations at different spatial scales. For each image three histograms are shown: one for the positive (bright) blobs; one for the negative (dark) blobs; and one showing the difference between these two histograms. Notice how this statistical description of the image makes explicit the difference between the two images, and makes explicit the nature of the different information available at different spatial scales in each.

(i) Isolating the segment

We start by isolating the segment from the rest of the image. We define the operation

$$\text{Segment (Data; } \mathbf{x_c}, \mathbf{y_c})$$

This is an Image operation: its output is an image which is zero everywhere except in the segment around the point $\mathbf{x_c}$, $\mathbf{y_c}$, where it is set to equal Data. We need the position vector $\mathbf{x_c}$, $\mathbf{y_c}$ in order to say which segment. This point could be found by random search, or it could be specified in advance.

Whether any given point belongs to the segment or not depends on whether it is connected to any other point in the segment. The rule:

$$\mathbf{x}, \mathbf{y} \text{ \underline{CONNECTED}} (\mathbf{x_1}, \mathbf{y_1}; \text{Image})$$

can be defined by

true: sign: value(Image; $\mathbf{x}, \mathbf{y}$) = sign: value(Image; $\mathbf{x_1}, \mathbf{y_1}$) and

$$|(\mathbf{x}, \mathbf{y} - \mathbf{x_1}, \mathbf{y_1})| < W$$

false: otherwise

where W is some arbitrarily small distance. We can define the set of all points in the segment recursively by the rule

$$\textbf{SEGMENT} = \{\mathbf{x}, \mathbf{y}, \mathbf{z} \text{ \underline{CONNECTED}} \textbf{ SEGMENT}\} \upsilon \{\mathbf{x_c}, \mathbf{y_c}, \mathbf{z_c}\}$$

The set **SEGMENT** is a set of vectors (hence the bold type), with each element having three components: two for its position and a third for its value.

We can obtain the set of points on the boundary from this set by applying a further rule to obtain a subset of **SEGMENT**. The easiest way to express this is to take the set of all points that are not in the segment. Let us write the set of all points in the image by the vector set **IMAGE**. The set **SEGMENT** is a subset of **IMAGE**, and the remainder after removing **SEGMENT** can be written as

$$\textbf{IMAGE}\backslash\textbf{SEGMENT}$$

The set of all points on the outline of the segment is the set of all points that conform to the rule

$$\textbf{OUTLINE} = \{(\mathbf{x}, \mathbf{y}, \mathbf{z} \text{ \underline{CONNECTED}} \textbf{ SEGMENT})$$

$$\text{and } (\mathbf{x}, \mathbf{y}, \mathbf{z} \text{ \underline{CONNECTED}} \textbf{ IMAGE}\backslash\textbf{SEGMENT})\}$$

(ii) Describing the Segment

Recall from Chapter 4 that the expression for the (weighted) mean value of an image is:

$$\text{mean}(\text{Image}; \text{Weight}) \Leftrightarrow \frac{\text{sum}(\text{Image} \times \text{Weight})}{\text{sum}(\text{Weight})}$$

With this we can immediately write:

$$\mathbf{centroid}(\text{Image}) \Leftrightarrow \mathbf{mean}(\mathbf{Position}; \text{Image})$$

which involves vectors because **Position** is an image where each value is a vector. **Position** is a two-dimensional value. The output of the image function **Position** is two values. I could have decomposed it into *X-position* and *Y-position*, each giving one value as output. Then

$$x\text{-centroid}(\text{Image}) = \text{mean}(\text{Image} \times X\text{-position})$$

$$y\text{-centroid}(\text{Image}) = \text{mean}(\text{Image} \times Y\text{-position})$$

This long winded notation is avoided by the use of vector quantities.

We can add further statistics such as the principal axis and the calculation of these quantities can be formalized along similar lines. How, once all the statistical descriptors have been calculated, should we organize them into a description?

For each segment we are going to make a sentence which will describe that segment. The sentence is a list of values of the statistics, which we defined in advance with a label. For example:

$$\mathbf{BLOB}(\text{mass}, \mathbf{centroid}, \text{principal axis}, \mathbf{sd}, \text{curvature})$$

Notice that we have used a vector standard deviation: this is the standard deviation, not of values, but of locations. It corresponds to the sd of the centroid.

We can write:

$$s_j \equiv \sum_{(x,y)} ((v_{x,y})^j)$$

where

$\equiv$ means "is equivalent to"

$(v_{x,y})^j$ means "the value at place (x, y) multiplied by itself j times"

and

$\displaystyle\sum_{(x,y)}$ means "sum over all (x, y) places in the image"

This terminology allows us to write the mass of the island simply as s_1, and the mean can be written as s_1/n, where n is the number of places, or area of the island. We can further write down the symbol:

$$\bar{s}_j \equiv \sum_{(x,y)} \left(v_{x,y} - \frac{s_1}{n} \right)^j$$

so that

$$\bar{s}_1 = 0$$

and

$$\bar{s}_2 = \text{variance of grey values in the island.}$$

We start by writing

$$m_{ij} = \sum_{(x,y)} (x^i y^j v_{x,y})$$

where

x^i means the value of the x coordinate at a place, multiplied by itself i times
y^j is similar

and the summation implies that we calculate the product of these three values at every place in the region and then sum them all together.

So, for example, the mass of the region can now be written quite simply as

$$m_{00}$$

It is convenient to use the value of the deviation from the mean rather than the simple value $v(x, y)$ and when we use the deviation from the mean, we can write

$$\bar{m}_{ij} = \sum_{(x,y)} \left(x^i y^j \left(v_{x,y} - \frac{s_1}{n} \right) \right)$$

It now follows that

$$\bar{m}_{00} = 0$$

The centroid of the segment can now be easily written as the point $(\bar{m}_{10}/m_{00}, \bar{m}_{01}/m_{00})$. The spread or standard deviation of the segment in the x dimension can be written as $(\bar{m}_{20}/m_{00})^{1/2}$ and the standard deviation in the y dimension $(\bar{m}_{02}/m_{00})^{1/2}$.

We can easily see that the sum of the first order moments about this point is zero:

$$\sum_{i=1}^{n} (x_i - x_c, y_i - y_c) v_i = \sum_{i=1}^{n} (x_i, y_i) v_i - \sum_{i=1}^{n} (x_c, y_c) v_i$$

$$= \sum_{i=1}^{n} (x_i, y_i) v_i - (x_c, y_c) \sum_{i=1}^{n} v_i$$

$$= \sum_{i=1}^{n} (x_i, y_i) v_i - \frac{\sum_{i=1}^{n} (x_i, y_i) v_i}{\sum_{i=1}^{n} v_i} \sum_{i=1}^{n} v_i$$

$$= \sum_{i=1}^{n} (x_i, y_i) v_i - \sum_{i=1}^{n} (x_i, y_i) v_i$$

therefore

$$\sum_{i=1}^{n} (x_i - x_c, y_i - y_c) v_i = 0$$

Now we can write the standard deviation in a direction r as:

$$\sigma_\theta^2 = \sum (v_i (x_i^2 \cos^2 \theta + 2x_i y_i \sin \theta \cos \theta + y_i^2 \sin^2 \theta))$$

or

$$\sigma_\theta^2 = m_{20} \cos^2 \theta + 2m_{11} \sin \theta \cos \theta + m_{02} \sin^2 \theta$$

Then

$$\frac{d\sigma^2}{d\theta} = -m_{20} \sin 2\theta + 2m_{11} \cos 2\theta + m_{02} \sin 2\theta$$

$$= (m_{02} - m_{20}) \sin 2\theta + 2m_{11} \cos 2\theta$$

If we equate this to zero, then we have

$$\sin 2\theta (m_{20} - m_{02}) = 2m_{11} \cos 2\theta$$

therefore

$$\tan 2\theta = \frac{\sin 2\theta}{\cos 2\theta} = \frac{2m_{11}}{m_{20} - m_{02}}$$

The standard deviations in the x and y directions are given by:

$$\sigma_x = (m_{20}/m_{00})^{1/2}$$
$$\sigma_y = (m_{02}/m_{00})^{1/2}$$

We can, in effect, rotate these to be aligned along and across the principal axis:

$$\sigma_c = \sigma_x \cos \theta - \sigma_y \sin \theta$$
$$\sigma_w = \sigma_y \cos \theta - \sigma_x \sin \theta$$

Of course, the sentence should ideally include the estimate of error for each value as well. The full description of an image is then a set of such sentences.

Finally, just a few notes about curvature to show how the ideas of the previous sections can be extended to other properties. We can write down the equation for a circle, centre $(0, 0)$, as

$$x^2 + y^2 = r^2$$

or centre (x_c, y_c) as

$$(x - x_c)^2 + (y - y_c)^2 = r^2$$

This can be rearranged to give

$$(x - x_c)^2 + (y - y_c)^2 - r^2 = 0$$

Now, if we have a set of points that did lie on a circle then it would also be true that

$$\sum_{i=1}^{n} (x_i - x_c)^2 + (y_i - y_c)^2 - r^2) = 0$$

Suppose that each point lay just off the circle by a small random error, e_i, then the sum would no longer necessarily equal zero. We have for each point a deviation given by

$$(x_i - x_c)^2 + (y_i - y_c)^2 - r^2$$

We can square this deviation and then obtain the mean square deviation. Just as before when looking at the principal axis, the expression for mean square deviation can be minimized with respect to the unknown parameters to find the circular arc that best fits the data.

References

Suggested further reading

Asada H. and Brady J.M. (1986) The curvature primal sketch. *IEEE Trans. Pattern Anal. Machine Intelligence* 8, 2–14.
Blake A. and Zimmerman A. (1987) "Visual Reconstruction". MIT Press, Boston.
Burns J.B. Hanson A.R. and Riseman E.M. (1984) Extracting straight lines. In: Proc DARPA IU Workshop, New Orleans. Reprinted in M.A. Fischler and O. Firschein (eds) (1987) "Readings in Computer Vision". Morgan Kaufman, Los Altos, CA.
Cooper D.B. (1979) Maximum likelihood estimation of Markov process blob boundaries in noisy images. *IEEE Trans. Pattern Anal. Machine Intelligence* 1, 372–384.
Julesz B. and Bergan J.R. (1983) Textons: the fundamental elements in preattentive vision and perception of textures. *Bell Systems Tech. J.* 62 II, 1619–1645.
Lowe D.G. and Binford T.O. (1982) Segregation and aggregation: an approach to figure-ground phenomena. Proc. DARPA IU Workshop, Palo Alto, CA. Reprinted in M.A. Fischler and O. Firschein (eds) (1987) "Readings in Computer Vision". Morgan Kaufman, Los Altos, CA.
Mott-Smith J.C. (1970) Medial axis transformations. In: B.S. Lipkin and A. Rosenfeld (eds) "Picture Processing and Psychopictorics". Academic Press, New York.
Nevatia R. and Babu K.R. (1980) Linear feature extraction and description. *Comput. Graph. Image Proc.* 13, 257–269.

Exercises

1. Now design a system for approaching a bright light, where there may be more than one in the field of view.
2. From an image we can obtain a number of **BLOB** descriptive sentences. Since these will all have the same parameters, we can compute the typical **BLOB** by averaging each parameter. Give some examples of situations where this might be a useful thing to do. Under what circumstances would some or all of these mean parameters change smoothly?
3. Under what conditions do the parameters in a **BLOB** sentence change together in related manners? This suggests a different way of parameterizing the sentence. What would the benefits of such a new approach be, and what are its disadvantages?
4. If a number of descriptive sentences of the same type are obtained from filtering at different spatial scales, what are the constraints on the parameter values that will be obtained at each scale? What use could these constraints be put to?

6

Visual Description

In the previous chapter, I have described techniques whereby an image description can be created. This description is an (unstructured) set of many sentences, each one describing one small region or aspect of the image. There is no guarantee that any one of these will contain all the information that is necessary for an action because it is likely that more than one sentence will have resulted from the image of any one thing in the scene. We must now explore ways in which the sentences of the description can be brought into a number of small sets one of which could contain all the information that will be required for an action or decision about an action. The structure that is created by doing this I will call a visual description. As with the preceding chapters, the emphasis lies with questions of how our understanding can be formalized rather than how these processes might actually occur in the brain or any robot vision system.

We start by seeing why this level of understanding is necessary, by examining a few simple visual actions.

6.1 Controlling Actions

We have already discussed how a whole image can be converted into a few numbers which can then be used to control simple actions. When using a set of descriptive sentences to control actions the same strategy applies, although there is an added richness due to the additional range of information available. It is possible to be selective by controlling actions towards small parts of an image where such parts themselves are determined by the contents of the image and therefore by the contents of the scene.

(i) Touching Something

In Chapter 1, I listed a few general types of visually guided behaviour. The most basic of these was touching something. In order to touch something it is necessary to have information about its location in three-dimensional space, that is its direction and distance, and information about its movement. What we need to do is to prepare a descriptive sentence holding these parameters and then send it to the apparatus that will carry out the action.

Figure 1.   Image of various things. In this image there are various things to which the actions of touching, grasping and lifting could be directed. The success of these different actions will depend on different properties of the visual descriptions. Beside the image is shown a set of blobs that were obtained by simple image algebra. All of these would lead to sensible touching. But in order to grasp and to lift, some of the things we need to bring together several different blobs into a single description. It is how this might be done that is the main concern of this chapter.

So far as we are concerned, touching something can be treated as equivalent to the creation of the appropriate sentence. The sentence might have the generic form:

TOUCH(**direction**; distance; ACTIVE)

The list to the touch action contains two parameters, ***direction*** and *distance* that are simple quantities (the first is a vector, the second a scalar), but also contains a Boolean, ACTIVE, which is essentially a control parameter. The sentence can be constructed with this set to false, so that nothing happens. When the time is ripe, it can be set to true so that the activity is started. In return, the parameter might be reset to false when the action is completed. It is more useful to use a control parameter which can take on a continuous range of values between 0 (false) and 1 (true). This fuzzy Boolean would then allow the action to be controlled in a graded fashion. For example, the calculation of the distance parameter, may involve a sequence of improving estimates. It would be inefficient to hold the action back until the sequence was completed, and a better strategy would be to allow the action to be initiated with some uncertainty early in the sequence. The control parameter could then be used to govern the approach of the finger.

Preparing a sentence of this sort is not very difficult, at least in principle. For a simple action like touching, most of the parameters are of the same form as those that are found in the image description. One could convert each **BLOB** sentence into an equivalent **TOUCH** sentence quite automatically by selecting the relevant parameters from the former. One could set the control parameter to take the value of the mass in each case, normalized by dividing each one by the greatest mass in the image description. If this were done then the action would be directed towards that blob with the largest mass.

(ii) Grasping Something

If we wish to grasp an object, then we shall need to issue an action description which is similar to that for touching, but has a new parameter.

$$\textbf{GRASP}(\textbf{direction}; \text{distance}; \text{width}; \text{ACTIVE})$$

The scalar parameter, *width*, is not quite the same as the other parameters. The width that is being expressed here is the width that the fingers should open. This is not likely to be specified by the parameters of any one **BLOB** descriptive sentence, but by the combination of the parameters of more than one **BLOB**. This creates two difficulties. The first one is to know which sentences to combine: we cannot now simply deliver an action sentence for each description sentence but must have a means for taking neighbouring sentences together. The second difficulty is then to know how to combine the parameters.

The difference between grasping and touching is that the object of the action is extended. It is sensible to talk about touching a point; grasping will only succeed if it takes into account the extent of the object. A further consequence of this is that there are usually several different successful ways of grasping something. The implication of this is that there are several different sentences to describe the proposed action all of which produce equivalent outcomes. The fingers may be held differently, but the same object has been achieved. In this respect the sentences are equivalent, but there is an important qualification to make. Try picking something up several different ways. I'm sure that you will find that the consequences can all be the same, but you will also notice that the room for error varies considerably. Some grips are good and others are less so.

This aspect, if predictable, can be signalled to the action mechanism through the control parameter, as can an estimate of the accuracy of the parameters that are being delivered. In this way, the visual system can provide a set of alternatives each of which has been partially evaluated, and then the most likely can be selected.

(iii) Lifting Something

In lifting something, a grip is applied to it which is sufficient to arrest it, and move it against a force such as gravity. A grip of this type requires that several opposing forces be applied to the object. The only way to pick up a football with one hand is to place that hand under the ball and push upwards so that gravity applies the other one of the opposing forces. With two hands, the ball can also be picked up by placing them on opposite sides. The number of available forces has a consequence for the constraints on how they can be used. Try picking up a selection of things with two fingers and then with all five, but without the palm and finally with all your hand. Try this with a range of different sizes and weights. You will see how there are severe constraints on where the fingers can be placed for success. Now try slippery ice cubes.

There are two important differences between touching or grasping something and lifting it. The success of lifting depends upon identifying where are the best grip points, as before, but also where the centre of gravity of the object lies. To estimate where the centre of gravity lies, we need to know the full extent of the object, not just its visible extent. If two somewhat separated parts of an image have very similar texture and colour patterns, or have other properties in common, then it is likely that they have both arisen from the one object. This has to be borne in mind when deciding where the centre of gravity might lie. When deciding how much force to apply, we need to know how rough the surface is. A rough surface is textured and will not give rise to a smooth image. The converse is not necessarily true but can be assumed to be more often right than wrong.

The action sentence that we create will contain all this information:

$$LIFT(Grasp(); \text{ Surface Quality}(); \text{ ACTIVE})$$

The sentence contains two parameters that are labels for further descriptive sentences. The technical term for this type of parameter is a *pointer*, because it points to the information. This notion of embedding a sentence within a sentence is a useful device. The *Grasp* sentence will have the same general form as we considered before, except that it has now to take into account the full extent of the object; the *Surface Quality* sentence will contain information about how rough the surface is, perhaps how hot or cold it is likely to be, and maybe other further qualities. All of this cannot be represented by a simple quantity, hence the convenience of using a pointer.

The construction of the **LIFT** sentence will require a further device for deciding which descriptive sentences should be used because spatial neighbourhoods will not suffice. We need to also combine somewhat more remote sentences if they are similar enough. The construction of the **SURFACE QUALITY** sentence will be based on the same descriptive sentences that are used to create the **GRASP** sentence, and we shall need a way of combining their different parameters to produce the appropriate new ones.

Recapitulation

This consideration of simple behaviours has identified a number of processes involving descriptive sentences that we need to understand. A large set of descriptive sentences will lead to a much larger set of potential actions and their descriptions. Somehow, some choices between these will have to be made. I do not propose to consider this.

(i)   Touching can be controlled more or less directly from basic image descriptions and needs no further consideration.

(ii)   Grasping requires that a set of sentences from neighbouring parts of an image be isolated and used to control the size of the grasp because no one sentence is likely to contain the information. The set of sentences will all be constrained in having very similar properties, and in particular their spatial locations will all be very close together (at least with respect to the size of the hand). The first process that we need is one to cluster together *neighbouring sentences*.

(iii) Lifting requires the identification of the various connected parts of the object. These are likely to be identifiable by similar surface properties and hence similar image properties, even when not necessarily close together in space. The second process that we need is one to cluster together *similar sentences*.

6.2 Relationships between Sentences

We started with an optical image, proceeded through various image algebraic processes and finally produced a set of descriptive sentences. From any one optical image it will often be useful to apply several different sequences of algebraic processes to produce several different sets of sentences, perhaps for example at different spatial scales. All these sets, which have no structure, can be very easily put together in a single all-inclusive image set. Our goal is to build from these image descriptions a set of descriptive sentences that represent potential actions in the scene.

The first step is to form from the image set a number of subsets, within each of which all elements can be treated as being likely to have a common physical cause in the scene. Ideally, the elements of a subset should all be relatively closely related, thereby increasing the likelihood that they all derive from a common cause. Notice that, because we are starting with such an unstructured device as a set, no relationships between elements are explicit. By making these relationships explicit, and thereby structuring the description to create a visual description, we can proceed towards our aim of descriptions of actions. So what is a relationship?

In everyday terms, I have relationships of various types with other people. I am closely related to some and less so or not at all related to others. Sometimes the relationships are temporary, sometimes they are more permanent. Some are strong relationships, others are weak. There are different causes and different functions for these relationships, some are family or business or social, others are purely coincidental. Relationships have a degree, have a time course, and have a quality and cause. The relationships between elements in a description are similarly complex.

Consider the relationships in a simple family. Each member is related to each other, and the relationships are described as *married to*, *child to*, or *parent to*. Each relationship exists, and may be described, because of some event or state in the world. The relationships plus the people involved, when taken together define new elements of description, the couple X, the children of X, the family X. These new elements stand for the people involved and their relationships.

So it is with descriptive sentences, where sentence A can be said to be *next to* sentence B or *similar to*, *connected to*, *surrounding* or *equivalent to*. These relationships have a number of specific properties. Some of them are transitive, which means that the relationship can pass on. If A is equivalent to B, and B is equivalent to C, then A is equivalent to C. Sometimes the relationships are symmetric, such as *next to*; others are not, such as *surrounding*. In the latter case there is an inverse, *surrounded by*.

The essence of all relationships is a condition or set of conditions that must be met. In order for two people to have the relationship *married to*, then one should be a man and one a woman; they should have made certain promises to each other, and so on. One condition specifies the types of things that may enter into the relationship. In order to assess whether A is related to B in the way prescribed, then we have first to check what A and B are: we must check types. Is A a man, and B a woman, or A a woman and B a man? We then check whether the property of the relationship exists: do the constituents have the appropriate configuration? In relationships between descriptive sentences the same considerations apply. The types of the sentences involved are, or may be, important, and their configuration must also be examined.

Once a relationship has been established, then we can use a new description to replace the descriptions of its elements. The new description will have qualities that depend both on the constituent elements and on the relationship itself. The new description has certain inherent properties that describe the constituents, but that are also dependent on the relationship. The couple X describes two people that have a certain configuration. Sometimes the new description so completely captures the important properties of the constituent elements that it can stand in place of them. The important consequence of *combining elements* is that the elements themselves are then unavailable, individually, afterwards. As we shall see in the next section, there are situations where this is appropriate, and the result is a single new sentence. On other occasions, the relationship may be relatively accidental and is not sufficiently powerful for its label to stand in place of the constituent elements. In this case the result is a set of sentences. By *associating elements* we are not committed to the relationship should it prove uninteresting or useless.

6.3 Combining Sentences

Starting with a set of **BLOB** sentences from an image description, we can use a selection of relationships to build up a richer, more diverse, description. The simplest type of relationship involves a condition on just one element. For example, if a blob in an image is elongated then we could describe it as a line. This means that if a **BLOB** sentence has two principal standard deviations that are markedly different, then we could make a **LINE** sentence to stand for the **BLOB**. The type condition requires one **BLOB**; the configuration condition requires a high ratio between the two sds.

The **LINE** sentence will have as parameters length, width and orientation that can be derived directly from the principal axis and standard deviations of the **BLOB** sentence. But it may be desirable to have other parameters such as how wiggly it is, that cannot really be measured until it has already been decided that a LINE sentence is being constructed. To deal with this type of requirement, it is convenient to be able to return to the image region itself and then create a further characterization.

TYPE(Mass	Centroid	Length/Width	Orientation)
BLOB(-520.15	-14.99,63.87	33.91,12.63	79.048)
BLOB(96.05	-7.77,113.69	5.65,3.64	89.082)
BLOB(395.33	-2.76,39.89	22.56,4.05	-89.451)
BLOB(241.83	-37.75,40.73	16.65,4.47	-86.654)
BLOB(375.20	-103.59,27.76	15.51,4.30	-85.770)
BLOB(-64.58	128.82,33.44	9.65,2.70	-88.639)
BLOB(-186.66	-131.44,32.85	9.27,4.96	-74.118)
BLOB(410.33	111.14,2.76	31.85,4.14	88.864)
BLOB(-191.17	-82.69,34.17	7.68,6.14	-34.876)
BLOB(-136.45	17.18,26.60	9.98,4.60	82.949)
BLOB(-78.52	-156.67,8.16	8.45,3.57	-76.287)
BLOB(119.84	-68.24,-4.59	5.16,4.09	-16.514)
BLOB(-160.47	-82.00,-29.18	12.43,6.37	87.867)
BLOB(151.56	-104.52,-42.31	13.81,4.16	-67.034)
BLOB(-101.51	-129.55,-47.54	12.27,4.20	-60.314)
BLOB(-146.24	140.79,-50.75	21.65,8.29	-16.361)
BLOB(-81.28	79.60,-55.57	15.66,2.41	-2.242)
BLOB(62.04	47.92,-71.32	9.16,3.38	1.782)
BLOB(106.56	110.39,-73.21	15.50,3.03	0.427)
BLOB(56.89	175.55,-76.46	7.76,3.13	4.614)
BLOB(364.81	-142.84,-97.39	32.41,8.01	-20.535)
BLOB(114.98	-29.86,-80.03	24.28,2.51	-2.285)
BLOB(-222.98	-158.07,-115.69	23.70,3.61	-13.406)
BLOB(-106.53	25.39,-116.69	25.07,2.08	-11.891)
LINE(395.33	-2.76,39.89	22.56,4.05	-89.451)
LINE(410.33	111.14,2.76	31.85,4.14	88.864)
LINE(-81.28	79.60,-55.57	15.66,2.41	-2.242)
LINE(106.56	110.39,-73.21	15.50,3.03	0.427)
LINE(114.98	-29.86,-80.03	24.28,2.51	-2.285)
LINE(-222.98	-158.07,-115.69	23.70,3.61	-13.406)
LINE(-106.53	25.39,-116.69	25.07,2.08	-11.891)

Figure 2. Blobs and lines. This figure shows the descriptions of the regions in the previous figure. Some can be described as lines, and the alternative descriptions of these are also given.

A more complicated relationship would involve two sentences. If two lines in an image meet at their end points, then we have a corner. The condition on the types is that they should be **LINE**s (which in turn requires that they be elongated **BLOB**s). The condition on their configuration requires that they have certain position and orientation relationships. Where these conditions are met a **CORNER** sentence can be created and used to replace the two **LINE** sentences. We could define a **RECTANGLE** sentence. The type condition would require four **CORNER** descriptions (four **LINE** descriptions might not touch). The configuration condition

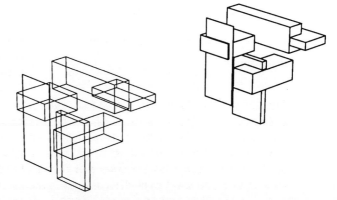

Figure 3. Three-dimensional rectangles. Although you can see a clear three-dimensional organization in this figure, it is instructive to think about the nature of the visual descriptions that could be produced. Give each line and each line end a unique label, and then consider what relationships between these elementary features are needed to create a description of the faces, and their relationships.

would involve *connected to* relationships. A **POLYGON** description would require an unspecified number of constituent elements. Notice that the type of a sentence is a shorthand for the relationship which itself involves simpler types in a specific configuration. This means that types have properties: for example, the type **LINE** has the property of elongation.

All sentences, whether simple, as we considered in the previous chapter, or more complex descriptions of actions or decisions, as I described in this chapter, are built up out of two basic types of element: symbols and quantities. Before describing the operations that can be performed on sentences, we must consider these elements.

(i) Symbols

Let's start by taking a sphere of radius r and centre $C_{xyz} = (x_c, y_c, z_c)$ as an example. It has the equation

$$(x - x_c)^2 + (y - y_c)^2 + (z - z_c)^2 = r^2$$

Another way of writing this, is to assume the three dimensions and note that for any point on or under the sphere surface p_{xyz}, the distance from the centre, C_{xyz} must be less than or equal to the radius. A way of writing this is:

$$|p_{xyz} - C_{xyz}| \leqslant r$$

The vertical lines either side of the difference mean that the absolute (positive) value of the quantity should be used.

We can now define the set, P, of all points in the sphere as the set of all positions that obey this condition for given values of C_{xyz} and r. P is the set of all points given by the mapping from C_{xyz} and r.

The concept of defining a set by a condition which holds true for all members and false for all non-members now allows us to proceed a step further. Let us call the conditional rule a symbol, which we can write down like this:

$$\text{sphere}(C_{xyz}, r)$$

This symbol defines a set for any particular pair of values for its two parameters, C_{xyz} and r. Because we can write the set down in an abstract form with two unspecified parameters, we have also and incidentally found a way of specifying the set of all spheres. This is a set of sets. Any member of this set of sets is a sphere; any member of the set defined by the symbol sphere is a point in three-dimensional space.

When we use symbols in a hierarchy where high order symbols refer to specific configurations of lower order symbols and so on, we are implicitly invoking a grammar. For instance, one can talk of a herd of elephants, but not an elephant of herds: the hierarchical symbols elephant and herd have allotted places in a grammar (although be careful here: the grammar is not ordinary English syntax).

The building blocks are the alphabet, a finite set of symbols, which for purely formal reasons includes a null symbol, corresponding to nothingness. Along with the symbols is a grammar, which is a finite set of rules which determine how the symbols of the alphabet shall be combined to form sentences. A complete grammar will contain rules that allow the construction of all valid sentences, and no invalid sentences.

Let us start with a simple symbol, such as point, and set out to describe some three-dimensional scene. The availability of an elemental symbol such as point guarantees us that anything in the scene could be described as a set of symbols.

One possible way to make a description of the scene is to create a list of all the points in the scene where there is solid matter. This description is complete in the sense that it has not omitted anything, It is however likely to be unwieldy and it hasn't captured anything particularly interesting or useful about the scene. From this description, we could tell whether a particular place in the scene was occupied by matter or not. We couldn't tell explicitly if the point was just an isolated blip or part of some extensive chunk of matter.

We need some more symbols in our alphabet. Recall the symbol sphere and how it was defined by a condition

$$|p - C| \leqslant r$$

If we could collect from our scene description a set of points, all of which conformed to this condition, and which completely filled the relevant space, then we could replace all those point symbols by one sphere symbol. To be precise, we are requiring that for a particular value of C and r there exists, within the set of points in our scene description, a subset which has two properties: (1) the position of each point lies within a distance r of the place C and (2) there exists no place which fulfils the first condition but which is not a member of the subset. This has described a so-called space-filling model of the sphere. We could apply the two rules to a cube and find a sphere of radius one-half of the side of the cube. In what is then left of each of the four corners of the cube we could find a smaller sphere, and so on until we had effectively filled the space of the cube with spheres of various sizes. This has provided a more economical description of the cube than we would have with just point symbols. Of course, a cube symbol would be still more efficient.

Clearly when used like this the presence of a sphere symbol in a description does not mean that there is a sphere in the scene. In order to have this correspondence between the symbol and a sphere there are some modifications required. We could change the rules which define the symbol so that they defined the outside surface of the sphere, in which case they would not apply at all to the cube. An alternative is to add an element to the grammar that will describe whether the matter corresponding to two sphere symbols is connected or not.

If the representation is a hierarchical model of the scene, then the extent to which its symbols are mappings for a particular subset of the image list is a measure of how adequately they might describe the scene. By allowing in our example the symbol point we have created a representation system that is sufficient to describe any spatial configuration. There is not a three-dimensional body that cannot be described as a set of points, although as we noted this symbol is not efficient: the representation produced is very cumbersome. For a scene that has plenty of spheres, the symbol sphere would be much more efficient. If we knew what was in the scene, or even likely to be in the scene, it would be a simple matter to design an efficient alphabet of symbols to represent that scene. In general, the more symbols, the more efficient the description will be, but it may be more difficult to find that efficient description. If the symbols are orthogonal, that is there is no overlap in their individual domains, then there is an unique representation, but if they are not, if they are redundant, as are point and sphere, then there are several valid representations, some of which are more efficient than the others.

Under what circumstances is an alphabet not orthogonal? The answer is that a flexible alphabet, designed to cope with a range of scenes which might contain novel bodies that perhaps do not even exist when the representation is being designed, is bound to be redundant. There have to be some very general purpose symbols, such as point to allow for the most unexpected, but for reasons of efficiency there also have to be some specific symbols, such as sphere. One can always replace the specific symbols in a given description by the general purpose ones, hence the multiplicity.

(ii) Quantities

An occluding edge gives rise to a luminance change that may be detected; its curvature may be calculated according to some rule, but this curvature needs to be made into a measurement. Just what does it mean to say that an edge has a particular degree of curvature? It is now necessary to consider the general theory of measurements.

How do we measure a curvature? We take a standard unit of curvature and then, starting from an origin (e.g. zero), count how many such units are required to make an equivalent curvature. An equivalent curvature is one which, when transferred to the right position, would replace exactly the curvature that is being measured. There are four arbitrary aspects to this: we are using an ordering of values; the standard unit defines a scale; and counting implicitly defines both an origin and a combination rule of how to continue the measurements (e.g. by addition). Taken together these aspects define a metric.

There are several possibilities for dealing with quantities in a submetrical fashion. For example, the definition of ordering on its own without scale, origin or combination rule could be used where it is only ever necessary to decide if a is greater than b. If we wish to know if the difference between a and b is greater than the difference between c and d, then we need also an origin and a scale. Finally if we wanted to know if the difference between a and b was twice the difference between c and d then we would also need a combination rule.

Try this experiment. Sing a note and then find it on a piano. Unless you have chosen a note that you can accurately identify, finding it on the piano involves trial and error. After a few attempts you will have converged on the correct note. Now sing another note, and repeat the process. Your attempts to find the right note will have demonstrated most of the functional aspects of metrics that we are going to be interested in.

There are all sorts of ways in which the origin of a metric can be set. Consider the case of edge blur. What is the quality of a "sharp edge"? It is one extreme of the range of received edge blurs: it is the smallest edge blur experienced. In order to know which is the smallest edge blur, all that is required is an ordering of edge blur values in the input. An ordering preserves only "greater than", "less than" information, not the magnitudes of differences. A system which organized itself with this rule for defining the origin for the metric of edge blur would not be affected by a deterioration in lens quality. There are many visual attributes that may be given a self-organizing origin like this. The mean curvature of lines and edges can be treated as an origin. In the output of a system with or without bias, this will correspond to a curvature of zero in the input. However, the mean is a metrical measure of central tendency because it is calculated from values of curvature. There are other measures of central tendency that only require that the ordering of values be maintained as for example the median.

The scale of a metric can also be self-organizing. This can be done by defining the extrema of the domain and then representing each point within as a fraction of the distance between beginning and end of the domain. This is rarely practical because most visual attributes do not have definite extreme values. Another related possibility is to use the standard deviation as a measure of the extent of the distribution and thence as a unit for the scale. The standard deviation is a metrical measure of dispersion, and is not really suitable as a result. Finally, the unit for a self-organizing scale could be given by the distance from the origin that is occupied by any arbitrary percentage of all the measurements.

The combination rule of a metric depends on what the measurements will be used for. For example, in the case of edge curvature or blur, there is no need for a combination rule because there will be no need to combine measurement, although comparisons will be needed. In the case of orientation, the domain has no boundaries: it is cyclic. Rotations of lines are additive, and so, therefore, should be the measurements. The scale and combination rule should be linear.

6.4 Associating Sentences

Sentences that arise from nearby parts of an image may have a common cause, but they may not. Sentences that are similar in some or most of their attributes may have a common cause, but they may not. For these situations we shall use a weaker mechanism for combining sentences which associates them into subsets. Each sentence can belong to several subsets, and we can then check which associations are the best.

Each sentence has a number, n, of parameters and, unless there was something degenerate in the image of the algebraic processes, none of the sentences will have the same list of parameters. All the sentences are different. The list of parameters assigns to each sentence a unique location in an n-dimensional space. We are concerned with discussing how to decide which sentences are near to each other in this space and which are similar to each other. Suppose that n had the value 1. In this case each sentence has a unique location in a one-dimensional space, a place along a line. What relationships are possible in this case? Of course there are many but they are all compounds of the simple relational elements *left of*, *right of*, *next to* and *distance to*. With these relational expressions, we can specify the relationship between any two elements in the description. Notice that there are inherently two ways of expressing the distance between two elements. One is ordinal by using, repeatedly, the *next to* expression to make a statement like 3 to the *left of*. The alternative is to use the *distance to* expression. This allows for the possibility that not all neighbours (*next to*'s) have the same separation on the line.

Relationships in One Dimension

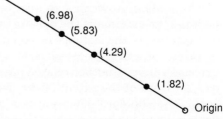

Figure 4. Relationships in one dimension. Sentences with only one parameter may be marked on a line at a position corresponding to the value of that parameter.

Relationships in Two Dimensions

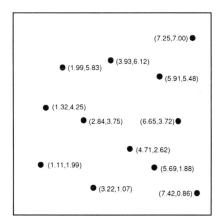

Figure 5. Relationships in two dimensions. Sentences with two parameters may be marked on a plane at a position corresponding to the value of their parameters. The scope for relationships is much increased.

For a two-parameter description, we can assign to each element a unique location in a two-dimensional space. To express the relationships between two elements we can use the one-dimensional relations in each of the two parameters independently, but we shall need another relational expression. It is possible for two elements to have the same value for one of their parameters, and so we can no longer be sure that every element has a unique place on each dimension. Therefore we need a *coincident with* expression.

(i) Neighbourhood Relationships

Elements in a description that come from neighbouring points in an image are likely to have a common cause, and it is therefore sensible to consider associating them. So, we shall consider how to define the neighbourhood relationship. It really applies with most force in the two or three dimensions of space, but there is no reason why other dimensions such as time should not also be considered.

A neighbourhood is a small area centred around a place, and the neighbours are the inhabitants of that area. The central idea is that of distance. In everyday terms, our neighbours are those people that live near us. In one dimension, the neighbours to a point on a line are the nearest points in each of the two directions (left and right). Distance in one dimension is defined as the difference between the values of two points along a line. This definition has two properties. If the two points are equally shifted, by adding the same value to each, then distance is unchanged. If the line is stretched, by multiplying each value, then distance is equally stretched.

In two dimensions, distance is usually defined from the differences between the two points on each dimension separately, Δx and Δy by the expression

$$d = (\Delta x^2 + \Delta y^2)^{1/2}$$

This has the property of shift invariance. If a length or distance is moved in any direction then its distance is unchanged. If the space is stretched uniformly in all directions then the distance is also stretched by an equal amount. Both these properties hold for a simpler expression that might be used:

$$d = (\Delta x + \Delta y)$$

which can be written rather clumsily as:

$$d = (\Delta x^1 + \Delta y^1)^{1/1}$$

which makes its relationship to the previous formula rather more clear.

We must note, however, that the first expression has a third property that the second lacks. If the length or distance is rotated through any angle then distance remains unchanged for the first but not the second. The first is calculated in a *Euclidean metric*; the second is calculated in a *city block metric*. The major difference between the two is the status of the two dimensions. These are at right angles, but in a Euclidean metric the two directions are treated as being arbitrary, having no more significance than any other pair at right angles to each other. In a city block metric, the two directions are the only ones along which you can travel, just like the streets in Manhattan. A more general measure for the distance between two points is given by the expression:

$$d = (\Delta x^a + \Delta y^a)^{1/a}$$

where a is constant. This is known as the Minkowski metric. The Euclidean metric and the city block metric are special cases where a equals 2 and 1, respectively.

Now we turn to the two-dimensional equivalent of the *next to* relation. In one dimension the relation can be defined as selecting the nearest element in each direction. If we adopt the same definition of *next to* as the nearest in each direction for two dimensions, then we are likely to include most of the elements in the complete description as being neighbours to our given point, because the only points that are ruled out are those that are truly aligned along the same bearing as a nearer point. Points are only excluded from the relationship by being occluded. The problem here is that each point occupies an infinitesimal region of our two-dimensional space, and therefore occludes an infinitesimal portion of the space beyond. We need to make each element of the description occupy a substantial region of the space. We are already prepared with the solution to this requirement. Each parameter in the sentence was calculated with an estimated error. If we use this error to define a region around its central location, then the sentence occupies an area of the space and thus occludes a substantial portion. Imagine that for each element in the description we make a mountain up

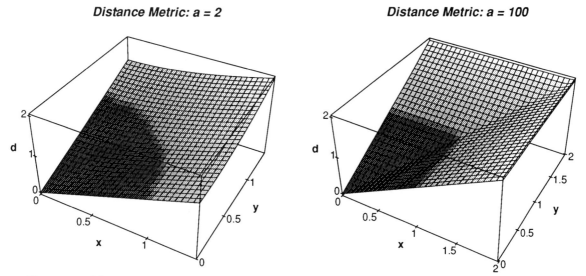

Figure 6. Distance metrics. These graphs show the distances between two points as a function of their relative locations in a two-dimensional space. The two ground axes of the graph are the quantities Δx and Δy, and the vertical axis is the distance between them. Several examples are shown with different values for a, the Minkowski metric term. The lower the height of the graph, the less distant the two points would be regarded. Notice that a difference in either dimension is sufficient to cause the two points to be regarded as separated.

from the two-dimensional space so that its height at any point (which becomes a third dimension) is a measure of the probability that the element is located at that point. The peak of the mountain is the best estimate of where the element is, and the breadth of the mountain is its error. Now, if we stand at the location of any element in the description we will only be able to see a few peaks, and these can be defined to be the neighbours of the element whose location we are occupying. We have defined a *neighbour to* relation.

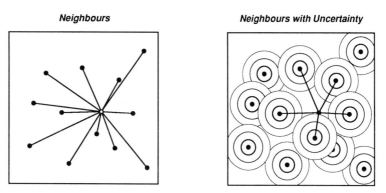

Figure 7. Neighbours in two dimensions. A number of points are marked in two dimensions. If we just took the nearest point in each direction, then all points would be neighbours of all points. By including the error with which the position of each point is known, and an error in assessing the relationship, we can reduce the neighbourhood about each point to a more desirable size.

For a system of calculating neighbourhoods in this way, the number of elements that are next to a given point depends on several factors. If the space is sparsely filled with points, then the neighbourhood will extend further, and the number of neighbours will be greater than if the space is dense. A sparse space is like an expanded dense space except that the error magnitudes remain unexpanded and thus occlude less of the area beyond. It is probably a drawback that the number of neighbours should increase as the space is made more sparse. A simple remedy to this is to combine the error due to the measurement of the parameters involved with a second error term that we could ascribe to the relationship and that was proportional to the distance involved. Adding the squares of the two errors, or multiplying the two errors would be suitable combinations. Now the number of neighbours will be roughly fixed and independent of the density with which the space is occupied. The relationship error term is a factor of the distance; but adjusting this factor, we can adjust the number of neighbours to expect.

The extension to n dimensions cannot be visualized, but is in all essentials the same. Distance in an n-dimensional space is given by the Euclidean formula:

$$(\Delta_1^2 + \Delta_2^2 + \Delta_3^2 + \cdots + \Delta_i^2 \cdots + \Delta_n^2)^{1/2}$$

where Δ_i is the difference in the ith parameter. However when we add numbers in different dimensions we are doing something very arbitrary. What is the sum of three apples and four grapes? It depends on why you are adding the quantities. One answer is seven fruits; another is 3 (weight of an apple) + 4 (weight of a grape). This latter example is called a *weighted sum*, and there is always the difficulty of choosing the appropriate set of weights in an expression like the Euclidean fomula.

The reason why this extension to n dimensions is rather arbitrary is because of the rotation property of Euclidean space. As something rotates, one of its dimensions becomes smaller and the others increase to compensate. Whilst this is quite acceptable when both dimensions are the same type as when they are both spatial, it may be much less acceptable more generally.

The least arbitrary approach is to use weights that make some aspect of the space uniform in all its dimensions. Applying a weight to one of the dimensions is like stretching the space in that dimension (if the weight is greater than one). Stretching a space decreases the density of points in that dimension, and it would be possible to select weights so that all dimensions had equal densities. If a self-organizing metric has been used on all dimensions, then a self-organized space has also been used and it should be fairly uniform.

Applying weights is also rather like assigning an importance, and there are several good reasons for doing this. The most general is where the parameter values is one dimension are much less reliable than in other dimensions. The estimated errors are high and it clearly does not make sense to weight this dimension as highly as the others.

The sentences involved must have the same list of parameters, in the same order, if we are going to calculate distances and neighbourhoods using all the parameters. It is, however, quite reasonable to use just a subset of the parameters and this allows different types of sentence to be associated in neighbourhoods.

(ii) Similarity Relationships

It is possible, often likely, that there will be instances where we will find two sentences that have very similar values for most of their parameters but perhaps one or two that are very different. The more parameters that two descriptive sentences have in common the more likely it is that they have a common cause in the scene.

We could set about examining this by ignoring each dimension in turn when we calculate neighbourhood relations, and then ignoring all pairs of dimensions and so on, but clearly the searching space becomes enormous. An alternative is to calculate distance with the following expression:

$$(\Delta_1^{-2} + \Delta_2^{-2} \cdots + \Delta_i^{-2} \cdots + \Delta_n^{-2})^{-1/2}$$

Low values of this correspond to high similarity. This is the same as the Euclidean formula, except that we are using powers of -2, rather than $+2$. As before there is a whole series of possibilities with different values for the exponent. Figure 8 shows the effect of using a negative power term. The surface in the figure tends to bow outwards, meaning that the similarity is less affected by a difference in one of the dimensions than is the distance measured with a positive power. Where there is a large Δ_i it will make very little difference to the overall result since the square of its reciprocal will be very small. Just as with the Euclidean formula, the above expression should be weighted in each dimension so that the terms are homogeneous.

I shall call the reciprocal of the quantity that is measured by this new formula, the similarity distance between the two descriptions from which it was formed. So for example, lines which are unusually close and are unusual in being parallel will have, all other dimensions being typically unrelated, a relatively high similarity. Measuring the extent to which two descriptions are similar then depends on being able to form accurate self-organized metrics for the dimensions of interest. It is not possible to say how similar the two orientations of 45° and 48° are without knowing how the values of orientation are distributed over the rest of the image.

It would be particularly useful to be able to use the logic of neighbourhood relationships in the context of similarity relationships. We saw how to define a multidimensional equivalent to the *next to* relation, which we called a *neighbour to* relation. What is an equivalent *similar to* relation? In calculating neighbourhood relations, we used Euclidean distance; we can replace the Euclidean distance by the similarity distance and thereby create similarity relationships. We can take a sentence from our original description and compute a similarity distance and error for each of the others. Then we can construct a set of neighbours which are *similar to* the sentence that we started with.

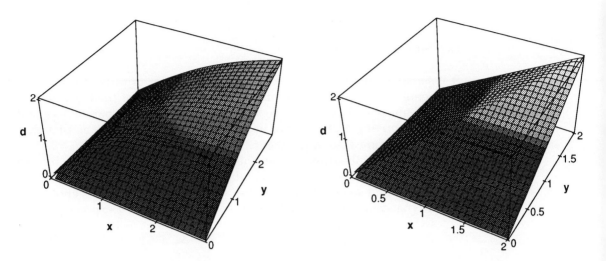

Figure 8.   Difference metrics. These graphs show the measure of difference between two points as a function of their relative locations in a two-dimensional space. The two ground axes of the graph are the quantities Δx and Δy, and the vertical axis is the distance between them. Several examples are shown with different values for *a*, the Minkowski metric term. The lower the height of the graph, the more similar the two points would be regarded. Notice that, compared with the distance metrics, a difference in both dimensions is required to cause the two points to be regarded as different.

We could use a subset of the list of parameters to compute similarity just as we did to compute distance, but this runs into a problem. When the sentences have different types, then this has to be considered before deciding how similar they are. The problem is to decide how to compare types or qualities.

How alike are chalk and cheese? This is a sort of nonsense question in everyday language. The answer depends on two different aspects of the context. In the first place we need to know why we are being asked. If the question is in the context of a discussion of food, then the answer will be different than if the context were considerations of whether they were man-made or not. Secondly, the answer also depends on the other things that might be included in the discussion. If the context were edibility, but the other items were granite, glass and cast iron, then the answer would be different than if the other items were haggis, tatties and neeps.

Similarly, in comparing the types of descriptive sentences, we need to examine what implied properties they have in common and compare this with the range of types that we are encountering. Types have implied properties by virtue of their definition. The types for lines and edges will have similar definitions and so examples of each will have similar properties, so will squares and rectangles.

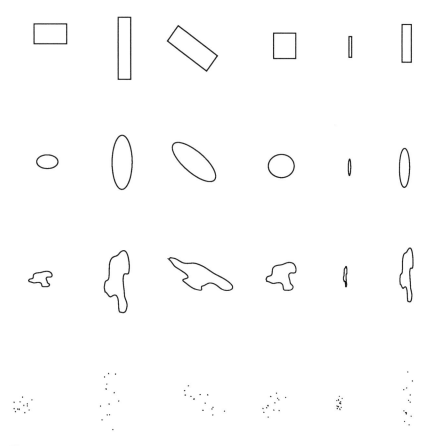

Figure 9. Examples of similarity. This figure shows a selection of image features. We would agree that those elements along a row are more similar than elements down the columns. What are we doing in saying this? The challenge is to discover what metric for similarity is being used.

6.5 Representing Associations: Visual Descriptions

In the previous section, I have described two ways in which small sets of sentences may become associated. Some of these associations will be purely accidental and contrived, whereas others will have captured a number of image components that have a common cause.

Let us start with two multidimensional descriptive sentences, and set out to represent the relationship between these two sentences. Each sentence has a list of parameters and the first requirement is that these should correspond so that we can calculate the difference between each. Because the discussion is restricted to numerically valued parameters, we can treat the sentences as vectors. In this case the vector difference between them is also a vector of the same dimension:

$$\textbf{Difference } (\Delta_1, \Delta_2, \Delta_3 \ldots \Delta_n)$$

This *difference vector* could be regarded as another sentence, but by treating it as a vector we can use the mathematically defined *modulus* of the vector, which is what I previously called the Euclidean formula. It is written as:

$$\| \textbf{Difference} \|$$

and is a scalar quantity. The *argument* of the vector can be used to specify the direction in the n-dimensional space of the difference. These two describe the parametric relationship between the two sentences, and can be used to describe the neighbourhood relationships.

The similarity relationships between two descriptive sentences can be treated in an analogous fashion. We can create a *similarity vector*:

$$\textbf{Similarity} \ (1/\Delta_1, 1/\Delta_2, 1/\Delta_3 \ldots 1/\Delta_n)$$

and this vector has a modulus, the reciprocal of which measures how similar the two sentences are, and an argument, which measures how they are similar.

For any one sentence, we end up with a small number of neighbouring sentences. Any one sentence and its neighbours can be taken as a set of descriptive sentences in their own right. We now have an intermediate description: one sentence describes one small region of an image; the whole set of sentences describes the entire image; and a smaller set of related sentences describes a neighbourhood of the image. All the sentences in the image description will belong to several such subsets and there may be as many neighbourhood sets as there are descriptive sentences. For any one sentence we can also extract from the image a subset of sentences that are neighbours in similarity space. Once again, each sentence will belong to several similarity sets.

If we take one of these neighbourhood or similarity sets, we can make the relationships between elements explicit by using the differences Δ_i as parameters in each sentence. In this way, one of the elements, say the central element, has all its parameters set to zero, and the others are described with respect to that sentence. In doing this we are shifting the origin of each dimension to be aligned with the sentence whose neighbourhood has been defined. We could choose any other location for the origin; obviously another sensible choice would be the centroid, in n dimensions, of the neighbourhood space. If we do this, then we shall need a special sentence describing the new origin of coordinates:

$$\textbf{Origin} \ (P_1, P_2, P_3, \ldots P_n)$$

We can write these new sets down in longhand by listing in any order the constituent sentences, or we can give each sentence a unique label and simply list the labels. A description of the neighbourhood will then take the form:

$$\textbf{NEIGHBOURHOOD} \ (\textbf{Origin} \ (P_1, P_2, P_3, \ldots P_n), \text{SET} \ \{a, b, c,\})$$

where each element of the set is a descriptive sentence

$$a = \textbf{BLOB}(a_1, a_2, a_3 \ldots a_n)$$

Notice that **NEIGHBOURHOOD** has the same form as that which we would use if we wished to write down a function to shift each element of SET from its relative position in the neighbourhood to its actual position in the image. **NEIGHBOURHOOD** is a descriptive structure which is made up from descriptive sentences. I will refer to it as a *visual description*.

The visual description contains a great deal of information, much of it in useful form. The size of extended objects can be obtained from a visual description in a way that it cannot from any one descriptive sentence. Where a property of an object such as its surface quality can only be inferred from several different image algebra processes, then the neighbourhood association will serve to bring them together.

6.6 Relationships between Descriptions

At the end of the previous section I defined a visual description as a set of sentences plus an origin vector. We now turn to consider relationships between these structures.

We have seen how it is possible to build up descriptions of neighbourhoods in images by associating sentences into sets of sentences. The overall image description that is created is highly linked by the existence of many elements that belong to more than one descriptive structure. By using both Euclidean and similarity distances, it is possible to arrange that links are strongest where the image relationships reflect physical relationships in the scene. Many of the links will be spurious but, hopefully, most of the useful scene relationships will be represented.

Each descriptive structure comprises a vector to represent the local origin of the structure and a set of sentences whose parameters are expressed with respect to the local origin. Relationships between descriptions depend on how their sets of sentences are related. We can make these relationships more explicit by creating an extra structure wherever the links are strong. By saying that the links are strong, what we mean is that the two sets we are comparing have a high proportion of their elements in common. There is a very convenient mathematical expression for this. The *intersection* of two sets S_1 and S_2 is defined as the set containing all those elements that are members of both S_1 and S_2 but no others. It is written

$$S_1 \cap S_2$$

The strength of the link between two structures is determined by the size of this intersection between their two sets of sentences. But the size is just a number and, as always, there is the question of how to evaluate numbers. In this case, we can compare the size of the intersection with the total number of elements in the two sets. Once again there is a convenient mathematical term. The *union* of two sets S_1 and S_2 is a set that contains all the elements of either or both S_1 and S_2. It is written

$$S_1 \cup S_2$$

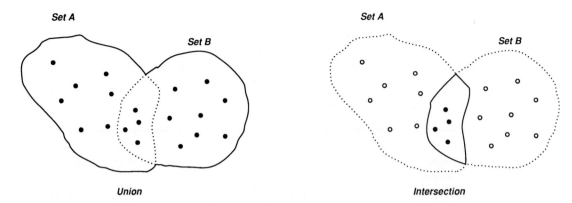

Figure 10. Venn diagrams for union and intersection of sets. Two sets are shown, and their union and intersection are illustrated. Each item in a set is represented by a small circle. The sets are marked by surrounding all their elements by a large outline. The union is the set that has the outline that surrounds all the elements in either. The intersection is the set that has the outline that surrounds only those elements in both sets.

The size of a set is called its *cardinality* and it is written

$$\text{card } (S_1).$$

A good measure of the strength of a link between two of our descriptive structures is given by

$$\frac{\text{card}\,(S_1 \cap S_2)}{\text{card}\,(S_1 \cup S_2)}$$

I shall call this quantity the *overlap* between the two structures. This ratio will take a value between 0 and 1, and will be larger in value the more elements the two sets have in common. Therefore it serves as a guide to indicate how strong the link between the two structures is and whether they might sensibly be combined. An important property of the overlap relationship that I have defined is that it is *commutative*. This means that

$$\text{overlap } (S_1, S_2) = \text{overlap } (S_2, S_1)$$

This result holds because both the union and the intersection operations are also commutative.

The central idea behind the definitions of union and intersection is the *identity* of elements of a set. It is necessary to be able to identify the common elements by noting that an element of S_1 is identical to an element of S_2. In our considerations, the elements are descriptive sentences:

$$\textbf{BLOB } (a_1, a_2, a_3 \ldots a_n)$$

and

$$\textbf{BLOB } (b_1, b_2, b_3 \ldots b_n)$$

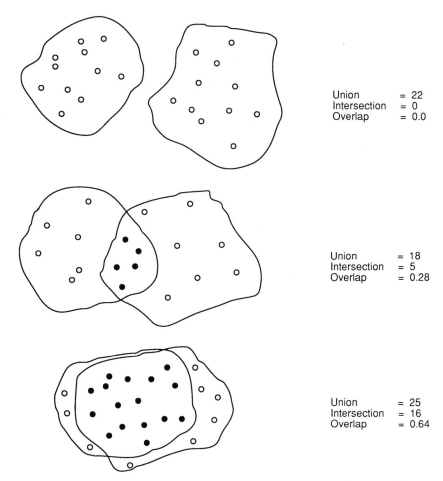

Union = 22
Intersection = 0
Overlap = 0.0

Union = 18
Intersection = 5
Overlap = 0.28

Union = 25
Intersection = 16
Overlap = 0.64

Figure 11. Venn diagrams for overlap of sets. Several pairs of sets are shown, and their overlaps are illustrated.

and these two are identical if

$$a_1 = b_1$$

$$a_2 = b_2$$

$$a_3 = b_3$$

$$....$$

$$a_n = b_n$$

Of course, the origins for the two sets from which these two sentences were drawn are important in determining the values of all these parameters and must be taken into account. The parameters, which are derived ultimately from the same image description, should be exactly identical.

Given a large overlap we can create a new descriptive structure from the union of its two constituents. The new origin will be the centroid of the

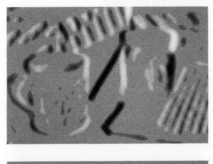

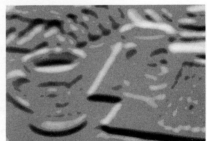

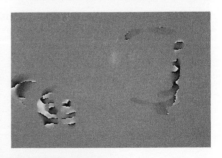

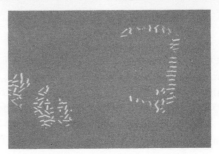

two old origins, and the new set of sentences will be the union of the two old sets, suitably transformed to the new origin. Notice that we combine the two structures by using the union operation. This operation does not split sets, whereas the intersection operation does.

The overlap between two structures does not depend on their two sets having the same number of elements and is thus less restricted than the element relationships that were discussed earlier. One consequence of this is that, given a large overlap between two structures we can create a new structure from them and then compare this with any other structure, again and again. There is a problem that arises here though, because the overlap operation is not *associative*, which means that, given three descriptive structures, the order in which we compare them matters. To put it formally:

$$\text{overlap}\ (\text{overlap}(S_1, S_2), S_3) \neq \text{overlap}\ (S_1, \text{overlap}(S_2, S_3))$$

except by coincidence.

6.7 Summary

In this chapter, I have described two ways in which sentences can be brought together to add some structure to the basic image description that is the starting point.

The first way is to construct a new sentence from one or more of the primitive sentences. This produces a sentence of another type and with a new list of parameters. The new list of parameters will provide information about the relationship between the various constituent sentences. We can write down the process as a compound condition, for example: "If there exist two lines, A and B such that one end point of A and one end point of B both have the same location, then there is a corner at that location".

There are more formal ways of doing this. We can define a **LINE** sentence to have the format (or grammar):

LINE (midpoint, orientation, length, width, mass)

and a **CORNER** sentence having a grammar:

CORNER (location, angle, **LINE**( ), **LINE**( ))

We can now be more explicit in our definition of the condition.

◄

Figure 12. An example of the function of visual description. This figure shows a pair of images taken in time. In between each one of the mugs was rotated about its centre, and the other was moved away from the camera. As in the example in Chapter 5, some information about the motion can be obtained from analysing the time derivative and two orthogonal spatial derivatives (e.g. in the x-direction and in the y-direction). The result motion blobs in the x-direction and in the y-direction. In order to discover from these images what motions have taken place, it is necessary to split the description into two parts one for each mug. In this case, spatial proximity is the most useful characteristic to use to achieve this.

If there exists two sentences, A and B, such that:

if   Label $(A) = $ **LINE**

if   Label $(B) = $ **LINE**

let   **ENDS** $(A) = \{(\text{midpoint }(A) - (\frac{1}{2}\text{ length }(A), \text{orientation }(A))),$

$(\text{midpoint }(A) + (\frac{1}{2}\text{ length }(A), \text{orientation }(A)))\},$

let   **ENDS** $(B) = \{(\text{midpoint }(B) - (\frac{1}{2}\text{ length }(B), \text{orientation }(B))),$

$(\text{midpoint }(B) + (\frac{1}{2}\text{ length }(B), \text{orientation }(B)))\}$

If there exists an element a from **ENDS** (a) and an element b from **ENDS** (b), such that

$$a \equiv b$$

then there exists a sentence

CORNER (**ENDS**$(a) \equiv$ **ENDS**(b), orientation $(A) - $ orientation (B),

LINE (A), **LINE** (B))

which is equivalent to

CORNER (**ENDS**$(b) \equiv$ **ENDS**(a), orientation $(B) - $ orientation (A),

LINE (A), **LINE** (B))

In defining the process as a compound condition whose clauses could either be true or false, we have a situation where the new sentence itself will either exist or not. It is much more feasible to use conditions which will be measured with a continuous variable which registers the likelihood that the condition has been met. In this example, the condition that there may be a common end point involves location parameters that will always be measured with some uncertainty or error. Consequently the condition may never be strictly satisfied. Where continuously valued conditions are used, the resultant sentence will have as a final parameter the cumulative likelihood. In this respect, it has a format which is closer to the action sentences with which the chapter began.

The second mechanism for bringing sentences together is by associating a number of them that are related into a small set. I have described two measures that can be used to determine which sentences should be associated. Each is based on the general principle of common cause. The first uses a metrical measure of distance to determine which sentences share a common neighbourhood. The second uses a measure of similarity. The visual descriptions that are produced have a local coordinate framework, which is represented by a special Origin sentence. This means that the parameters of the other sentences in the visual description then can record their distance from or similarity to the Origin sentence which can be regarded as a type of prototype for the visual description.

We start with a sentence A which has a list of parameters. This is part of an image description which contains many other sentences, some of which will be of the same type as *A* and therefore have the same dimensions on each of their list of parameters. Others will have a different type and may only have a few parameters in common with *A*. A distance between *A* and any other sentence can only be calculated for dimensions that they have in common. The simplest property is two-dimensional location. The similarity between *A* and any other sentence is computed in an analogous manner.

Given a number of visual descriptions arising from an image there will be several that overlap. I have shown how the degree of overlap can be calculated and how the two sets can be combined if the overlap is high.

The outcome of visual processing of this type is a set of visual descriptions, some of which will hold most or all of the information that is pertinent to a particular action. For some actions, such as touching something, or grasping and lifting something, the object of the action can be anything. In this case very little further processing is required and the action description can be created.

References

Ahuja N. (1982) Dot pattern processing using Voronoi neighbourhoods. *IEEE Trans. Pattern Anal. Machine Intelligence* **4**, 336–343.

Barrow H.G. and Popplestone R.J. (1971) Relational descriptions in picture processing. *Machine Intelligence* **6**, 377–396.

Guzman A. (1968) Decomposition of a visual scene into three-dimensional bodies. Fall Joint Computer Conference, Vol. 33.

Jolicoeur P. (1988) Curve tracing operations and the perception of spatial relations. In: Z. Pylyshyn (ed.) "Computational Processes in Human Vision: An Interdisciplinary Perspective". Ablex, Norwood, NJ.

Mahoney J.V. and Ullman S. (1988) Image chunking defining spatial building blocks for scene analysis. In: Z. Pylyshyn (ed.) "Computational Processes in Human Vision: An Interdisciplinary Perspective". Ablex, Norwood, NJ.

Kanade T. (1980) A theory of origami world. *Artificial Intelligence* **13**, 279–311.

Serra J. (1986) Introduction to mathematical morphology. *Computer Vision, Graphics Image Proc.* **35**, 283–325.

Ullman S. (1984) Visual routines. *Cognition* **18**, 97–106.

Zahn C.T. (1971) Graph-theoretic methods for detecting and describing gestalt clusters. *IEEE Trans. Comput.* **C20**, 68–86.

Exercises

1. What is the minimum information that would be necessary for a machine to pocket a ball in a game of pool? Think of this in terms of the actual action it will have to make, and the decisions that it will have to make before it can start its action. You can suppose that the balls on the table will be represented by blobs of differing colours.

2. How might a primitive symbol for a circle be defined? How about a spiral?

3. It is easy to make patterns that are recursive, so that the same structure repeats itself at ever finer scales. Any book on fractal geometry will contain examples. Consider what the visual description of such a pattern might be.

4. What types of symbol would be most useful in describing the visual image of a tree? The answer to this question depends on the reason for making the description. Take several different reasons, and see how different the descriptions might want to be.
5. Take a set of randomly placed dots and compute neighbourhood relationships between them. Try the effect of giving them differing degrees of spatial uncertainty, and see how many neighbours each has. What effect does changes in the exponent in the distance metric have?
6. Make a collection of different types of leaf. Decide on two or three different measurements to make, such as length, weight, colour. Now use the similarity formula to determine which leaves are most similar. If you have several different examples of each species then use the within species variability as a measure of the uncertainty. Try different values for the exponent in the formula.

7

Visual Interpretation

In the previous chapter the idea of visual descriptions was introduced. These represent relationships between the sentences of a description and hopefully some of the visual descriptions will contain all the information that is necessary for some types of action. In that chapter I considered touching, grasping and lifting things. There are no specific constraints on the objects of these actions. Just as it is possible to touch anything, so it is possible to derive a *Touch* sentence from any (or all) visual descriptions. It is possible to derive a *Grasp* or *Lift* sentence from each and every visual description, although sometimes, of course, the parameters will be beyond the scope of the effector mechanism.

There is a whole category of actions which do not share this broad applicability or scope. I can greet a colleague, but prefer not to greet the shadow of a tree. The range of objects of the greeting action is restricted to a specific class. Membership of this class can be determined from visual information, but we shall need a new mechanism to allow the property to be made explicit. The visual information will be compared with a description of a set of conditions that it should meet in order for the action to be appropriate. This set of conditions will be called a *visual model*, a term I will elaborate below. The visual description will be assessed to see if it *matches* the *model description*. A *decision description* is produced, recording the result of the assessment. This decision description then provides the information with which the action description is created.

It is tempting to think of matching some incoming data to a stored description of a face or a predator as being equivalent to "recognizing" an object, being able to name it, to assign it to a category, to associate a meaning with the image source of the object. This is far too narrow a consideration of the purpose of visual models. There are situations where the conditions of a model specify, not a thing or object, but rather the physical property of something. This is particularly useful for the properties that are not fully specified in any one aspect of an image, but are jointly specified by a series of different cues. Depth is a good example of this. A model can be used to specify how and under what conditions motion parallax, stereopsis, shading and so on can be used to measure the distance to an object.

A great deal of visually controlled behaviour relies on forward planning. The most appropriate actions in any particular situation and the way in

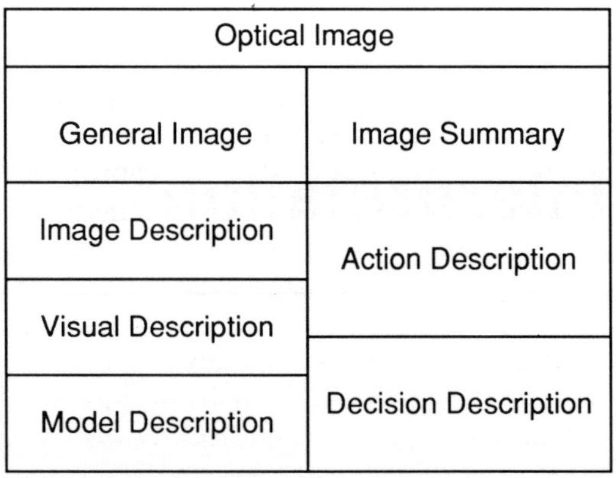

Optical Image	
General Image	Image Summary
Image Description	Action Description
Visual Description	
Model Description	Decision Description

Figure 1. Terminology. This diagram puts the various types of information representation into their connectivity relationships.

which they should be co-ordinated and sequenced can really only be determined when the alternatives have been established. Central to the planning of behaviour is the ability to provide extra visual information about the things in view. If a description that has been created from a part of a visual image matches a description of a predator that has been stored in memory, then an urgent chain of responses can be set in progress, even if the predator does not look generally dangerous.

We are dealing here with ways in which the visual description can be interpreted. Visual descriptions and the behaviours that they themselves can support involve only the most general of assumptions about the nature of matter, light and space. Visual models can be regarded as a mechanism for introducing much more specific assumptions about the significance of what is contained within a visual description.

7.1 Visual Models

The term model is a familiar one. A model is a device which retains some important characteristics of a real thing, but is more convenient to use because it lacks some unimportant factors. A model car looks like a car, perhaps has some of the moving parts of a car, but does not have the inconvenience of the size and exhaust fumes of the real thing. Under certain circumstances it can stand for the real thing.

A scientific model is used to provide a convenient description of a state of nature. A scientific model is supposed to exhibit properties that are equivalent to those found in nature. In practice, all scientific models have restricted domains and, of course, it is important to know what the limits of the model are. Generally, a model can only be regarded as an approximation to a state of nature and it will also have a degree of uncertainty. A scientific model functions both as a concise descriptive device and as a means of predicting what will happen next in a given circumstance. Generally, the better the model, the more specific and reliable the predictions that it makes. Visual models play an analogous role. Any reasonably sophisticated visual system is concerned with representing approximations to certain aspects of states of nature. The needs for these representations are all inherently related to being able to form appropriate concise descriptions and predictions about the properties of the domain.

In mathematics, a model is a similar device although the term is defined rather more precisely. Given a rule that specifies one mapping from set A to set B, a model for that mapping achieves the same mapping, but by a different rule and perhaps only for a subset of A. For example, take the mapping rule of multiplying a number by itself: squaring. This applies to the set of all real numbers. Its domain is the set of real numbers $\mathbb{R}$ and its co-domain is the set of all positive real numbers $\mathbb{R}^+$. A mathematical model for this mapping would be to take the logarithm of the number, add this to itself, and take the antilogarithm. The model only applies to the set $\mathbb{R}^+$, and is thus not complete, but if multiplication is not convenient, then it is a useful model. Visual models play an analogous role here also. A mathematical model is a process: give it some data and it will produce a result that is equivalent to that that would be produced by the mapping that is being modelled. A visual model of the relationship between the scene and the image has the same logical status. As the observer moves about the scene, the image changes in ways that can be modelled.

In both cases, models are also abstractions rather than instances. The scientific model of gravity has "spaces" in it into which one can place specific bodies and forces. The mathematical model of a processs can be given any data to start with. Once the model has been given the specific details of a situation, then it can be used to make a description.

(i) Models of Objects

Actions have objects; some actions require specific objects. In order to decide whether a given visual description indicates a suitable object for a particular action, a model of the conditions that specify the object will be needed.

Consider this example of faces. A person's face tells us a good deal about that person: their age, their gender, their race, their emotional state, and even their identity. As a surface, a face has a number of specific characteristics. It is nearly symmetrical about a vertical plane; it has a fairly specific shape; within its outline, a number of features are laid out according to a fairly specific plan; and it is deformable but may only change shape in a fairly specific fashion. Faces are constrained things and these constraints serve to set faces apart from other things in the environment.

There are several specific consequences of these surface characteristics for images of faces and for visual descriptions of faces. Any face can give rise to a number of different images and thence to a number of different visual descriptions, depending on viewing direction, illumination conditions and the expression on the face. However, these different images and descriptions are all constrained. Seen front on and with fair illumination, the image of a face will be nearly symmetric about one specific axis. As illumination varies in its direction, the image and its description will depart from symmetry in a fairly specific way. The axis of symmetry and degree of symmetry both change as the viewing direction changes. The features of a face will cause the image to have a fairly specific structure; eyes are always below the hairline and above the nose. This structure will change, as the face deforms, but always in a constrained manner.

A visual model of a face would specify all the various constraints. The simplest domain within which to do this is obviously three-dimensional space, in which case, having specified the state of nature represented by a face, the model must also specify the effect of the processes that map a three-dimensional face into a two-dimensional image. It would then be possible to match an instance of an image of a face to the model and thereby form a decision sentence describing the instance of the face. The reasons for matching occur at several different levels. Given a description of an image, it can be matched with a generic face description, thereby deducing that it is an image of a face. The face can then be described by giving its size, its shape and elongation, its age. All of these obviously come in degrees. The face can be matched with a more specific description of a female face; an oriental face; my own face; etc. Each of these matches also has a degree which has significance for the planning of subsequent behaviour. Each different reason or level of matching is useful for a different set of actions.

The consequence of matching data to a model can be represented in a decision description such as:

FACE(**direction**; orientation; size; **EXPRESSION**(); MATCH)

Compare this with the **LIFT** sentence from the previous chapter. Both have some straightforward parameters. The **LIFT** sentence had a pointer to **SURFACE QUALITY**, this one has a pointer to **EXPRESSION**. Finally the **FACE** sentence contains a parameter, MATCH, which records the degree to which the data fit the model. This parameter could be used to register the accumulation over time of evidence that the sentence is accurate. If the sentence is to be used to control an action, such as greeting the owner of the face, then this fuzzy Boolean parameter can be used more or less directly as the ACTIVE parameter in the equivalent

GREET(**FACE**(); friendliness; ACTIVE)

This example allows us to see how, by creating the **FACE** description, we can then access information about the type of greeting that we should be using. The **FACE** description is an example of a *decision description* and the **GREET** description is an example of an *action description*.

(ii) Models of Properties

Most visual systems with a modicum of intelligence and ability to react adaptively will be making actions that involve three-dimensional geometry and are made against a range of forces such as inertia, friction and gravity. Neither three-dimensional geometry nor these forces are fully specified by simple image properties, but they are reflected in a number of partially correlated properties. The situation of having multiple sources of information, but each individually being weak and inconclusive, is possibly widespread.

There are very many different partial cues to depth available: stereopsis, motion parallax, texture gradients, surface shading, occlusion, and probably many more. The problem of assessing depth from multiple cues is the simplest example to consider, and it has all the difficulties that are generally characteristic of the creation of visual models for dealing with the properties of objects. Information about distance in the third dimension is very often necessary for visual behaviour that involves the third dimension. Some typical examples are threading a needle, grasping a mug, and running through a forest. In each case, it is possible to devise methods that would have some degree of success without employing three-dimensional descriptions, but explicit information about the third dimension will be useful.

That information about the third dimension can be obtained from various different sources. Let us work through the examples so that we can see what the general strategy should be. In the case of threading a needle, texture cues to depth are not very helpful, and neither are shading cues. On the other hand stereopsis and motion parallax cues are both potentially very useful. Of these two, motion parallax has the drawback that it requires some relative motion and this may not be desirable given the fine degree of hand positioning that is required. This leaves stereopsis and occlusion as the preferred cues to depth for threading a needle.

In the case of grasping a mug, there are two types of depth information that are required. It is necessary to know how far away the mug is, and it is also necessary to know the width of the mug or its handle so that the hand may be opened appropriately. We are concerned with the relative positions of mug and hand, but in this case there is no need for the hand to be kept nearly still and so motion parallax can also be used. We are also concerned with the shape of the mug. If this is smooth and featureless, then neither stereopsis nor motion parallax will be very useful or reliable but shading information and the shape and size of its outline will be good sources of information. If it is textured on its outer surface then texture gradients will be of some help.

Finally when running through a forest, the prime needs are navigational. It is very useful to have depth information for selecting a route and avoiding obstacles, and also for finding where to place the feet so as not to fall over. This is a situation where the observer is in relatively fast motion and so motion parallax is the obvious choice of depth information.

What we have been doing here is assessing, from the nature of the task, which sources of information are most suitable. Stereopsis is most accurate for short distances from the observer; motion parallax is most reliable if there is a reasonable amount of movement; texture gradients are useful when the texture is not very self-similar under scaling; shading information is best when surfaces are smooth and featureless; and so on. In most situations all the various depth cues will be correlated, but by no means in complete agreement. Each is based on some specific assumption about the nature of the world and the various assumptions will be valid and invalid in different situations. The uncertainties or estimation variable errors within each cue will be different. More seriously, the manner in which each cue is calibrated can lead to systematic distortions.

The logic behind all of this examination of depth recovery is based on two types of rule. The first type of rule specifies the conditions under which the different depth cues are most valid and useful. The second type of rule specifies how to combine the different estimates of depth in different situations.

Visual models can be used to specify how parts of visual descriptions can be allowed to interact. Very often it is rather general physical properties of the environment that need to be modelled. The representation of three-dimensional geometry is a good instance of this. Depth recovery is only the beginning of the process of three-dimensional analysis. It is inherent in the construction of the third dimension, from its projection onto a flat two-dimensional image, that depth estimates will be subject to error. The resultant three-dimensional information is unlikely to conform to Euclidean geometry and this must severely limit its usefulness. However, by creating a model of the relationships intrinsic to three-dimensional Euclidean geometry, it is possible to identify the discrepancies and correct them by making small and specific changes to the visual description. The computational problem lies in finding the smallest overall adjustment that will cause the description to conform to the rules of geometry specified by the model. In general this type of procedure is known as constraint relaxation.

7.2 Model Descriptions

Models specify the conditions that a visual description should meet in order for its interpretation in terms of certain further descriptions to be valid. Models can then specify how the new description should be formed: what its parameters should be and how they relate to the parameters of the earlier visual description. The most convenient form to represent the conditions that are specified by the model is as a model description with a very similar structure to a visual description. The conditions will involve a set of elements that the visual description should contain and by implication a set of elements that the visual description should not contain. The conditions will also involve a set of relationships between the elements. For example, a model for the letter F will contain a set of elements such as:

3 line ends
1 two way junction
1 three way junction

The absence of a four way junction in this set implies that any letter containing such would probably not be an F. This set of elements is enough to specify F from all other capital letters, but does not distinguish the letter from its mirror image. It is necessary to specify the spatial relationships between the elements in a model description. The spatial relationships in the model can be specified by giving each of the elements in the model description a list of parameters. If this is done then the model description becomes a set of descriptive sentences, closely analogous to a visual description.

There are two problems that would arise with models like this. Firstly, the visual processes are always subject to some variability. The chances of finding an F that corresponds precisely to a model of this sort would be slim. However, an important aspect of visual descriptions is the fact that all the parameters can be recorded along with an estimate of their precision. We can use the same mechanism in the context of a model: the error terms with each sentence of a model can be used to specify a *tolerance*. Secondly, not all Fs have the same shape, size and orientation. A model description should also allow for certain types of change in the relationships of the elements.

7.3 Matching Descriptions

The significance of matching descriptions to allow the access of non-visual information is considerable, but the matching process itself is far from trivial. The descriptions have as their fundamental elements, sentences which have qualitative aspects (**LINE**, **BLOB**, **CORNER**, etc.) and quantitative parameters (length, orientation, distance, etc.). We can discuss qualitative matches where we are only interested in the qualitative aspects of the sentence, or we can discuss quantitative matches, where the match between parameters is also a concern. In two-dimensional Euclidean geometry there are three types of match that are found useful. Two descriptions are in *identity* if they have the same of sentences, with each sentence in one being identical to one in the other description.

Two descriptions are in *congruence* if they have the same list of sentences with each sentence agreeing in all angles and distances, but not in overall rotation and position. By relaxing the matching requirement on some specific parameters, the process will be given *invariance* with respect to their domains. Typically, the parameters that might be match invariant are those that govern the layout of the image. *Similarity* of descriptions shares the features of congruence, but allows for a greater range of invariance.

Because the scene has one dimension more than the image, there are congruent descriptions in the scene domain that are not congruent in the image domain. Similarity of descriptions therefore allows for effects like foreshortening. This sounds simple. There is an algebraic description of how foreshortening works. We can easily create a description of the image of a foreshortened cube that could be used for matching. However, the application of the principle of similarity matching for the recognition of other properties is less simple when these are not described as a set of geometric invariance transformations. The images of various rough surfaces cannot be related to each other by a geometric transformation in the way that the images of all

Similarity   **Congruence**   **Identity**

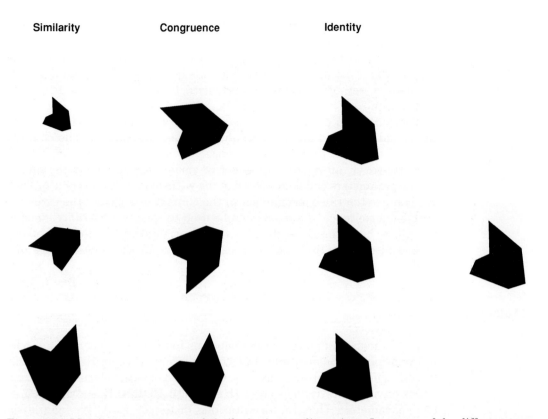

Figure 2.   Identity, congruence, and similarity in two dimensions. Instances of the different types of match are give for simple geometrical figures.

cubes can. What the images of rough surfaces have in common is a statistical quality and so it is statistical descriptions that have to be matched.

In matching, we are asserting a relationship between two sets of descriptive sentences. Just as an action could be represented by a sentence that specifies what the action is and a parameter list to give information about the specific instance, so can we represent a matching decision by a sentence that specifies what the match was made to and what degree and nature of relationship exists. This representation is the decision description.

(i) Qualitative Match

We start by looking at the details of a qualitative match. The visual description comprises a vector origin and a set of sentences; each sentence has a symbolic type and a list of parameters. The model description has a similar structure: a vector, whose role will become clear later and a set of sentences each having a type and a list of parameters. For a qualitative match, all we are concerned with is whether the two sets have the same composition of sentence types. For this we can reduce the elements of the two sets to just their types, although we must be careful to keep different

Figure 3. Similarity of textures is not as easy to define. The textures in this image are all similar in some respects and not in others.

instances of the same type distinct. Strictly speaking, this is called a multi-set. There are three component subsets that determine whether the match is good or bad. The first is the number of elements that the two sets have in common. Writing S_V for the set derived from the visual description and S_M for that from the model description, we can denote the set of common elements by the intersection

$$S_V \cap S_M$$

and obtain the cardinality of this set to tell us how many elements the two sets have in common. This will range from zero up to the size of the set S_M. The second component of the match concerns the number of elements that are in the model description but that are missing from the visual description. Technically the set of these elements is termed the difference between S_M and S_V and is written

$$S_M/S_V$$

The cardinality of this set will vary from zero up to the size of the set S_M. The third component of the match is the set of supernumerary elements that are present in the visual description but are not to be found in the model description:

$$S_V/S_M$$

The cardinality of this set will range from zero up to the size of the set S_V.

These three components are all closely related. The three sets that are formed in this way will have no elements in common. This means that the sum of their three cardinalities will equal the cardinality of the union of the visual description and the model description:

$$\text{card}\,(S_V \cap S_M) + \text{card}\,(S_M/S_V) + \text{card}\,(S_V/S_M)$$
$$= \text{card}\,(S_V \cup S_M)$$

The union of the two difference sets is called the symmetric difference and is written

$$S_V \triangle S_M$$
$$= (S_M/S_V) \cup (S_V/S_M)$$
$$= (S_M \cup S_V)/(S_M \cap S_V)$$

and so we have:

$$\text{card}\,(S_V \cap S_M) + \text{card}\,(S_V \triangle S_M) = \text{card}\,(S_V \cup S_M)$$

For a perfect match the cardinality of the intersection of the two sets S_V and S_M should be the same as the cardinality of S_M alone, and the cardinality of the symmetric difference set should be zero, as should the cardinality of the two earlier difference sets. This is just a long way of saying that S_V and S_M should be the same. It is more than likely that they will not, and a measure of how nearly the same would be useful. More generally the higher the cardinality of the intersection and the lower the cardinality of the

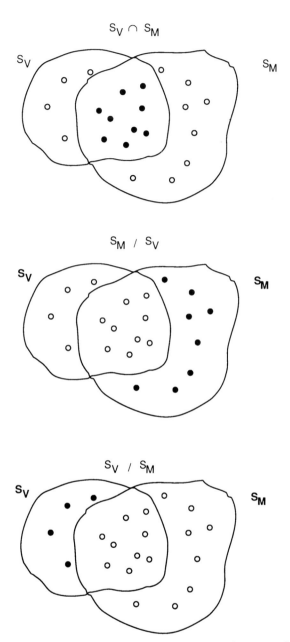

Figure 4. Venn diagrams of the three components in a match. This figure uses the standard Venn diagram notation to illustrate the three components that need to be considered in assessing the degree of a match.

symmetric difference, the better the match. A simple measure of how good the match is can be provided by evaluating the expression

$$\frac{\operatorname{card}(S_V \cap S_M)}{\operatorname{card}(S_V \cup S_M)}$$

This quantity ranges from 0.0 (no match) to 1.0 (perfect match). It is worth noting that the expression is commutative, which means that we are treating the two sets S_V and S_M as equals:

$$\text{match } (S_V, S_M) = \text{match } (S_M, S_V)$$

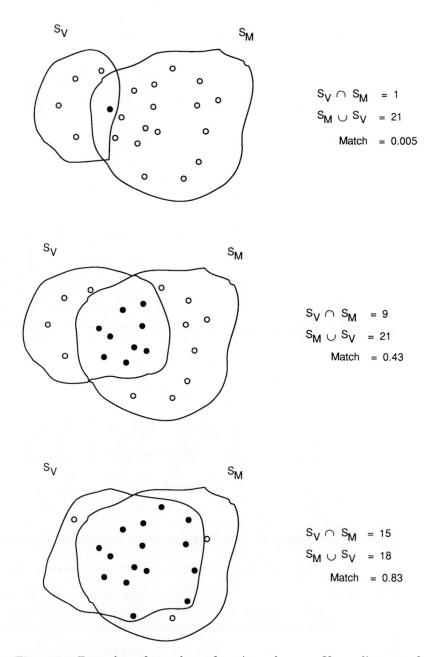

Figure 5. Examples of matches of various degrees. Venn diagrams for matches of various degrees are shown.

(ii) Quantitative Match

We now turn to a consideration of a quantitative match, which requires that the two descriptions match for both the types of the sentences and their parameters. Let us start by examining what is involved. We shall use the same expression for the goodness of the match:

$$\frac{\mathrm{card}\,(S_{\mathrm{V}} \cap S_{\mathrm{M}})}{\mathrm{card}\,(S_{\mathrm{V}} \cup S_{\mathrm{M}})}$$

But this use of set theory implies that the elements can be compared to decide which elements the two sets have in common. If we are only dealing with distinctive types then the process of deciding whether two elements, one from each set, are the same is trivial. However we are now concerned with continuously valued attributes: are two lines of length 5.0 and 5.1 to be treated as the same? The way that this question should really be asked is: how similar are two lines of length 5.0 ± 0.05 and 5.1 ± 0.01? There are two important changes in this question. First, we are now talking about degree of similarity, and second we have included the error or tolerance of the parameters.

In Chapter 6, I described two different ways in which a relationship and its degree could be assessed between two sentences: the neighbourhood distance and the similarity distance. In that case both sentences were drawn from the same set and ultimately from the same image. We could use either of these two measures now to assess whether two sentences, one from a visual description and one from a model description, could be the same. In working through this I shall use the neighbourhood measure.

Let us take two sentences, one, M, from a model description and one, V, from a visual description. We have two parameter lists (vectors):

$$(m_1, m_2, m_3, \ldots, m_n)$$

$$(v_1, v_2, v_3, \ldots, v_n)$$

and two uncertainty lists (vectors), a tolerance from the model and an error from the image visual description:

$$(t_1, t_2, t_3, \ldots, t_n)$$

$$(e_1, e_2, e_3, \ldots, e_n)$$

The difference list (vector) is given by

$$(m_1 - v_1, m_2 - v_2, m_3 - v_3 \ldots m_n - v_n)$$

and the joint uncertainty is given by the square root of the sum of squares:

$$((t_1^2 + e_1^2)^{1/2}, (t_2^2 + e_2^2)^{1/2} \ldots (t_n^2 + e_n^2)^{1/2})$$

We can use this to scale the difference list (vector), giving

$$\Delta_{\mathrm{V}} = \left(\frac{(m_1 - v_1)}{(t_1^2 + e_1^2)^{1/2}}, \frac{(m_2 - v_2)}{(t_2^2 + e_2^2)^{1/2}} \cdots \frac{(m_n - v_n)}{(t_n^2 + e_n^2)^{1/2}} \right)$$

The modulus of this difference vector, which is also the Euclidean distance between the two vectors, scaled by their uncertainties can then be used to estimate how close the two sentences are to being the same. The modulus of the difference vector will be zero if the two sentences are identical and has a greater value the more different the two sentences are. From the modulus, we can calculate the quantity

$$m_v = \frac{1}{1 + \Delta_V}$$

which ranges from 0 (completely dissimilar) to 1 (identical).

This raises a new difference between qualitative and quantitative matches. In both cases we are seeking to extract the intersection set of the two descriptions, but previously we could make a Boolean decision about the identities of elements. In the present case, the decision m_v has a continuous value between zero and one. We could set some arbitrary threshold above which the two elements were regarded as identical, but there is a better approach.

The starting point is to describe a different type of set. The sets that we have been considering so far have all had the property that any given element either belonged to them or it didn't. Set membership has been a Boolean function. There is another type of set, known as a *fuzzy set* in which the elements belong with some value between 0 and 1 inclusive. The operations of union, intersection and symmetric difference are all defined on fuzzy sets, as is the cardinality function. It is often easiest to think of fuzzy sets as sets in which elements have a probability of membership, although this is neither how they are defined nor is it always appropriate because there are operations that do not behave like the corresponding probability operations.

In determining the degree of qualitative match we used the expression:

$$\frac{\mathrm{card}\,(S_V \cap S_M)}{\mathrm{card}\,(S_V \cup S_M)}$$

We will now make the two sets that are formed from S_V and S_M, i.e. their intersection and their union, fuzzy sets and define their cardinality to be the sum of the membership variables, each having a value between 0 and 1 inclusive. With this value for membership we can form the fuzzy sets for the intersection and symmetric difference and hence calculate the degree of match.

So far it has been assumed that the pairing of elements for matching is a relatively obvious process, and for qualitative matches this will normally be true. For quantitative matches it is not necessarily so obvious and the consequences of making a mismatch are rather more serious. When we calculate Δ_V, we take one element from each of the two descriptions and the problem is knowing which elements to take. We can take one element from the decision description and then find that element from the visual description that is closest in value. This can be repeated for all of the elements in the decision description or until the elements in the visual

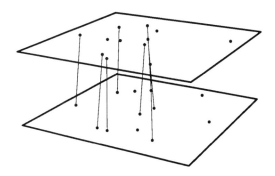

```
{  {-0.95, -0.17},  {0.51, -0.85},    {-0.062, -0.9},
   {-0.2, -0.78},   {-0.69, 0.45},    {-0.54, -0.16},
   {-0.38, 0.72},   {-0.027, 0.089},  {-0.5, -0.18},
   {-0.12, 0.53},   {-0.32, -0.14},   {1.0, 0.53}      }

{  {-1., -0.27},    {0.51, -0.79},    {-0.14, -0.81},
   {-0.3, -0.8},    {-0.74, 0.45},    {-0.039, -0.13},
   {-0.34, 0.77},   {0.035, 0.16},    {-0.54, 0.63},
   {0.91, 0.081},   {0.19, -0.61},    {0.42, 0.95}     }
```

Figure 6. The matching process. This figure shows two sets of vectors to be matched. The process of deciding which vector to pair with which can take a great many trials. This can be seen more easily by examining just the list of co-ordinates and trying to make the match.

description have been exhausted. There is the risk that this will pair some of the earlier elements that we try with the best partner for some of the elements that are yet to be tried. It is really necessary to investigate all possible ways of matching the two sets and then taking the best overall. This is a long-winded process, the number of possibilities for a decision set of size r and visual set of size n, is

$$\frac{n!}{(n-r)!} = \frac{n(n-1)(n-2)\ldots 3.2.1}{(n-r),(n-r-1)\ldots 3.2.1}$$

For $n = r = 12$, this gives 479001600 possible pairings! However when $n = r = 6$, the figure is reduced to 720. So that if it were possible, for example, to exploit a symmetry in the visual description to effectively halve the number of elements that needed to be matched, the savings could be enormous.

7.4 Organizing Descriptions

The fundamental difficulty in the matching process is the vast number of combinations in which two descriptions can be compared. Because the two descriptions are sets in which no element takes precedence or has a specific place, all possible mappings between the two sets have to be considered.

This leads to the situation that is commonly and graphically known as the combinatorial explosion. Set operations like intersection and union are combinatorially and computationally expensive. The equivalent operations on a list, where each element has a place in an ordering, are much more constrained and thus faster. It is therefore very desirable to exploit any way in which the elements of a description can be reduced in number or ordered into a list.

The benefits of reducing the number of elements to be compared derive directly from the combinatorics of the situation and below I shall consider some ways in which this can be accomplished. The benefits of putting the elements into a list are a little less obvious, but are much greater. If we have two strict lists, then we can compare the first element from each, the second element from each, and so on. It is rarely practical to put the elements into an exactly corresponding list because of errors and uncertainties in processing leading to missing or supernumerary elements or mislocations. However, a list, even with these qualifications, is a very much easier structure to match than an unordered set.

(i) Reducing Numbers: Symmetry and Self-similarity

There is a great benefit in being able to reduce the number of elements in a description, and I now turn to consider some of the ways in which this can be done. There are some simple and rather uninteresting ways that could be used to great effect, like using the coarsest spatial scale convenient and using the smallest image size suitable. There are also some more interesting ways which involve organizing the elements.

Figure 7. Bilateral symmetry. The pattern in this figure has a degree of bilateral symmetry, but it is not perfect. There might be many situations where this would not particularly matter.

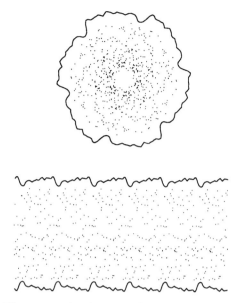

Figure 8. A selection of richer symmetries.

Bilateral symmetry in an image offers a very simple type of organization where some elements are paired. All elements that do not straddle the axis of symmetry should be paired; those that do lie on the axis should themselves be symmetric. This is equivalent to saying that if the description is compared with itself after all the elements have been transformed in a manner that would be equivalent to taking the mirror of the original image, then there should be a high degree of correspondence. The task to find the symmetry is to discover the axis about which the transformation should occur. This need not be too difficult because the axis is bound to pass through or close to the centroid of the whole description.

Obviously, the richer symmetries with more than one axis can be treated in similar ways. There are two rather special cases of higher degree symmetry. One is where all the axes of symmetry pass through the same point and the other is where all the axes are parallel creating a linearly periodic pattern.

The general principle in using symmetry is that if a pattern can be found to be similar to itself under a transformation (like reflection) then the number of descriptive elements can be reduced. Another potential transformation of this type is that of shrinking or expanding: changing spatial scale. A number of natural patterns are self-similar under this transformation.

(ii) Ordering into a List

A list is a structure in which elements have explicit relationships denoted by their relative positions. These relationships provide another type of organization that can powerfully constrain the number of combinations that need to be examined to decide a match.

We can very easily make a list from a set of single-valued parameters by using numerical order. This in turn is based simply on the Boolean operations of *greater than* and *less than*. We can draw the process of one-dimensional ordering as a mapping from one line to another. On the first line the points are unevenly distributed; on the second line, the ordering, they are all equispaced. Whilst there are very many mappings from one line to the other, there is only one which meets the constraint that none of the lines of the mapping should intersect and cross over. This is the one which orders the points.

Now turn to consider an ordering of a two-dimensional attribute, such as image position. The ordering should be based on the two-dimensional equivalents of *greater than* and *less than*. The simplest way of making such equivalents is to use these two relationships independently in the two dimensions. For clarity's sake, we can call one of the dimensions x, running left to right, and the other y, running bottom to top. So there are four ordering relationships, *left of* and *right of, above* and *below*. We can order all the points according to their x value, or according to their y value, or even some combination such as $(x^2 + y^2)^{1/2}$. But all of these are still one-dimensional orderings. How do we make a two-dimensional ordering that still has both the x and y ordering properties?

We can draw the process of two-dimensional ordering as a mapping from one plane to another. Once again the points are irregularly dispersed in the first plane and are evenly spaced in the second. As before, there are many different mappings that would be possible, but this time few if any of them will have any actual intersections. Seen from some angles, some lines will appear to intersect, but it will usually be the case that one passes in front of the other. Of course, seen from either of the two dimensions along which we are ordering, such cross overs would not be acceptable, but this is then likely to lead to a situation where no ordering is possible.

Figure 9. Ordering mapping in one dimension. None of the mapping lines cross over, if they did order would not be preserved. There is only one ordering mapping for a given set of data.

The principle of an ordering is that each element is placed in the list at index j so that its value V_j satisfies the two criteria.

$$V_j > V_i \qquad \text{for } j > i$$
$$V_j < V_i \qquad \text{for } j < i$$

If each value is a vector with two components $x,\ y$ then it would be most fortunate if there existed a single indexed (i.e. one-dimensional) ordering such that for all j

$$\left.\begin{array}{l} x_j > x_i \\ y_j > y_i \end{array}\right\} \qquad \text{for } j > i$$

$$\left.\begin{array}{l} x_j < x_i \\ y_j < y_i \end{array}\right\} \qquad \text{for } j < i$$

but an ordering of this type could not be guaranteed.

Clearly there is a great advantage in finding a one-dimensional ordering whenever possible. For example, if the elements have a parameter giving their size, then this could be used on its own. Generally, however, the most useful dimensions with which the image may be organized are the two spatial dimensions of the image. Instead of using a single dimension there are several ways of treating the two as one.

An axis of symmetry provides an intrinsic direction along which elements or pairs of elements can be ordered. The ordering is unlikely to be unique

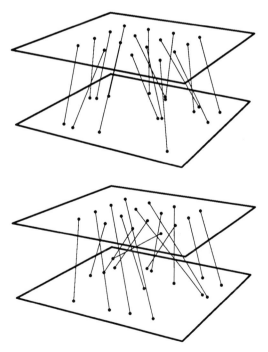

Figure 10. Ordering in two dimensions. For most patterns in two dimensions, there are more than one mapping relationships that do not cross over.

because there are not guaranteed to be extra constraints on those elements that are off the axis. This would mean that two or more elements could have the same place in the ordering. Thus symmetry has two beneficial effects. It reduces the number of elements to be compared by pairing elements together. It also provides an ordering.

Symmetry is useful because it provides a single axis or dimension along which a spatial ordering can be imposed. Movement also provides a similar axis. When we've seen an animal move, then we can say what its front legs are and what its back legs are. The direction of movement is locally a single dimension and thus can be used to create a useful spatial ordering.

In a similar way, if the image of something is long and fairly straight then it becomes possible to treat its spatial layout as having one predominant spatial dimension along its line of elongation. This dimension can be used for ordering the elements.

(iii) Hierarchical Organization: Spatial Scale

Spatial scale has a use in organizing a description which is closely related to ordering, that of creating a hierarchy. In an ordering, each element is defined to be either *less than* or *greater than* each other element. In a hierarchy, each element is defined to be *less than* some of the others and *more than* some others but has no defined relationship to yet others. In an ordering all of the other elements are defined to either *less than* or *more than*, in a hierarchy some pairs of elements do not have a defined relationship.

If an image is analysed at several different spatial scales then there are a number of potential organizations that may result. Suppose that we start with just one blob at some large spatial scale. If we could continuously reduce the scale of analysis, then we would find that this one blob would split into a small number of new, smaller blobs. These in turn would split and so on. The number of blobs that we were dealing with would progressively increase, but each new blob would develop within the confines of an earlier, coarser blob. This provides a hierarchical ordering of the blobs, and the sentences that describe them. For a pattern that is not constrained, the rate of emergence of new blobs will be relatively constant as scale changes and the number of blobs will be inversely proportional to the spatial scale.

Figure 11 illustrates this for a one-dimensional case. Any horizontal line through the plot in the figure is a representation of the image at a particular spatial scale. The vertical lines in the plot show where in space the zero crossings are found. At the bottom is the result of the smallest amount of smoothing; at the top is the largest amount. This plot, which is called a *scale–space diagram*, illustrates how the number of zero crossing varies with increasing smoothing. Notice how the positions of the zero crossings change with increasing smoothing. The zero crossings do not cross over each other. They do not split or suddenly appear as spatial scale increases, although they do merge. This behaviour has been formulated mathematically as the *diffusion equation*.

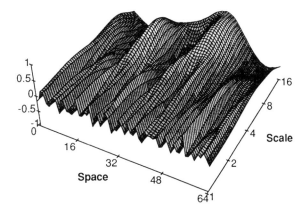

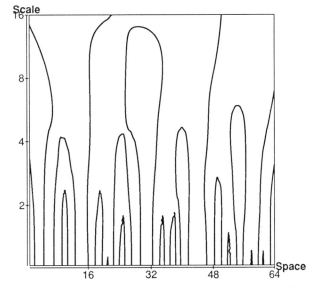

Figure 11. Hierarchy from spatial scale. The top of this figure shows a scale–space diagram. Across the figure is space, and into the figure or up corresponds to increasing spatial scale. At any one spatial scale, the cross section shows the convolution of a random image with the appropriate Laplacian of Gaussian filter. Notice how the structure changes smoothly. At the bottom is shown the type of hierarchy that can result from spatial scale changes.

If we only use Gaussian smoothing then there is only a restricted set of patterns to which the structure of an image must conform. Basically, in one dimension the space–scale diagram comprises arches and vertical or near-vertical lines.

The scale–space diagram is not a function of position: for some positions there will be no spatial scales at which zero crossings exist; for others there will be several spatial scales at which zero crossings are found. It is strictly a two-dimensional Boolean function: specify a spatial position and a spatial

scale, and the diagram provides a result true/false for the presence of a
zero crossing. The scale–space diagram for a two-dimensional image is a
three-dimensional Boolean function. Think of it first as a vertically stacked
sequence of maps, each recording the locations of zero crossings at a
particular spatial scale. The higher you are off the ground, the larger the
spatial scale of analysis.

Now think of the scale–space diagram for a two-dimensional image as a
transparent block which is opaque at points where the Boolean function is
true. The diffusion equation guarantees that all the various opaque bits will
form continuous surfaces within the transparent block. Just as in the
scale–space diagram for a one-dimensional image the possible patterns of
lines are constrained, so the pattern for surfaces in the scale–space diagram
for a two-dimensional image is constrained.

A hierarchy of this sort is a useful organization for matching. We can
start by matching at the coarsest scale, where there are few elements. Each
matched pair of elements at this level has a few children that can be matched
quite separately from the children of any other elements.

7.5 Transforming Descriptions

A visual description has an origin sentence which aligns the description
with the region in the image from which it comes. This provides a rather
general way in which many transformations of a description can be achieved.
The transformations of shifting the description, of rotating it in the image
plane and of scaling it in size can all be achieved by simply altering the
multidimensional origin. It is important to realize that this only works if
all the parameters are coded in a relative fashion and also that only
transformations in the same space as the origin are possible. For example,
if the parameters include positions of blobs with respect to the local origin
and a local mean distance from the origin, lengths with respect to the mean
length, and curvatures with respect to the mean curvature, then a shrinking
transformation may be applied by reducing the local mean distance, the
local mean length in proportion, and increasing the local mean curvature
in (inverse) proportion. In other words, every parameter that has a distance
dimension must be altered in an equivalent fashion.

The hallmark of this technique is the way in which all the elements of
a description are treated quite equivalently and quite independently,
according to very general rules. We now turn to consider ways in which
more specific transformations of the description can be undertaken. There
are three main situations where specific transformations will be useful.
These are where the illumination direction of something varies, where the
viewpoint varies, and where the thing itself can articulate or deform in
shape. In each case the consequences for the image are quite profound. For
any given thing, there is a continuum of images that correspond to
movements which involve the third spatial dimension. These cause non-rigid
or non-affine transformations of the two-dimensional image, and result in
transformations in the image description. The individual sentences of a

Figure 12.   Rotation in three dimensions: this figure shows a series of frames from the projection of a complex shape rotating about a vertical axis. The image effects of the rotation are not simple, although there is a definite pattern to the appearance and disappearance of particular parts of the shape.

description can be altered and extra ones may appear, or some may be lost. These transformations are for the most part smooth, but do have singular points where a discrete change in the image structure occurs.

The location from which something is being viewed is specified by a two-dimensional direction and a one-dimensional distance. The effect of viewing distance is to scale the image of the thing in size. However the effects of changing viewing direction are more complex and depend heavily on the structure of the thing itself.

A sphere is the only object which does not have an image that changes with viewing direction and this is because it is rotationally symmetrical about all axes that pass through its centre. Something like an egg that is rotationally symmetric about one axis will have an image that doesn't change as the observer moves around that axis, but does change if the observer's movement revolves around any other axis. Anything that does not contain rotational symmetry will have an image that always changes with any change in viewing direction. If a thing has a surface that is everywhere convex and has no holes then it will only occlude itself around its occluding boundary in the image. If, on the other hand, it contains local concavities or holes then there will be further self-occlusions within the occluding boundary in the image that depend on viewing direction.

Take a cube as a simple example. A fairly standard view of a cube will have one vertex pointing towards the observer with three lines radiating from this to three corners on the occluding contour. The occluding contour, a hexagon, has six corners, of which these three are alternating members. Opposite sides of the hexagon are roughly parallel (perspective and fore-shortening ensure that they are not exactly so) and also parallel to one of the lines from the vertex. As the viewpoint is changed the vertex moves about within the hexagonal occluding contour. The lines remain connected to the same corners, and so change their lengths and orientations. The sides of the hexagonal occluding contour remain parallel to the lines from the vertex and so change also their orientations and lengths. Occasionally the view will go through a more drastic change as a new vertex becomes the nearest one to the observer.

If we wish to be able to identify a cube from any viewing angle, then it is necessary to specify the variations in its image that can arise. This specification can be given by just a few conditional rules, one for each topological state.

(a) If the outline is square then there should be no further visible lines or vertices.

(b) If the outline has six sides, then alternate corners should be joined by lines to a vertex in the centre. Each line should be nearly parallel to two of the sides of the outline and so on.

For more complex shapes, then there will be a greater number of conditional rules because there will be more topological states of the image. These conditional rules, dependencies between elements in a description, define the specific way in which the image can transform as the direction that it is viewed from changes or as the illumination changes.

The difficulty that is created in this situation has two aspects. On the one hand, the different topological states have somehow to be identified as having an equivalence. The other aspect is more subtle. Take the three inside lines in the image of a cube. Because we do not have any reason to expect one preferred orientation for the cube, we have to allow a high degree of tolerance for the orientations of the lines. Each line can appear at any orientation. No matter what the general orientation of the cube is, however, the relationship between the orientations of the lines and the orientations of the outer lines is very closely constrained. Moreover, there is a constrained relationship between the set of orientations and the corresponding set of line lengths. We have a situation where some properties of the model description are more constrained than others. In the case of a rectangle, right-angled corners are necessary, a ratio of 2:1 on the lengths is not. This adds a new degree of complexity to the structure of the model description. In this situation a hierarchical model could help by specifying at one level the relatively fixed relationships and at another level the less fixed relationships.

In fact the hierarchical representation of a description is particularly useful in the case of representing a complex three-dimensional form. The key idea is to note that any two points in a hierarchy have a degree of relationship that is determined by their remoteness from a common ancestor. One may be the actual ancestor of the other, in which case they are very closely related; a common ancestor may be only one generation above; or it may be right at the start of the hierarchy. Similarly two points on a three-dimensional object, or rather their projections in the optical image, may be closely coupled so that if one is visible then the other one will nearly always be. Or they may be so arranged so that if one is visible then the other is most unlikely to be so. By using the structure of the hierarchy to mirror these relationships, the one model can serve for all views, allowing for the joint probabilities of occurrence. As a thing in the world changes in position and angle with respect to a viewer, different branches in the hierarchy will become matched in turn to the object, but in an orderly sequence and with the visual description occupying a contiguous region of the model description.

In practice the situation will always be a little more complex than this so that several visible parts may be multiply represented. Consider the case of an ordinary dice with the numerals 1 to 6, one on each face. There are a number of different viewpoints from which the number 3 can be seen, and accordingly we shall have a number of different contexts within which it appears in the hierarchical representation. The hierarchy allows for the various combinations of numerals in view at any one time, but also and quite naturally represents the fact that the numberals 3 and 4 cannot both be seen at the same time. There is no branch of the hierarchy on which both appear together except through a common ancestor at the topmost layer. A hierarchy that can stand as a representation of the numerals on the dice, plus their spatial relationships, is given in Fig. 13 and the reader may care to examine the form of this representation or model description to see how it works.

The essential point is that a hierarchy provides a natural and simple format for expressing the relationships between the different possible views of something by making explicit what parts of the description are related and usually appear together, and also which parts are not related and never appear together. In so doing, the hierarchy also makes explicit how things

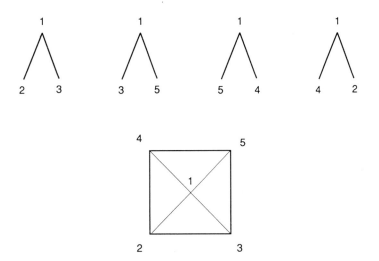

Figure 13. A model representation for the numerals on a dice. At the top of this figure, lines connect combinations that can be seen at the same time. There are only vertical lines. Beneath this there is another representation of the same structure, but with a higher dimensionality. This now has horizontal lines. Any one triangle of this structure can be visible at one time. For a simple geometric shape like a dice, there are no parts that will become occluded together as it rotates.

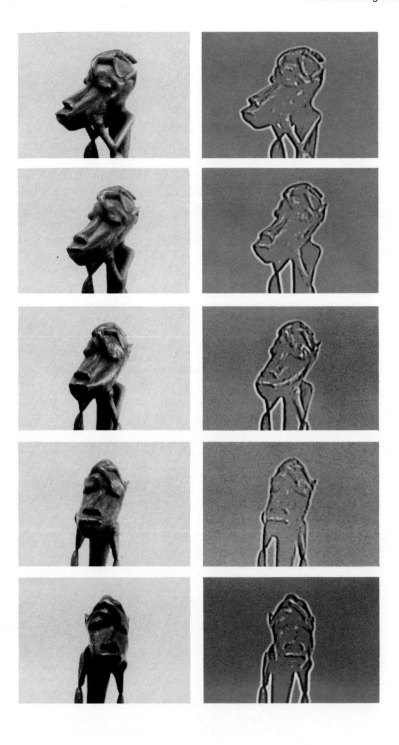

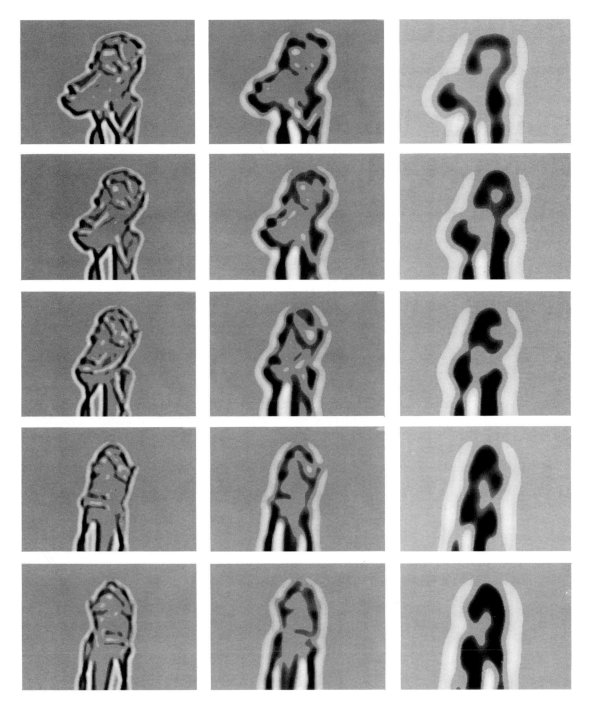

Figure 14. Visual matching for a three-dimensional thing. This figure shows a sequence of images obtained as a rigid three-dimensional thing was rotated in front of the camera. Beside each image in the sequence are shown processed images of the same thing at various scales. A visual model of the thing would need to make explicit the relationships between all these different images.

may change in their visual appearance, and particularly, what the natural progression should be as the thing or the viewpoint moves.

Hierarchies were originally introduced as a means for speeding up the matching process. Whilst they certainly have this property, they have this new property as a bonus. It is important to realize that hierarchies provide the natural means for understanding, at an intellectual and scientific level, the nature of matches between images from particular viewpoints to the things themselves.

7.6 Summary

Certain actions are not appropriate for direction towards all or any things that might be represented by a visual description. The objects of these actions must meet certain conditions to make the action reasonable, safe or wise. We can use a visual model to specify the conditions that have to be met and then measure the degree to which any visual description matches up to the conditions in the model. A decision description can be used to represent the outcome and it in turn can then provide the information for an action description.

Matching with visual models can be used in two rather different situations. On the one hand the object of an action can be modelled and the match can be regarded as a process that detects the presence of the specific object. On the other hand the model can be used to specify the conditions which determine how a property of an object should be measured.

Visual descriptions are relatively bland, making no distinctions in the information content of different dimensions and attributes. A match between two descriptions is made on the basis of an equal treatment of all the various qualities and quantities. Visual models can be used to help organize a description so that the efficiency of the matching process can be increased. The central idea is to give all the elements of the description a place in a list so that it is explicit which elements between two descriptions are to be compared. Unless all the dimensions of its various attributes are very highly correlated, there will be a choice of different possible orderings, depending on which dimension is selected.

In some cases, two or more dimensions will be coupled, such as the two spatial dimensions of the optical image. In these cases, the two-dimensional coordinate system is rather arbitrarily oriented and there is an infinite range of pairs of orthogonal directions. A two-dimensional ordering is computationally awkward, and it is accordingly useful to have a model which will allow the expression of the two dimensions as one. Symmetry, direction of elongation, motion and others provide the pattern.

Visual models can also be concerned with transformations of things in the world that have characteristic and specific effects on the two-dimensional image and its description. Movements in the third dimension, articulations and non-rigid changes in shape, and variations in illumination all produce effects in the two-dimensional image that cannot easily be generalized. It is far simpler to invoke models of the changes in image descriptions that these produce. As some solid chunk of matter moves in space, its image description changes. The changes are sometimes continuous and sometimes not as new elements are added or old ones lost. Relationships between descriptive elements tend to be less variable in their behaviour and it is for this reason that visual models are appropriate.

The common pattern to these applications is the idea that one can take parts of descriptions or whole descriptions and apply a model to them so that the result is a new set of descriptions that have been changed in a rather specific fashion. The consequence is still a visual description from which behaviour is generated as before. Visual models are programmable processes rather than data.

References

Suggested further reading

Biederman I. (1985) Human image understanding: recent research and a theory. *Computer Vision, Graphics Image Proc.* **32**, 29–73.

Brooks R.A. (1981) Symbolic reasoning among 3D models and 2D images. *Artificial Intelligence* **17**, 285–348.

Hoffman D. and Richards W. (1985) Parts of recognition. In: A. Pentland (ed.), "From Pixels to Predicates". Ablex, Norwood, NJ.

Hummel R. and Zucker S. (1983) On the foundations of relaxation labeling processes. *IEEE Trans. Pattern Anal. Machine Intelligence* **3**, 267–287.

Kanade T. and Kender J.P. (1983) Mapping image properties into shape constraints: skewed symmetry, affine transformable patterns and the shape from texture paradigm. In: J. Beck, B. Hope and A. Rosenfeld (eds), "Human and Machine Vision". Academic Press, New York.

Koenderink J.J. (1984) On the structure of images. *Biol. Cybern.* **50**, 363–370.

Longuet-Higgins H.C. and Prazdny K. (1980) The interpretation of a moving retinal image. *Proc. Roy. Soc. Lond.* **B208**, 385–397.

Pentland A. (1988) The parts of perception. In: C. Brown (ed.), "Advances in Computer Vision". Lawrence Erlbaum Associates, Hove.

Roberts L. (1965) Machine perception of three-dimensional solids. In: Tippet *et al.* (eds), "Optical and Electrooptical Information Processing". MIT Press, Cambridge, MA.

Rosenfeld A., Hummel R, and Zucker S. (1976) Scene labeling by relaxation labeling operations. *IEEE Trans. Systems, Man Cybern.* **6**, 420–433.

Ullman S. (1979) "The Interpretation of Visual Motion". MIT Press, Cambridge, MA.

Ullman S. (1989) Aligning pictorial descriptions: an approach to object recognition. *Cognition* **32**, 193–254.

Yuille A.L. and Poggio T. (1988) Scaling and fingerprint theorems for zero-crossings. In: C. Brown (ed.), "Advances in Computer Vision". Lawrence Erlbaum Associates, Hove.

Exercises

1. Examine the set of Roman letters (the alphabet), in upper case and lower case. Is it possible to define a small set of symbolic primitives, such as line intersection, that would allow a qualitative match to distinguish between all the different letters? How sensitive to changes in font would these features be?

2. Faces have a basic structure that has many of the types of organization that are useful in vision. Consider what a model for a face would be. How would this model be used to create a decision description for the gender, age, race, identity of the person?

3. Try experimenting with the expression for a quantitative match. Take a set of random dots, and then add a small extra random perturbation to the position of each one, thereby simulating positional error. Compare the resulting positions to the positions of the dots in the original, assuming differing degrees of positional error. Try using exponents other than the standard value of 2 (see previous chapter).

4. In the limit of no external knowledge, the task of finding a bilateral symmetry can be as computationally complex as the matching process it is supposed to help. What simple assumptions can be made to speed the process? Where is the axis likely to lie?

5. Try experimenting with the scale–space diagrams for different types of pattern. How is the distance between a blob appearing and splitting distributed across spatial scales?

8

Studying Human Vision

How should we set about studying human vision? The essence of vision is that information is taken from the image and used to control actions. A sensible starting point is to discover what information the human visual system is capable of extracting from images. But we have to be careful. As soon as we start considering human vision, there is a strong tendency to confuse phenomenological experience with the information-processing side of our vision. Throughout this book the emphasis is on the manner in which vision makes information available for particular tasks and decisions. This emphasis must continue now.

I can show someone a stereoscopic display and ask if they can see depth in it: if they say no, what can I infer? It's tempting to deduce that they cannot use stereoscopic differences to see the depth, but, of course, they might just have misunderstood the question. To improve matters. I could show the person three displays: two without and one with the stereoscopic information. Now we can ask the subject to identify the odd one out. If the subject can identify the odd one out, then we can be sure that the information that defines the difference between them is available. We can interpret what the subject says at this level without much risk of being wrong. We're still not learning very much however.

We want to know how much and what kind of information is actually used and how it is recovered from the image. The key is to note that the more variable a person's vision is, the less information it is providing. In the limit, a completely blank screen has no information: if we require someone to read the words on a blank page, their behaviour will be totally random, will have infinite variability and they will have extracted no useful information from the page. At the other extreme, if I asked you to read the words on this page, your behaviour would be highly predictable, would have very low variability. In the first case the subject has no information; in the second, plenty. So we can measure how much information a visual system is getting by assessing its variability. There are some circumstances where we can observe the variability directly, but it is more usual to infer it by measuring how sensitive the visual system is to small differences in stimuli. Clearly the more variable a system is, the less sensitive it will be to a small change in the input. It then follows that the variability of a system can be inferred from a measure of how much change in the input is needed to produce a reliable change in its output.

At first inspection the sheer power of our vision is overwhelming—how can we study the reliability and accuracy of a system that hardly ever makes an error? When was the last time you walked into something because your vision did not warn you of its presence? One place to start is the absolute limits of vision.

How much contrast is just necessary to detect a pattern? Let's consider how we might measure this. The simplest way that could be thought of unfortunately will not suffice, but it is instructive to see why. We could set up a blank screen at some intermediate luminance and then provide a dial to turn to increase the pattern contrast. Then we simply sit a subject in front of the screen and tell them to set the pattern to be just visible and measure the setting they select. This is called the *method of adjustment*. As the subject turns the dial and increases the contrast of the grating, evidence for the presence of the grating accumulates both through the eyes and through the hand that is turning the dial. At some point the evidence is sufficient for the subject to admit its "truth" and the setting is made. I have deliberately used this word to emphasize how extra-visual factors, such as a criterion, are involved in such a decision. Technically speaking, the design is contaminated by bias. The setting any particular subject makes is determined by both visual information and that subject's willingness to switch from saying "No" to saying "Yes". This is a measure of the subject's phenomenal experience, which is not necessarily closely related to the actual visual information available for behaviour.

We have to give the subject a simpler and less ambiguous decision to make. Suppose that there are two screens, only one of which contains the pattern, and the subject doesn't know which. With this design we can ask the subject which screen contains the pattern stimulus. The response can either be correct or incorrect. If we switch the pattern randomly from side to side, it is possible to measure how reliably correct the subject is compared with the physical reality. This is called the *method of two alternative forced choice* (2AFC). We can choose a range of pattern contrasts that lie between zero contrast, where the subject will be responding at chance, and a level at which the subject can reliably detect the pattern. If we test each pattern a number of times, we will then be able to draw a graph showing per cent correct as a function of contrast. This technique is called the *method of constant stimuli*, and the graph is an example of a *psychometric function*.

There is very little bias in this design. It is not up to the subject to decide how much grating has to be visible to support a decision that it is present. We the experimenters infer that quantity by finding out how much contrast is needed for the subject to meet some criterion performance level. The important point is that the decision criterion is under the experimenter's control, not the subject's, and therefore can be kept constant.

8.1 Two Basic Designs

There are two fundamental designs, each of which can be used with a number of modifications.

In the first design, the subject is required to detect a particular *increment* in stimulus value, ∂s, from a *pedestal* value s. Of course, s could take the value of zero, in which case the task requires the subject to *detect* the presence of ∂s alone. In the most complete version of this design, the subject is shown three stimuli: two have a value of s and one has the value of $s + \partial s$. The subject is required to report which is the odd stimulus. The advantage of doing the experiment this way is that the subject's verbal understanding of the cue is not necessary. It can be done as a three alternative forced choice, but it is probably better to tell the subject that the odd stimulus will only ever be two of the three possibilities. The subject then knows that the third stimulus is a reference. The third reference target is very often omitted, so the subject is shown s and $s + \partial s$ and asked to detect which is which.

The second basic design also uses three stimuli. Two of these are the *reference* stimuli and are shown to the subject with values $s + \partial s$ and $s - \partial s$, where ∂s causes a clearly visible change in the stimulus. The other, the *test* stimulus, may either have the value of $s + \partial s$ or $s - \partial s$. The subject is told which is the test stimulus and asked to *discriminate* whether the increment, ∂s, is positive or negative. Three stimuli are needed in this case to ensure that there is no doubt which is the test stimulus and what the value of the reference s looks like. It is frequently possible to use only one reference stimulus rather than two.

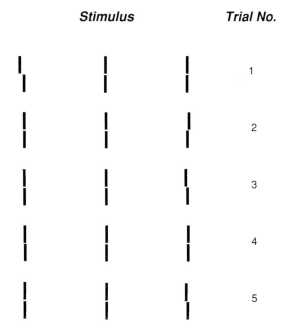

Figure 1. The first basic psychophysical design. The subject is shown three stimuli and asked whether the leftmost or rightmost stimulus is the odd one out. From trial to trial the target stimulus is randomly assigned to either position. By varying the size of the increment cue, it is possible to obtain a psychometric function that plots the proportion of trials on which the subject reports that the target is in the rightmost position, as a function of the cue size.

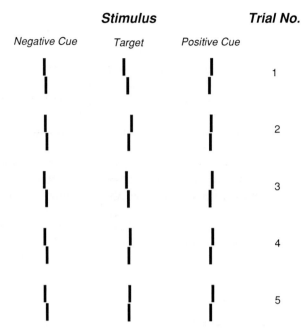

Figure 2. The second basic psychophysical design. The subject is shown three stimuli and asked whether the central stimulus has a positive or negative cue value. The outer two have a positive and a negative cue for comparison purposes. From trial to trial the sign of the cue is randomly assigned. By varying the size of the increment cue, it is possible to obtain a psychometric function that plots the proportion of trials on which the subject reports that the target is positive, as a function of the cue size.

The first design is concerned with measuring sensitivity to an increment, by requiring the subject to detect which of several stimuli has a known increment. The second design is concerned with measuring sensitivity to an increment by requiring a subject to discriminate the unknown sign of the increment in a known test stimulus.

8.2 The Subject's View

It is important to consider the procedure from a different point of view: that of the subject. There is a considerable art in creating the circumstances in which subjects will give of their best, although much of this is a sort of folklore. One might be sceptical of a body of knowledge obtained when subjects are treated to get "good data", but such scepticism is without cause. Good data means accurate measurements that are not erratic but can be readily repeated. Being a subject in a psychophysical experiment can be an experience similar to torture by tedium taking superhuman efforts to maintain some degree of concentration and willingness to co-operate with the instructions. It is difficult to get good data under adverse circumstances. Mild but continuous distraction such as music or light conversion often helps, when timing aspects of an experiment are not critical. It is as if there is unconscious vision that can be released by preventing the subject concentrating too much.

Subjects bring a number of preconceptions into an experiment. They tend to regard the process as a test of themselves, thank goodness, although this can mean that realization of having made an error can be distressing. Subjects will always use the strategy for doing a task that seems most reliable, almost regardless of instructions and the possibility that different subjects will use different strategies is always a concern.

If you give subjects two responses, two buttons to press or whatever, then they will tend to use them roughly equally and an experiment should be designed with this in mind if an artificial bias is not to be introduced. If a series of near-threshold discriminations are being made, subjects tend to lose confidence in their memory of what the cue is and it is a good practice to mingle easy judgements with the difficult near-threshold ones.

8.3 Psychometric Functions

The value of the cue, ∂s, determines the probability of a subject using a particular response. When ∂s is near zero, the probability of either response is near 0.5. It is a frequent practice to measure the proportion of trials on which the subject makes a correct response. At a ∂s of exactly zero, there is an interesting dilemma because the subject will always be incorrect. The problem lies in our use of the term "correct". It is better practice to assume that the *subject's decision is always correct*, and that what is being measured is the *reliability of the information that is provided*. This is just inferred from the probability that the subject will use one of the two response categories as a function of the value of ∂s. When ∂s is zero, then this probability will be nearly 0.5.

Suppose that a particular value of $s + \partial s$ is transmitted by the visual system as an internal parameter t:

$$t = s + \partial s + e$$

where e is a random variable of fixed mean, μ_e, and standard deviation, σ_e. This means that, for a given value of ∂s, there is a distribution of likely values of t with mean $s + \partial s + \mu_e$ and sd σ_e. Any one instance of the test $s + \partial s$ gives a particular value of t, which is compared with a reference of value s without error. The probability of a particular response, as a function of t, the internal parameter, switches suddenly from 0 to 1 at $s + \mu_e$.

$$P(R^+) = 1 \qquad t > s + \mu_e$$
$$P(R^+) = 0.5 \qquad t = s + \mu_e$$
$$P(R^+) = 0 \qquad t < s + \mu_e$$

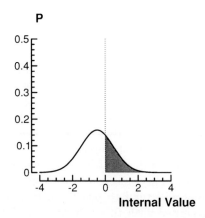

Figure 3.   The process of stimulus mapping into vision. A stimulus of value $s + \partial s$ is presented to the subject, and gives rise to an internal representation or effect that has a probability density function, as shown. The internal effect is then compared with the decision criterion which is also shown as a vertical dotted line. The probability that the subject will respond "greater than" is then given by the area under the density function that is to the right of the decision function (shaded).

The probability of a particular response as a function of $s + \partial s$ is then given by the convolution of the step decision function and the error distribution $p(e)$. This convolution is equivalent to the integral of $p(e)$.

$$P(s + \partial s) = \int_{-\infty}^{s + \partial s} p(e)\mathrm{d}e$$

If $P(e)$ is the normal or Gaussian probability distribution then this function has the form of an S-shaped sigmoid curve, rising from 0 monotonically to 1. It is steepest at the point where the probability is 0.5, which is where ∂s is equal to $-\mu_e$. Its steepness at this point is inversely proportional to σ_e. If we measure the probability of a particular response as a function of $s + \partial s$, it is possible to plot a series of values that should lie on such a sigmoid curve. The values can be analysed by fitting a curve that has two free parameters, μ_e and σ_e, to the data by standard curve-fitting procedures. These two parameters are the bias and the standard deviation of the subject's error response distribution. The more sensitive the subject is to the dimension under consideration, the smaller the parameter σ_e will be and the steeper the psychometric function will be. The experimentally measured function relating probability of a particular response to the stimulus value, $s + \partial s$, is called the *psychometric function*.

The psychometric function, P, can be written down as

$$P(s + \partial s) = \int_{-\infty}^{s + \partial s} \exp\left(\frac{-(e - \mu_e)^2}{2\sigma_e^2}\right)\mathrm{d}e$$

or we may write

$$s' = \frac{s - \mu_e}{\sigma_e}$$

$$\partial s' = \frac{\partial s}{\sigma_e}$$

$$p(s + \partial s) = erf(s' + \partial s')$$

or

$$z(s + \partial s) = s' + \partial s'$$

where z and erf are standard statistical functions. The z function is called the normal deviate function and it corresponds to plotting the probabilities on probability graph paper. Usually this gives a straight line in place of the sigmoid psychometric function; below we shall meet a situation where this is not true. A simplification can be made if the bias is zero.
If

$$s' = \mu_e$$

then

$$z(\partial s) = \partial s'$$

or

$$z(\partial s) = \frac{\partial s}{\sigma_e}$$

There are various terms that are used to describe the parameters of a psychometric function. The values for the bias and error rate that are obtained could be attributed to either the decision function or the internal

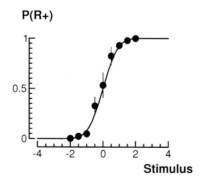

Figure 4. A typical psychometric function. The proportion of trials on which the subject responded "greater than" is plotted as a function of the magnitude of the cue. A smooth sigmoid curve has been fitted to the data and is also drawn.

error function. It is usual to assume that the decision function contributes little to either and that we are essentially measuring the internal error function. Before proceeding, a word about the term "threshold". It is frequent to quote thresholds for a discrimination task. It is sometimes equated to σ_e, the error rate and the reciprocal of the sensitivity. In this case it is equivalent to the increment, ∂s, that will raise the probability of response from 0.5 to a probability of 0.83. If the bias of the system is zero, then this is equal to the value of ∂s at which the probability of a particular response is also 0.83, because the value of ∂s at which the probability is 0.5 will be zero. The term threshold is sometimes used to describe the value of ∂s at which the probability of response reaches some criterion level, say 0.75 irrespective of bias. When this is done the value obtained confounds bias and sensitivity.

Recapitulation

The sensitivity of the visual system to a stimulus difference is best measured with a *forced choice design*. The design may be organized either to measure sensitivity for the detection of an increment in a particular stimulus parameter or to measure the sensitivity for discriminating the sign of an increment.

The function relating the probability of a particular response to the value of the increment is called a *psychometric function*. The simple psychometric function has two parameters, the *bias* and *error rate* or *sensitivity*.

8.4 An Example Experiment

An example will help to make the business of psychophysics easier to understand. I shall describe here a small part of a series of experiments that I am currently doing. The subject is shown a display which contains two patterns such as that in Fig. 5. In this instance the right-hand one is just two vertical lines, side by side and separated by emptiness. The left-hand pattern has eight vertical lines, all parallel and occupying much the same horizontal extent as the left-hand pattern. The subject is asked to judge which pattern, left or right, occupies the greater horizontal extent. In this instance it is the left-hand pattern, although the subject will not know this. If the subject cannot see a difference in the extent of the two patterns, then he is forced to guess.

From trial to trial the side which contains the greater interval will be changed randomly. The magnitude of the interval difference, the cue, will also be varied from trial to trial ensuring that responses at a fair range of different points along the psychometric function will be obtained. Ideally, the subject will find roughly half of the trials easy and half difficult, with the two categories randomly intermingled. Since in this case it is expected that the two patterns, filled and empty, will be treated differently by the human visual system, they are also randomly assigned to left or right side of the display to avoid confounding an effect of left/right sides of the screen and the filled/empty intervals which would otherwise be correlated.

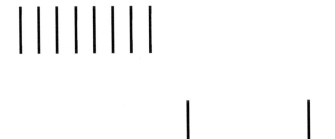

Figure 5. The stimulus for the sample experiment described in the text. The subject is required to judge which of the two spatial intervals is greater. In the experiment this would vary from side to side in a random fashion. The pattern that was made of many lines would also vary from side to side, so that the effect of the filling lines could be assessed independently of any other factors.

The subject is given two buttons with which to indicate his response at which time a new stimulus is displayed. At the end of 64 trials a psychometric function is computed from the proportion of "left side" responses obtained at each of several physical test distances. The psychometric function is plotted in Fig. 6. The vertical bars through each data point represent estimates of the standard error, given by

$$\sqrt{\frac{p(1-p)}{n}}$$

where p is the proportion correct, and n is the number of responses that were collected.

Beside the psychometric function I have added a graph which shows, for each stimulus condition, the median response time. The median response time is that response time at which there is an equal number of faster and slower responses. It is a good estimate of the typical response time because it is unaffected by any extremely slow responses when the subject may have been distracted.

The data are given for two different but related experiments and for two subjects: one (RJW) with many years of experience in doing psychophysics and the other (SW) undertaking a first ever experiment. There are many typical results in the data, and I now select a few to draw attention to.

(i)   The standard deviations of all the four psychometric functions are all similar at about 5% of the standard distance. This is a fairly typical value. It is also quite usual for the two subjects to be in close agreement. This is the reason why psychophysical measures can often be made with a small number of subjects.

(ii) In the case where the test and standard stimuli were the same, the bias of the psychometric function is nearly zero for each subject. This is the point of subjective equality (PSE) and when it corresponds to the point of physical equality, then we deduce that the two stimuli are both being distorted equally. It is not the case that

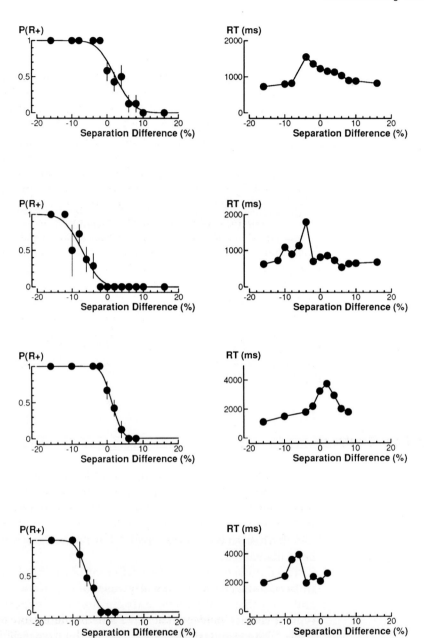

Figure 6. The psychometric functions. This shows some psychometric functions from the sample experiment. The data points are represented by round symbols, and the smooth curve drawn between them shows the best fitting cumulative error function. Each symbol has a vertical bar drawn through. The length of this bar is equal to two standard errors. Beside each psychometric function is drawn a plot of the median response times. Two psychometric functions are shown for each of the two subjects. For each subject the upper data is from a condition where the two stimuli both comprised only two vertical lines, as in the right side of Figure 5. The lower data is for a condition exactly as in Figure 5, where one of the stimuli was made up of eight lines and the other of two lines.

the two stimuli are perceived veridically, we cannot say how they are perceived.

(iii) Where the test and standard stimuli are different, the mean of the psychometric function is significantly different from zero. This means that two stimuli of physically the same length appear to have different lengths and that two stimuli that appear equal in length have physically different lengths. This is a visual illusion. It is worth noting about the subjects are in agreement about the sign of the illusion, but not very closely about its magnitude. This is also a fairly typical finding, which is due in part to the variable willingness of subjects to use one response more often than the other. For this reason, adaptive procedures that select stimuli for testing on the basis of earlier responses are preferable.

I leave it to the reader to decide what conclusion(s) may be drawn from this experiment. In practice, the whole run of 64 trials would be repeated several times by each subject and the data combined. The biases are estimates of the mean of a distribution and can be combined by simple arithmetic averaging. The standard deviations have to be combined by taking their root mean square. This is because the variance of a distribution can be averaged, but the standard deviation cannot. In psychophysics of this type is it unusual to find any critical difference between subjects and two or three subjects are usually considered to be sufficient if their data are in agreement.

8.5 Low Contrast

I have given the cumulative Gaussian function as a formula for the psychometric function. This is, in many ways, the most straight-forward model that can be adopted. It is one of several alternative forms that have been used, and I shall now describe the other main formulae. They are all used in measurements of contrast discrimination or detection.

(i) Sensitivity to Contrast Detection

We will now consider some data on the detection of contrast in human vision that were reported by Foley and Legge (1981). Figure 7 shows a typical psychometric function, relating the proportion of correct responses to the contrast of the stimulus. The ordinate (vertical axis) shows proportion correct, which in this case is equivalent to the proportion of trials on which the observer made one of the two possible responses. The abscissa (horizontal axis) uses the Michelson definition of contrast in terms of the maximum and the minimum luminances in the image:

$$C = \frac{L_{\mathrm{max}} - L_{\mathrm{min}}}{L_{\mathrm{max}} + L_{\mathrm{min}}}$$

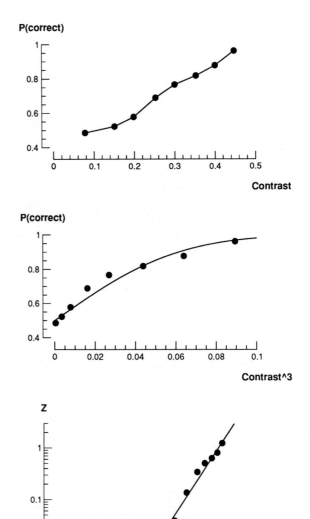

Figure 7. Psychometric function for contrast detection, as measured by Foley and Legge (1981). The data are only plotted as proportion correct, and therefore range from 0.5 to 1.0. The data points are plotted alone at the top. The standard function for a psychometric function does not provide a good fit to the data, but a modified expression which involves a monotonic transformation of the stimulus quantity does fit. This is shown in the middle panel. At the bottom is drawn a plot of the data and the model, using the normal deviate as scale for the ordinate.

The experimental data do not fit the normal psychometric function, as given above, very well at all. However, Foley and Legge found that the data are well fitted to a modified form of the function:

$$z(\partial C) = \frac{\partial C^k}{\sigma_c}$$

where $z(\partial C)$ is the normal deviate of per cent correct for contrast ∂C, as before. The only difference between this and the normal form is that the stimulus variable cue is raised to a power before being used in the normal way. This function therefore has an extra free parameter, k, which is found to be roughly constant between 2.5 and 3. As before the term σ_c is the inverse of the sensitivity.

The psychometric function for contrast detection can be fitted with several other algebraic expressions. For contrast detection, it is usual to use a *Weibull function* of the form

$$W(c) = 1 - \exp[-(c/\alpha)^\beta]$$

This expression has two parameters, α and β. The exponent, β, corresponds to the steepness of the function on a log–log plot. It is found to be a roughly constant value of around 3, irrespective of many experimental factors. The parameter, α, corresponds to the horizontal position of the function on a log–log plot.

It is appropriate at this stage to comment on the important concept of linearity and non-linearity. A system is *linear* if its outputs obey simple addition so that

$$R(a + b) = R(a) + R(b)$$

which says that the response to an input of $a + b$ is the same as the sum of its separate responses to a and to b. If this rule does not apply, then the system is *non-linear*. The transduction of contrast is clearly non-linear.

(ii) Sensitivity to Contrast Differences

Suppose that we show a subject two stimuli of slightly different contrasts and ask which has the greater contrast. In this way we can measure the psychometric function for *contrast discrimination*. From this we can assess the sensitivity to *contrast increment* for a range of *pedestal contrasts*. A typical psychometric function for this type of experiment is shown in Fig. 8. The data are taken from the same source as that for the psychometric function for contrast detection: same subject, same mean luminance, same cosine wave stimulus, same procedure. The only difference is the presence of a 0.004 pedestal contrast, which happens to correspond to that contrast which itself on its own can be correctly detected on 75% of trials.

Notice that the psychometric function now has a different form as well as being much steeper. The data show quite clearly that the visual system is more sensitive to an increment in contrast when there is a small pedestal present. There is now no evidence in this new psychometric function for a non-linearity of contrast. The two psychometric functions are plotted together on transformed axes in the figure, with the vertical axis plotting the logarithm of the z-transformed per cent correct scores and the horizontal axis plotting the log of contrast. If the psychometric functions are of the general form

$$z(\partial C) = \frac{(\partial C)^k}{\sigma_c}$$

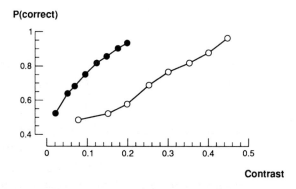

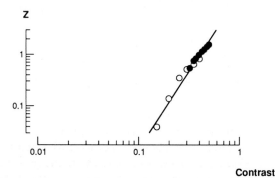

Figure 8. Psychometric function for contrast detection in presence of a contrast pedestal. This shows the contrast detection psychometric function that was obtained by Foley and Legge when the experiment was conducted with all stimuli presented on a 0.004 contrast pedestal (filled circles). The data points are shifted to lower contrast values, indicating a higher sensitivity in this condition. The open circles show the data from the experiment without the pedestal.

then the data should lie on straight lines of slope k:

$$\log\,(z(\partial C)) = k \log \partial C - \log \sigma_c$$

The figure shows that this is more or less the case. In fact if we plot the psychometric function, not as a function of the increment contrasts but as the sum of increment and pedestal contrasts, then the two psychometric functions for detection and discrimination lie on a single line. The implication of this is that the improvement in sensitivity when a small pedestal contrast is introduced can be attributed to the accelerating non-linearity in the transduction process.

Legge and Foley (1980) measured how the threshold increment contrast varies with pedestal contrast. The detection threshold non-linearity causes this function to have a dip at low thresholds for reasons that I have just been considering. This facilitation in threshold is followed by a subsequent progressive rise in increment threshold, indicating a second non-linearity. This second non-linearity conforms very approximately to:

$$\partial C \propto C$$

Increment Constrast

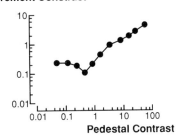

Pedestal Contrast

Figure 9. Weber's law for contrast. This shows the variation in contrast discrimination thresholds as a function of the pedestal contrast. The pronounced dip in the function is a well-established feature. The data are taken from Legge and Foley (1980).

This function is known as Weber's law and appears to be common to many sensory attributes. There have been many accounts of Weber's law, and the interested reader is referred to the book by Laming (1986). For the present it suffices to remark that Weber's law may reflect the way in which sensory magnitudes are either coded or compared within the nervous system.

It is quite normal to use a log–log plot for data from experiments of this type. There are several reasons for this practice. The log–log plot allows a wide range of values to be shown: many natural phenomena are based on power laws of various types, and these are easily seen on log–log plots; and for most psychophysical procedures, the standard error of measurement is proportional to the measurement itself. On a log–log plot, the error bars will all be roughly the same size. If the standard error of a variable, z, is given by ∂z, and we then transform z to $\log(z)$, then the error is also transformed, but not in the same way. This can be seen by treating the error as a derivative of z:

$$z' = \log_{10}(z) = \log_e(z)/\log_e(10)$$

therefore

$$\frac{\partial z'}{\partial z} = \frac{1}{\log_e(10)} \frac{1}{z}$$

therefore

$$\partial z' = \frac{1}{\log_e(10)} \frac{\partial z}{z}$$

8.6 *d'*

Sensitivity of a threshold is a way of expressing the amount of stimulus difference that is required to allow a subject to reach a criterion level of discrimination, which depends on how sharply discrimination varies as the stimulus difference changes. This is measured by collecting data with which a psychometric function can be plotted. To collect a psychometric function, the stimulus difference is varied along a continuum, and responses are recorded.

There are situations where it is interesting to know how discriminable two stimuli are, even when they are not easily placed on a simple continuum. The fact that they are stimuli, i.e. two-dimensional images, means that there are many continuous transformations from one to the other, and so, in principle, there are many opportunities to collect psychometric functions between the two. However these may well be quite inconvenient or even contrived, and under such circumstances when it is possible to use only two stimuli, d' (pronounced d prime) is used to express their discriminability.

The calculation of d' is based upon the percentage of correct discriminations between the two stimuli. The general idea is to express the distance between the two stimuli in terms of the standard deviation of the uncertainty or variable error with which they are represented within the observer's visual system. So, two stimuli that can be discriminated on 83% of trials differ by one standard deviation and have a d' of 1.0. Calculation of d' is usually simplified by assuming that the uncertainty distributions for the two stimuli have the same standard deviation.

8.7 Internal Noise

The most basic assumption in doing psychophysics is that there is a source of error or noise within the system. This noise source sets one of the limits on performance, and the psychophysical techniques can be regarded as making measurements of this noise source, although as we shall see in the next chapter, they are by no means restricted to doing just this.

There is another way of measuring the internal noise which is worth mentioning because it leads us, in the next section, to a consideration of efficiencies. The essence of the technique is to add noise to the stimulus and measure how much worse it makes the psychophysical sensitivity. In practice, this can be achieved by using a range of different degrees of stimulus noise and then using linear regression. We start by supposing that the threshold, which is the standard deviation of error responses, e_t, is determined by the standard deviation of all the noise in the experiment, e_n:

$$e_t = k_e e_n$$

We can square each side of this equation

$$e_t^2 = k_e^2 e_n^2$$

so that the terms are now variances. Now, the total noise in the experiment is made up of the noise that we are interested in but don't know, the internal noise, e_i, and the noise that we have added to the stimulus, e_s. If we assume these two are independent, then their variances add to give the total noise variance:

$$e_n^2 = e_i^2 + e_s^2$$

We can substitute this, giving

$$e_t^2 = k_e^2(e_i^2 + e_s^2)$$

If we write v for variance instead of e^2, then the equation looks like

$$v_t = k_v(v_i + v_s)$$

This equation is linear, that is, it is the equation of a straight line, with two unknowns which are k_v, the slope, and v_i, the intercept. By measuring v_t at various v_s values, and fitting the data using linear least squares regression, we can then obtain estimates for these two unknown quantities. The square root of v_i is then the internal noise level (expressed as a standard deviation).

The figure shows an example of orientation discrimination for a texture stimulus where the noise is represented by an orientation variance. The subject is shown a target as illustrated. Most of the lines have been drawn

Figure 10. Orientation texture patch. This shows a selection of stimuli from an orientation texture experiment described in the text.

from a population with a mean orientation that is horizontal. Those in a small patch are drawn from a different population with a mean that is not horizontal. The orientation cue, the mean of the path, is varied from trial to trial and the subject is asked to judge whether it is oriented clockwise or anticlockwise from horizontal. In each case a number of different degrees of orientation variance are illustrated. Thresholds are measured at a range of different orientation variances, and are plotted in two ways in Fig. 11. The data are shown as variances on linear axes, with a straight line drawn through the data to represent the least squares regression line. This line has the equation

$$v_t = k_v(v_i + v_s)$$

and consequently at the vertical axis, corresponding to $v_s = 0$, we then have

$$v_t = k_v v_i$$

In other words, the threshold obtained ordinarily without stimulus noise depends on two factors. By measuring performance at a range of different values of v_i we can assess both quantities.

We can interpret both these terms in this experiment. The internal variance term is a measure of how variable the orientation of individual lines is registered within the visual system. Since the experiment can be easily regarded as involving an estimate of the mean orientation, then we can treat the standard deviation of the subject's error response distribution as being analogous to the standard deviation of estimates of a mean, σ_m. This quantity is related to the number of estimates, n, and the standard deviation of the distribution, σ_t, by the expression:

$$\sigma_m = \frac{\sigma_t}{\sqrt{n}}$$

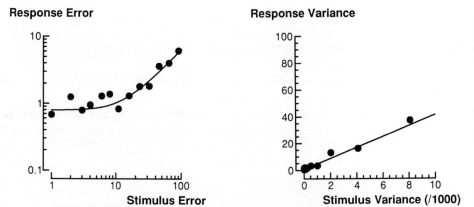

Figure 11. Orientation thresholds as a function of stimulus variance. The results of an experiment that measured orientation sensitivity for a patch of texture, as a function of the orientation variance of the stimulus. The data are plotted in two forms: variances on linear axes and standard deviations on log–log axes.

The second term from our model to the data of the experiment, k_v, can be related to the number of estimates, which in this case becomes the effective number of lines from the target patch that are used. We could now construct a device that would completely emulate the human performance by giving it an orientation variance to match and then limiting the number of lines that it could use to match.

It is more conventional to use logarithmic scales for the data because the error bars on the data points tend to be uniform in size. On such a plot, the vertical position of the curve depends only on k_v, and the point of highest curvature of the line through the data corresponds, roughly, to σ_i. The way in which the data are plotted is secondary to the main point which is to show how the equivalent internal orientation variance (or uncertainty) of the visual system can be measured. Of course, this measure depends on the task used, and I leave it to the reader to think about that.

8.8 Efficiences

One difficulty which often arises when trying to compare psychophysical data concerns the units with which the data are expressed. The use of one set of units can have consequences that are far from obvious, but that can tend to obscure any real trend in the data. The use of efficiencies can avoid this situation. A similar situation might arise when two different measurements in different units are to be compared. There is no common metric, so how can the measurements be compared? Once again, efficiencies which are dimensionless (i.e. they have no units) can be used.

Consider the set of data on curvature discrimination shown in Fig. 12. The data are taken from an experiment where the subjects were shown two lines on each trial and asked to indicate which line had the greater curvature (Watt and Andrews, 1982). From each run, a psychometric function could be plotted and a measure of curvature threshold was calculated. The figure plots this threshold as a function of the mean curvature of the test stimuli. Curvature of a line can be expressed in many different ways, two of which are used on the figure. You can see that the same set of data when plotted in two different metrics can show quite opposite effects. Does curvature discrimination get better or worse as line curvature is increased?

Suppose that we could devise an ideal machine that could formulate the best estimate of line curvature from a given stimulus. We could see how this ideal device fared in the experiment and compare its performance with the human data. We must work through this step by step. Start by assuming that there is some small, random spatial error in the physical stimulus, so that each point in the physical stimulus is displaced at chance within a small area of uncertainty. This is rather like the internal noise experiment. The problem now is to decide what the most likely curvature of the physical stimulus is on any one occasion. We have met an analogous problem in Chapter 5. We have a set of samples and we wish to calculate the maximum likelihood estimate of the curvature. In fact what we now want to know is

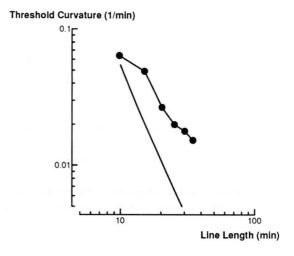

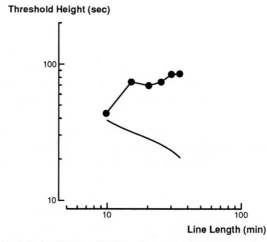

Figure 12. Curvature discrimination plotted two ways. This figure shows the same set of data on curvature discrimination plotted two ways. At the top, the line curvature (1/radius) is used. Beneath this the arc height (the distance between the midpoint of a chord joining the ends of the arc and the midpoint of the arc itself) is used. In one case the performance appears to improve as line length increases, in the other it appears to worsen. The performance of an ideal machine is shown on the same axes, from which it can be seen that there is no discrepancy. The data are taken from Watt and Andrews (1982).

how this estimate is itself distributed: what the standard deviation of curvature estimates is. This would be equivalent to the curvature threshold for the ideal device. For a given length of line and curvature, and a given level of spatial error, we can predict the best possible threshold that could be achieved: an ideal threshold.

The next step is to compare the actual human threshold with the ideal threshold. The obvious way to compare the two is to take their ratio: divide the ideal threshold by the actual threshold. This ratio has no dimension, which is what we require, provided that the two thresholds are in the same units. The ratio will always be less than one; to achieve a value of one, the human subject would have to be performing at an ideal level. There is another rationale for using this ratio which lets us treat it as an efficiency. Fisher, the statistician, has defined information as the reciprocal of variance. The ideal threshold, squared, is the reciprocal of the information content of the stimulus; the actual threshold, squared, is the reciprocal of the amount of information used by the subject. The ratio of these two is an efficiency.

Returning to the psychophysical data of the figure and the paradox of the two different trends, we can compute ideal thresholds using the two different measures of curvature and these are shown in the figure. Since the vertical axis has a logarithmic scale, the ratio of the two thresholds is given by the separation of the two points on the graph (because $\log(a/b) = \log(a) - \log(b)$). Now it is clear that the efficiency falls similarly in the two cases and the paradox is resolved.

There is another reason for being interested in efficiencies. Imagine a device for pumping water out of a deep coal mine. A steam engine is coupled to a pumping mechanism. We can measure the efficiency of the steam engine, and having done so, we can then be sure that the efficiency of the whole device, no matter how good the pump mechanism, will not exceed that of the steam engine part.

Of course, human vision is a much more complicated system than this, but the same principle applies. Suppose that we wished to test the hypothesis that curvature discrimination is done on the basis of the output of line orientation analysis. This is a reasonable suggestion that we can examine by measuring the efficiencies of orientation judgements and curvature judgements. If curvature judgements have a higher efficiency than orientation, then the hypothesis is untenable.

8.9 Measuring Appearance

It cannot be denied that a visual stimulus has an appearance. This phenomenon is really outside the scope of this book, and I believe remains something of a conceptual stumbling block. Visual appearance is closely related to consciousness and it remains an open question what the functional significance of consciousness might be. For this reason, we must be cautious in interpreting experiments where the object of study is ultimately visual appearance. Unfortunately a great many interesting experiments fall into this category, including nearly all of the studies of visual illusions.

The two typical paradigms that are employed are matching and probing. In a matching experiment, subjects are required to adjust the appearance of one test stimulus until some specific aspect of it matches a second, standard stimulus. The stimuli might be two different luminance patterns, perhaps a sharp edge and a blurred edge, and the subject would be asked to set the contrast of the sharp edge so that it matched the contrast of the blurred edge. In a probing experiment, subjects are shown a stimulus, perhaps an arc of a circle with a gap in it, and a probe, which in this case might be a spot. They are asked to position the probe stimulus so that it matches where the arc would be if the gap was bridged.

Whilst both of these are interesting experiments, they are not easy to interpret. In the case of a probe design, the major difficulty is the fact that the presence of the probe is bound to interfere with the property that is being measured. It does not provide a transparent measure of the appearance of the stimulus without the probe, and analysis of the results that are obtained have to take this into account. The matching design has several problems of interpretation. Once again the property that is being measured may be affected by the measurement process; if the appearance of something depends on its spatial and temporal context, then this becomes an unavoidable obstacle. There is also a more general problem in knowing what the subject has actually done. A ridiculous example will make this point. Suppose we give a subject a stimulus which is red on one half of the field and green on the other. We want to know the "chromatic contrast" of this stimulus and accordingly provide the subject with a similar black and white stimulus and then require the subject to adjust the contrast of this latter until it matches the contrast of the former. I'm sure that subjects could be persuaded to do this and quite possibly they would each be fairly self-consistent. It's far from clear what the data would mean. Clearly the visual system delivers measurements of various aspects of the two stimuli, and presumably one of these has been set to match, but how can we find out which one? Although this is a mildly ludicrous example, the same difficulty can be traced in most matching experiments.

The root difficulty lies in the lack of a theory of visual appearance. The general approach is rather along the lines of "picture inside the head". The image is transformed and generally processed, but is delivered to conscious experience in some form of reconstruction, maybe lacking some of the undesirable properties of image, such as being made of luminance rather than surface reflectance. This seems unlikely and rather simplistic, but we do not know for sure and so experiments based on visual appearance remain difficult to interpret.

8.10 Reaction Times

Much psychological knowledge has been obtained from measurements of subjects' reaction times and patterns in multiple choice tasks. The drawback to these measures is that they can only be analysed in a qualitative manner because there is no adequate theory of how reaction times are generated.

Psychometric functions can be accounted for, in detail, by simple propositions. The first was that there is uncertainty in the mappings between the physical stimulus and the internal representation upon which the subject makes a judgement. The second is that individual judgements are uncorrelated. With these simple propositions it is possible to measure the sensitivity and bias of the system involved. The first proposition seems plausible and even perhaps unavoidable; the second proposition is less likely to be fair but the sequential correlations between judgements are unlikely to interact with specific conditions in a task.

However, when we turn to consider reaction times, we need far more complex and questionable propositions before an equally quantitative analysis can be attempted. What factors alter a reaction time? A simple answer is the amount of processing required to generate a response. Anyone familiar with the computer operating system Unix will know that the time taken by a process can vary for reasons that are not directly observable, but that depends on what the processor was doing concurrently. Obviously no experiment can ever claim to have the full resources of the subject, but can only rely on having a fair proportion of the important resources. A reaction time can also depend on how ready the subject is to process the stimulus and to generate and execute the response. This, in particular, gives scope for a considerable degree of sequential correlation between responses.

None of this is intended to deny that reaction times, if they could be interpreted as dynamic indicators of processing, would be interesting and useful. The typical high level of serial correlation in responses is a problem, and the absence of a good statistical theory renders them difficult to interpret. My own opinion is that studies based on reaction times should be treated much as one would regard a region on a map which was marked with the legend "Centaurs abide here". The point is that present information is not to be relied on too heavily, but rather as an indication of something of interest and perhaps, adventure.

8.11 Summary and Comments

This chapter started with a general discussion of how to study human vision. I rejected the phenomenal approach and adopted an approach based more directly on visual actions. The ideal design is where subjects are asked to identify which of a number of stimuli is the odd one out, although this can usually be simplified. A discrimination experiment will lead to a psychometric function which shows the variability of response as a function of the size of the cue. From this function, we can determine the subject's sensitivity and bias.

By adding noise to the physical stimulus and measuring performance changes, it is possible to assess the equivalent internal noise or uncertainty. This is a technique that has proved most useful in understanding some of the basic properties of human vision.

Very often, it is misleading or even illogical to compare thresholds obtained under different stimulus situations. When this is the case, it is useful to measure efficiency of performance instead. This may be compared across quite widely differing stimulus situations.

Once we have collected the basic data, then we need to interpret it. Recall the data on contrast detection, as an example. The data on contrast detection clearly show a non-linearity in the transduction of contrast, so that the internal effect of contrast is a positively accelerating function of contrast, at least for very small contrasts. The evidence for this non-linearity is very strong. What is its cause? I will examine four potential answers to this question. Notice that the examination has to be at two levels, one of which concerns the actual evidence, the other of which concerns our understanding of vision.

The first possible cause for the transduction non-linearity is just that it exists. It is there because that is the way that nature works. There is no objection to this answer on logical or empirical grounds. It may be an arbitrary property of the system, but it may not. If it is not, then we won't be able to claim a full understanding until we know what benefits it offers the visual system.

A second possible explanation for the non-linearity comes from the work of Pelli. He has shown that such a non-linearity would be expected if the visual system were *uncertain* of what the signal was. If the visual system is uncertain about the stimulus then, of course, it doesn't know what to look for. As evidence for the existence of the stimulus begins to accumulate, so too does information about where it is and what its form is. This allows the visual system to improve its performance more rapidly than in simple proportion to contrast.

The third potential case is that the system needs to have a non-linear threshold device so that it can determine where in the image there is no variation in luminance. If the image is noisy, or more importantly in everyday viewing conditions, the internal signal is subject to *intrinsic noise*, which is noise generated in the system itself, then it is necessary to set a criterion signal strength, below which any activity is deemed to be noise. In its simplest form, such an internal threshold would appear as a neutral 0.5 region in the decision function. It would not appear as a discontinuity in the psychometric function because of errors in transduction. Obviously, this would lead to misses where the signal was subthreshold; it would also commit false alarms where the noise exceeded threshold, and these errors will tend to smooth out the psychometric function.

The fourth possible explanation for the contrast transduction non-linearity is that it is a by-product of the detection mechanism. Recall that I described in Chapter 5 how different measures of the presence or absence of a signal had different error rates. Provided that we can treat the effective visual signal as a derivative of the retinal image, then zero level will correspond to no contrast and non-zero to the presence of contrast. A particularly sensitive measure is the integral of the signal between adjacent zeros. When the noise contains components of higher frequencies than the signal, this measure exhibits a positively accelerating non-linearity that matches the data. Stated simply, the reason for this non-linearity is that each point on the signal is subjected to its own decision: is it positive or negative? This is a type of thresholding in its own right, but it is then followed by a second device which adds it into the overall decision if its sign matches that of its neighbours. As the signal increases in amplitude, more and more points are recruited, and hence the accelerating non-linearity.

In this chapter I have set out to discuss how we can study human vision. Since it is my desire to understand vision as a system that is purposeful, the techniques of neurophysiology are not very relevant to my goals since they do not allow me to observe the whole system at work. This is a personal statement that makes no comment on the worthiness or interest of data obtained by neurophysiology: it is just of little help to my enterprise at present.

I have described the basic techniques of psychophysics and how they can be interpreted. In the next chapter I will describe how these techniques can be used to explore the nature of our vision by seeking variations in performance as circumstances change. Many readers will feel that I have given a typical psychophysicist's view of performance measurement and have not described methods concerned with factors other than thresholds in a very favourable light. My main reason for doing this lies in the number of assumptions that need to be made before valid conclusions can be drawn. Frequently, these assumptions are not articulated. Following on from this, the conclusions themselves are often relatively weak, being little more than a restatement of the result: discrimination A is faster/less error prone than discrimination B. Psychophysical methods, when used rigorously, should lead to quantitative conclusions that only rest on a few, clearly stated assumptions.

References

Psychophysical techniques

Cornsweet T.N. (1962) The staircase method in psychophysics. *Am. J. Psychol.* **75**, 485–491.

Guilford J.P. (1954) "Psychometric Methods". McGraw-Hill, New York (Especially Chapters 2 to 6).

Laming D.R.J. (1973) "Mathematical Psychology", Chapters 3 and 4. Academic Press, London.

Senders V.L. and Sowards A. (1952) Analysis of response sequences in the setting of a psychophysical experiment. *Am. J. Psychol.,* **65**, 358–374.

Taylor M.M. and Creelman C.C. (1967) PEST: efficient estimates on probability functions. *J. Am. Stats. Assoc.* **41**, 782–787.

Watt R.J. and Andrews D.P. (1981) APE: adaptive probit estimation of psychometric functions. *Curr. Psychol. Res.* **1**, 205–214.

d′

Laming D.R.J. (1973) "Mathematical Psychology", Chapter 5. Academic Press, London.

Tanner W.P. and Swets J.A. (1954) A decision making theory of visual detection. *Psychol. Rev.* **61**, 401–409.

Efficiences

Andrews D.P., Butcher A.K. and Buckley B.R. (1973) Acuities for spatial arrangements in line figures: Human and ideal observers compared. *Vision Res.* **13**, 599–620.

Barlow H.B. (1962) A method for determining the overall quantum efficiency of visual discriminations. *J. Physiol.* **160**, 155–168.

Barlow H.B. (1980) The absolute efficiency of perceptual decisions. *Phil. Trans. Roy. Soc. Lond.* **B290**, 71–82.

Barlow H.B. and Pelli D.G. (1987) Statistical efficiency of natural and artificial vision. *J. Opt. Soc. Am.* **A4**, 2291–2457 (special issue).

Watt R.J. and Andrews D.P. (1982) Contour curvature analysis: hyperacuities in the discrimination of detailed shape. *Vision Res.* **22**, 449–460.

Contrast

Foley J.M. and Legge G.E. (1981) Contrast detection and near-threshold discrimination in human vision. *Vision Res.* **21**, 1041–1053.

Legge G.E. and Foley J.M. (1980) Constrast masking in human vision. *J. Opt. Soc. Am.* **70**, 1458–1471.

Laming D.R.J. (1986) "Sensory Analysis". Academic Press, London.

Suggested Further Reading

Geisler W.S. (1989) Sequential ideal-observer analysis of visual discriminations. *Psychol. Review* **96**, 267–314.

Exercises

1. A good test of how well the principles of psychometric functions have been understood is to program a simulation of the subject in an experiment. The program will generate a series of stimulus levels randomly (or according to some adaptive procedure), and the simulation will then generate a response. The response should be subject to an error response distribution.
2. Try different error response distributions. Use a standard random number generator to obtain a uniform distribution, and then transform this to get Gaussian and other distributions.
3. Assess the effect of different numbers of trials on the eventual precision with which the parameters of the psychometric function can be assessed.
4. Try using different power law transformations of the stimulus parameter.

9
Psychophysics and Image Algebra

In this chapter and the next two I shall show how the fundamental techniques of psychophysical measurement that I explained in Chapter 8 can be used to obtain some insights into the ways in which human vision works. The main argument of these chapters is to show how this can be done, although I have selected topics that also give a cross-section of the range of interests of present day research. The three main criteria that I have employed in selecting the topics of research to be examined in detail are:

(i)   the techniques involved must be rigorous enough to allow fairly firm conclusions to be reached;
(ii) the experiments must be intrinsically interesting and related to a computational rather than a phenomenological understanding of vision;
(iii) the topic must be well enough studied that it is possible to make some sense of the data.

In presenting the experiments that follow, I have ordered them in terms of their level of explanation, along the lines of Chapters 4–7 of this book, although it must be borne in mind that every experiment involves several levels.

In this chapter, the first topic that I shall describe concerns the initial filtering stages of human vision. A great deal of research effort went into gaining some understanding of these processes, and even after 20 years there are still some important unanswered questions. Two of these, filter output combination and dynamic selection of filters, are considered in the second and third topics. A natural context for considerations of the dynamics of spatial filtering operations is found in the analysis of visual motion, and this topic follows as the fourth. Finally, I describe some intriguing experiments that have the distinction of using the task of reading rather than the more usual task of button-pushing forced choice, so beloved of experimenters and loathed by subjects.

9.1 Stimulus Configuration and Contrast Detection

Although the general characteristics of the contrast detection process are presumably fixed properties of the human vision system, the threshold itself varies considerably with the spatial and temporal pattern of the stimulus. These variations are important because from them it has proved possible to discover significant information about the initial transformations in the visual system.

There have been two approaches to the measurement of the effects of configuration. One has been concerned with the spatial and temporal impulse functions of the visual system. The other has been concerned with the Fourier domain properties of spatial and temporal effects by using stimuli that are most easily and directly expressed in terms of spatial and temporal frequencies.

(i) Spatial Impulse Functions

One way of measuring the spatial properties of the detection process is to use as targets spots of varying diameter. Figure 1 shows how contrast threshold varies with spot size. It has been a regular practice to describe this function by three laws. For spots that are very small, *Ricco's law* states that threshold is inversely proportional to the area of the target. *Piper's law* states that, for slightly larger spots, threshold is inversely proportional to the square root of the target area. For larger spots there is a *Null law*, i.e. no effect.

Inspecting the data suggests that these laws are a rather heavy interpretation of what is really a smooth function. At the right of the figure the same results are shown as the total flux at threshold (intensity multiplied

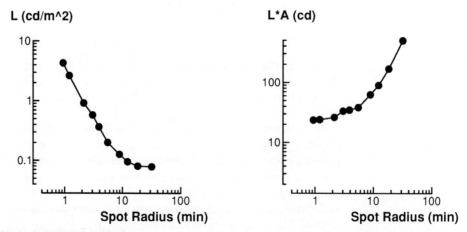

Figure 1. Spatial integration and contrast detection. The effects of target size on contrast detection thresholds are plotted. Two different scales for threshold are used: simple luminance difference threshold, and flux (luminance × area) difference. The thresholds are constant flux for radii up to 10 arc min, and constant luminance difference for larger stimuli.

by the disc area) as a function of the spot radius. A more simple description of the data is that up to a radius of about 10 arc min, flux is a constant at threshold; beyond 10 arc min, luminance is a constant at threshold.

How can we interpret this observation? A simple account can be readily offered by hypothesizing that the system integrates luminance in the optical image over a radius of about 10 arc min. Light falling beyond this range is irrelevant and cannot influence the threshold, hence luminance is the important factor for large discs. Integration over a fixed radius is equivalent to convolving the image with a disc-like function such as a two-dimensional Gaussian. We have found an algebraic operation on the image which, if applied to the stimuli in these experiments, produces a response which is always the same at threshold.

There is one other interesting aspect of the data on Ricco's law. This concerns the effect of mean luminance. An increase in mean luminance causes the size (width) of the integration region to decrease. At low luminances photons are both relatively rare and relatively random (photon noise is proportional to the square root of mean luminance). It is therefore sensible to attempt to collect them over a relatively large visual angle. At higher mean luminances the number of photons increases and the photon noise is a smaller proportion of the absolute number, and so a smaller integration region (giving better spatial resolution) can be tolerated.

(ii) Spatial Frequency Functions

Another way of discovering how light is spatially integrated by the human visual system is to measure the contrast sensitivity to a cosine-wave grating as a function of its spatial frequency.

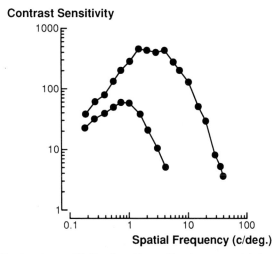

Figure 2. Contrast sensitivity functions. Contrast sensitivity (reciprocal of contrast threshold) is plotted as a function of spatial frequency for cosine-wave grating stimuli. Two different mean luminances are shown. The data are taken from Campbell and Robson (1968).

The basic logic is that an impulse can be made by adding together cosine waves of all frequencies and all of the same amplitude. The spatial response of the system to an impulse is equivalent, in the Fourier domain, to the variation in the response of the system to a cosine wave as a function of spatial frequency. The *contrast sensitivity function* (usually abbreviated to CSF) is the name given to the variation in contrast sensitivity with spatial frequency. It is the Fourier transform of the impulse function of the system at threshold.

The CSF is shown as measured at two mean luminances. The major effect of mean luminance is on the sensitivity to high frequencies: try reading a newspaper at twilight. There is very little change in sensitivity at low spatial frequencies. This is the same effect as the spatial integration over larger areas at lower mean luminances.

9.2 Independent Filters

Starting with the CSF, it is possible to predict the contrast sensitivity to any arbitrary waveform. However the rule whereby the prediction can be made is surprising. A pattern will reach visibility when its contrast has reached a value such that at least one of its cosine components is present at an amplitude at which it would be independently visible on its own. A pattern made up of, for example, six cosine waves will be visible if and only if one or more of them would be visible alone.

This is only approximately true, but it does suggest that each spatial frequency or narrow band of spatial frequencies is being detected independently. This is the same as suggesting that there are several, perhaps many, spatial filters of different spatial scales each operating independently over the image. The initial proposal of this kind came from Campbell and Robson (1968), who found that the contrast sensitivity for a square-wave grating was a factor of 1.28 higher than that for a sine-wave grating of the same frequency (provided that the frequency was more than 1 c deg^{-1}). This is close to the factor, $4/\pi$, which is the ratio of the two contrasts of the fundamental cosine component in each of the two patterns. The implication of this result is that the different components of the square wave are being detected by different mechanisms. A natural question to follow this is to ask how far apart the components should be in spatial frequency for their detection to be done by different mechanisms. The answer to this should give some information about the individual filters.

I now describe two different ways that have been used to assess how broadly tuned individual filter mechanisms are.

(i) Gain Adaptation

It has been found that the visual system is adaptive and changes its spatial characteristics to match the distribution of inputs. One instance of this has already been described: spatial summation tends to occur over larger areas at lower mean luminances. The property also appears to apply in a restricted sense to the individual spatial filters. Blakemore and Campbell (1969) found that prolonged inspection of a cosine-wave or square-wave grating of a particular spatial frequency (the adapting stimulus), led to a *threshold increase* in the detection of gratings of similar spatial frequency (test stimuli), but had no effect on gratings of widely different frequency. It was possible to measure the spatial frequency tuning of the effect, which shows a selectivity which is consistent with the presence of multiple spatial filters of various spatial scales.

It is not possible however to treat the spatial frequency tuning as a direct measure of the Fourier transform of the spatial filter. It is not known whether the adapting stimulus causes one or more spatial filters to change their sensitivity. There is little or no adaptation at the frequency of the third harmonic, suggesting that only one filter is adapted. There is actually a significant *threshold decrease* at spatial frequencies about one octave away from the adapting frequency. This suggests that there is interaction between the gains of the different spatial filters. It is not known exactly what is being changed by the adaptation process. Is it the filter threshold non-linearity, or is it the gain of the signal before the threshold?

(ii) Scale-specific Contrast Non-linearities

In Chapter 8 I described two contrast non-linearities. First, threshold contrast increment is decreased in the presence of a small pedestal contrast, but threshold contrast is increased in the presence of a large contrast pedestal. In that section, I was considering the case where the spatial configuration of pedestal and increment were spatially the same. What happens when they are not?

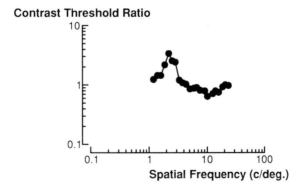

Figure 3. Gain adaptation. This figure shows the elevation in contrast detection thresholds after adaptation to a cosine wave of frequency $2\,\mathrm{c\,deg}^{-1}$, as a function of test spatial frequency. There is a marked rise in threshold immediately around the adaptation spatial frequency. The data are taken from Blakemore and Campbell (1969).

Contrast Threshold Ratio

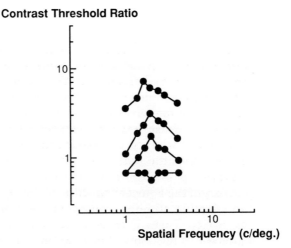

Spatial Frequency (c/deg.)

Figure 4. Scale-specific contrast interactions. This figure shows the effects on contrast detection thresholds for a cosine-wave target in the presence of a second cosine wave of various contrasts. For low contrasts (lowest curve) of the second cosine wave, there is a spatial frequency-specific reduction in thresholds; for higher contrasts (upper curves) there is a broader elevation in thresholds. Data are taken from Legge and Foley (1980).

Legge and Foley (1980) did an experiment in which subjects were asked to detect the presence of a cosine grating with a spatial frequency of $2\,\mathrm{c\,deg}^{-1}$. At the same time there was always present another grating with a spatial frequency of $1\,\mathrm{c\ deg}^{-1}$. We can think of the latter as being a pedestal contrast and the $2\,\mathrm{c\ deg}^{-1}$ grating as a test increment. Now, if the two are detected independently, then the contrast of the pedestal should not have any effect on threshold for the test, whereas if the two affect the same mechanism, then there should be interactions leading to contrast threshold being decreased at low pedestal contrasts and raised at high ones.

When the pedestal becomes independently visible, then the threshold for the increment begins to rise exactly as when the pedestal and increment have the same spatial frequency. This behaviour is typical of all frequencies within one octave either side of $2\,\mathrm{c\,deg}^{-1}$. On the other hand, Legge and Foley found that the threshold reduction for low contrast pedestals only occurs when the spatial frequencies of the two stimuli are very much less than an octave apart. The spatial frequency tuning of the two effects is different.

Summary

I have described several different techniques each leading to the suggestion that there is a spatial scale selectivity in some aspect of the processing path between the visual stimulus and a subject's contrast detection response. Moreover in each case the selectivity is narrower than the bandwidth of the entire visual system. The implication is that, in order to cover the full spectrum, there have to be a number of independent mechanisms, each selective for a different range.

However, the bandwidths estimated by the different techniques do not agree: they range from $\frac{1}{2}$ octave to $2\frac{1}{2}$ octaves. A clear instance is the finding in the one study by Legge and Foley of a narrow bandwidth for the reduction of contrast increment thresholds by low contrast pedestals, but a broader bandwidth for the elevation of the same thresholds by high contrast pedestals. There are many possible explanations for these discrepancies. There may be different bandwidth filters employed in the different tasks. More plausibly, the detection mechanism may have its own spatial characteristics.

In general, a problem with the various techniques is that they rely on somewhat arbitrary assumptions about the threshold process. There is, it is usually posited, an array of devices whose outputs are each a single number, a variable, which determines whether a visual stimulus has been seen. In the earlier chapters I have stressed that spatial filters are devices that produce as output a (transformed) image, i.e. a two-dimensional function not a single variable, and so the spatial variation of response within the output image should be taken into account.

9.3 Combining Filter Outputs

The spatial filters each produce a two-dimensional response function, which is the result of convolution of the filter with the image. For each dimension that the filters vary along, such as spatial scale, we must add another dimension to this response function. The total filter outputs are thus a multidimensional space, comprising at least two dimensions of space, one of spatial scale and one of orientation. This space could be sampled and it sometimes seems convenient to consider the filter outputs as being a multidimensional matrix of coefficients to be selected and used by subsequent processes at will. This convenient theory has a restricted utility as is shown by some evidence of interactions between widely separate spatial frequencies and therefore perhaps different filters.

In this section I shall consider two experiments. The first is concerned with contrast detection, as before, but manifests an interaction between remote spatial frequencies. The second experiment shows that when the output of the filters is used to judge the characteristics of an edge, the human visual system cannot independently access any particular filter's output.

(i) Probability Summation

Suppose that stimulus a is detected by device A because it raises the output of that device just to threshold. Now stimulus b is added into a. If the device also responds to b, then less of stimulus a should be needed to raise the output of the device to threshold. The extent to which two different stimuli can co-operate in setting a threshold could thus be used to indicate the range of stimuli that the device responds to. This approach has proved difficult to develop because even when the two stimuli are not detected by the same device, they may co-operate in the setting of a threshold by *probability summation*. Probability summation is a technical term for the situation where two chances are better than one.

If the probability of stimulus a being detected on its own is p_a, then the probability that a will not be detected is given by $(1 - p_a)$. Similarly, if stimulus b has a detection probability of p_b, then the probability that b will not be detected is $(1 - p_b)$. The probability that neither a nor b will be detected is then

$$(1 - p_a)(1 - p_b)$$

and so the probability that either or both will be detected is

$$1 - (1 - p_a)(1 - p_b)$$

This is bound to be greater than p_a on its own, as can be seen by rewriting it as

$$p_a + p_b - p_a p_b$$

If this is greater than p_a, then it is implied that

$$p_b - p_a p_b > 0$$

i.e.

$$p_b > p_a p_b$$

i.e.

$$1 > p_a$$

which is necessarily true.

There are well-documented effects of probability summation on grating contrast detection. The interested reader should read the papers by Graham (see references). I am more interested here in direct interactions between filters.

(ii) Filter Interactions in Contrast Detection

There is an exception to the rule that contrast thresholds can be raised by the presence of a high contrast pedestal only if the two stimuli have spatial frequencies within an octave of each other. Henning *et al.* (1975) first demonstrated that the contrast threshold for a grating at $1.9\,c\,deg^{-1}$ could be elevated by up to a factor of 10 when in the presence of three gratings of frequencies 7.6, 9.5, and $11.4\,c\,deg^{-1}$ (4, 5 and 6 times the target spatial frequency). This obtained even though the $7.6\,c\,deg^{-1}$ grating on its own had only a weak effect on the same threshold.

When these three gratings are added together a pattern is produced which has a fundamental period corresponding to a frequency of $1.9\,c\,deg^{-1}$ even

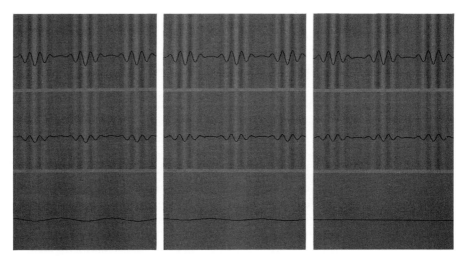

Figure 5. This shows examples of the stimuli used in the Henning *et al.* (1975) experiments. Grey level images and cross-section plots are shown. Across the page are three contrast levels of the cosine wave target and down the page are three levels of the masking waveform.

though there is no energy at that frequency. The pattern is like a $9.5\,c\,deg^{-1}$ grating whose contrast is slowly modulated at a frequency of $1.9\,c\,deg^{-1}$. This is technically known as *amplitude modulation* (AM). It seems, from the results, that this modulation can interfere with the detection of a grating at the same frequency. More recent experiments by Nachmias and Rogowitz (1983) have shown that the effect occurs only when the amplitude modulation has the same phase as the target grating.

Some of the details of these results could be accounted for by a non-linear transduction of intensity, such as a logarithmic transformation. However,

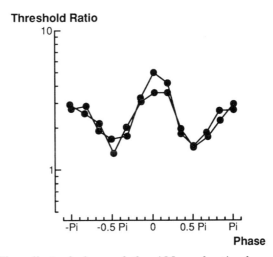

Figure 6. The effect of phase of the AM mask stimulus relative to the detection threshold. Data are taken from Nachmias and Rogowitz (1983).

many details cannot, and it seems more likely that the results reflect the manner in which the output of spatial filters are combined.

(iii) Filter Interactions in Characterizing Edges

Another rather similar situation occurs when subjects are asked to judge the location of a luminance edge. Accuracy for this task is normally very high, and can be assessed by using a Vernier scale type of stimulus. Typically subjects would be shown a line or edge with a lateral break midway along it and then asked to judge whether the upper half of the line was to the left or right of the lower half of the line. This is a task that can be done in several different ways and a certain degree of caution is required in interpreting some of the results that have been obtained. It is often remarked that the spatial offset thresholds that are obtained, typically 5 arc seconds, are less than the size of the receptor elements themselves. Whilst this sounds impressive, the fine performance was shown by Andrews *et al.* (1973) to be due to the relatively efficient use of information from a great many receptors and is not particularly interesting.

Westheimer and various colleagues found that the precision of localization judgements could be decreased by placing flanking lines on either side of the target (e.g. Westheimer *et al.*, 1976).

The results showed a maximum interference when the distance between the target and each of the two lines was about 2 arc min. This pattern of results can be attributed directly to the response of a small, high spatial frequency filter (Watt, 1984). As an explanation this seems adequate and leads to the deduction that the smaller filters might be used for relative

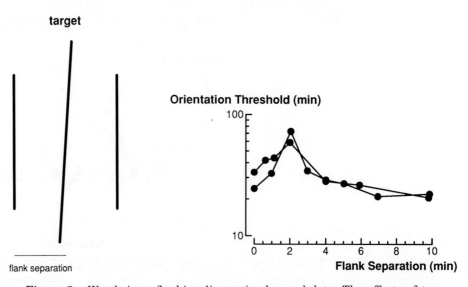

Figure 7. Westheimer flanking lines stimulus and data. The effects of two flanking lines on orientation sensitivity are shown as a function of their distance from the target. Data are taken from Westheimer *et al.* (1976).

location judgements. However this is a situation where the visual system could do better than it actually does, if it were to use a larger filter for the 2 arc min separations between target and flanking lines. That the visual system does not do this is a very interesting result.

Watt and Morgan (1984) showed that when the localization target is made up from a relatively narrow band of spatial frequencies, then it can still be localized very accurately, and that the precision does not depend very markedly on the centre frequency of the spatial frequency band. The same conclusion may be reached from a related experiment in which the effect of Gaussian blurring on localization precision was assessed. A considerable degree of blurring is needed before the sensitivity to location is adversely affected. Clearly many different filters can be used to measure relative location, and all with roughly the same precision.

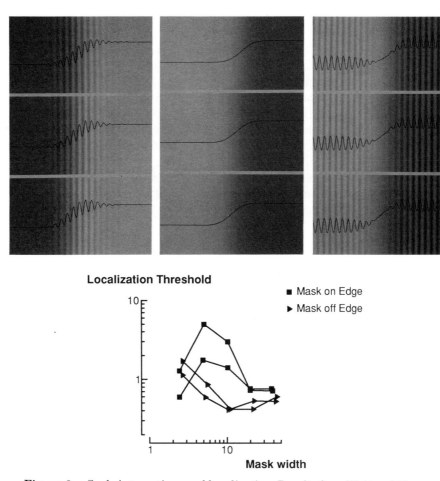

Figure 8. Scale interactions and localization. Results from Watt and Morgan (1984) on the sensitivity for localizing a coarse scale edge in the presence of fine scale irrelevant detail. Sample stimuli are also shown for the three basic conditions: no mask, mask on edge and mask off edge. In each case the offset moves leftwards down the page.

Watt and Morgan also examined interactions between the filters. They measured the precision with which a blurred edge (which gives rise to a significant response only in large size filters) could be localized in three different conditions. The first condition was for the edge on its own; the second was for the edge plus an irrelevant patch of high spatial frequency which was placed over the mean location of the edge but did not move with the edge; and the third condition was for an edge plus two high frequency patches, one either side of the edge. Compared with the first condition, thresholds for the second condition were very much raised and thresholds for the third condition were very much reduced. The high frequency patterns, which provided no cue and should be irrelevant, appear to act like an inertia in each case, indicating that the coarse scale filters cannot be accessed independently of the fine scale ones.

Summary

These experiments lend further support to the general hypothesis that the various different filters of different spatial scales cannot be accessed independently of each other. As a result of these experiments a model of the next stage after filtering was proposed by Watt and Morgan (1985). A detailed account of this model is beyond the scope of the present work, and the interested reader is recommended to read the book by Watt (1988) which explores both the model and some of its implications for computational and cognitive research into vision. For the present it suffices to state that the model proposes that the outputs of filters be combined wherever they have the same sign at the same location. This accounts for the results that I have described.

9.4 Dynamic Influences on Spatial Scale

It is reasonable to suppose that the dimensions of space and of time are intrinsically interwoven in our visual system. Temporal events in an image sequence or continuum occur at determined locations at space; most things change in their spatial characteristics as time progresses. It is therefore interesting, but not particularly surprising, to learn that the spatial characteristics of the visual system depend on the time course of the stimulus.

(i) Time Course of Contrast Detection

The time course of the appearance and disappearance of a stimulus is a function of time that can be considered much as its spatial configuration can be. It is possible to use the temporal frequency of cosinusoidal luminance or contrast variations in time to analyse the temporal characteristics of the system.

Sensitivity

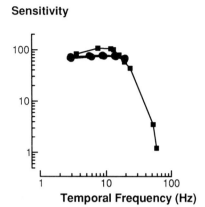

Temporal Frequency (Hz)

Figure 9. Temporal contrast sensitivity function. Contrast sensitivity is plotted as a function of temporal frequency for a flickering stimulus. Data taken from Kelly (1972) and Moulden *et al.* (1984).

Psychophysical experiments have generally followed one of two approaches. The first approach is to adopt a spatially neutral stimulus, such as a blank field field or a large circular spot. The second approach is to take a particular stimulus thought to interact spatially with only one filter and thereby measure the temporal properties of that filter. The two approaches result in the broadly similar conclusion that there exist two types of temporal response. One is a relatively high temporal frequency band-pass response which therefore transduces only rapid changes in the image. The other is a lower temporal frequency low-pass response which also responds to slowly varying changes in the image and has some DC response. These are often referred to as *transient* and *sustained*, respectively.

Note that both mechanisms respond to the abrupt onset and offset of a stimulus (even if the stimulus is only on for an infinitesimal period). The sustained mechanism does not however respond to stimuli that flicker at high rates: it has a temporal resolution of about 50 ms. The transient mechanism does not respond when nothing in the image is changing: it can be thought of as producing something like a first temporal derivative of the image. The sustained mechanism is, of course, a little slower in its response to a change than is the transient mechanism.

The two mechanisms appear to have different spatial properties. The transient mechanism is selective for lower spatial frequencies than the sustained mechanism.

(ii) Time Course of Spatial Discrimination

The same general trend can be shown for a different type of task where the visibility of a target is not the question. Watt showed how to infer the spatial scale of filtering from measures of the precision with which a number of different geometric properties of a line could be judged. Any device that has some intrinsic noise but that is able to use the information available

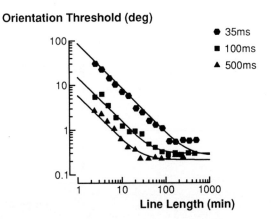

Figure 10. Exposure duration effects on orientation discrimination. This shows some data taken from Watt (1987), which gives the effect of line length on orientation thresholds for three different exposure durations.

with reasonable efficiency will show changes in precision as the length of the line is changed. These will be characteristic of the spatial scale at which the analysis is being conducted. As a short line is blurred, i.e. examined at a coarse spatial scale, it will tend to become a round blob from which estimates of length, orientation and curvature, for example, are difficult to make and highly error prone. If a long line is blurred to the same extent, however, it will still have an elongated appearance and the same judgements will be easier and more accurate. This means that for a particular system the way in which precision of judging, say orientation, decreases as the length of the stimulus line decreases, can be used to calculate the spatial scale of the system.

Watt (1987) used this technique to measure the effective spatial scale of the visual system at various exposures. The various different models used for the various different tasks all provided good models for the experimental data as well. Given this, it was then deduced that the spatial scale effective within the visual system decreases over time. For perhaps as long as a second, the spatial scale of the visual system, as assessed by these geometric tasks, is inversely proportional to time.

(iii) Context Effects

This result is placed into a functional context by some intriguing results obtained by Weisstein and colleagues. The essence of the experiments was to measure d' sensitivity for the discrimination between lines of different orientations under a number of different conditions. These different conditions were designed to provide an indication of the state of the system. The condition of most interest here concerns the effect of blurring the target because this can give some indication of the spatial scale of the system as has been described above.

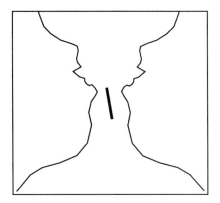
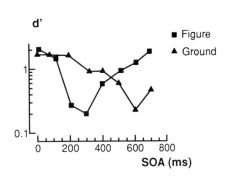

Figure 11. The stimulus used in the experiment by Weisstein and Wong (1985). The target line is the short near-vertical line in the centre. It could also appear in the surround. The question of interest is whether the target is processed differently when it is seen as lying on a figure or in the background. The data on the effects of onset asynchrony for the target and the rest of the stimulus are also shown.

The major innovation of these experiments was the way in which the target lines were placed in a number of different contexts. The simplest experiment to describe was reported by Weisstein and Wong (1985). They showed subjects a figure known as the Rubin ambiguous figure. This can either appear as a vase, so that the central area is seen as the figure, or as two opposed faces, so that the central area is seen as a background. Which configuration is seen tends to change from moment to moment. The question posed by Weisstein and Wong was: does the spatial scale of vision vary depending on whether the target line occurs in a region which is being seen as figure or as background? Obviously, by flashing the target in one of the face regions or in the vase region, and by separating responses obtained when the vase was seen as figure from those when the faces were seen, the experimenters could establish the effects, independently, of all the variables. Taking everything else into account, the basic finding was that lines presented in figure regions received processing at a finer spatial scale than did those in background regions. This result is intriguing because it obtained two different results for exactly the same physical stimulus.

Williams and Weisstein (1981) examined the effect of perceived three dimensionality on the spatial scale of visual processing. Their subjects were required to judge the orientation of a short line that could appear in three different contexts, differing in how readily the overall pattern could be seen as a three-dimensional thing. They found superior performance for the case where the line was easily interpreted as being part of a three-dimensional solid. They found that even just a moderate degree of blurring, affecting principally spatial frequencies above about $5\,c\,deg^{-1}$, obliterated this context effect. Blurring just the target line has this effect also, but blurring the context pattern alone has very little effect on performance at all. A time delay of about 200 ms between target offset and context onset was also sufficient to obliterate the context effect.

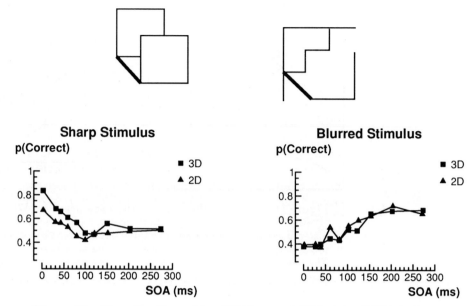

Figure 12. The stimuli used by Williams and Weisstein (1981) to assess whether there is a difference in the processing accorded to a stimulus when it is part of a recognizable three-dimensional thing. Data are shown for a sharp focused stimulus and a blurred stimulus.

Taken with the Wong and Weisstein result, a rather complex picture emerges. It is clear that figures, especially those with good three-dimensional interpretations, preferentially receive finer spatial scale processing. It is also clear, however, that information at coarse scales is used to select these preferentially treated areas of the image because blurring the context alone does not radically affect the pattern of results. This relationship between the coarse scale analysis and the structure of the image and of its potential origin in three-dimensional things remains to be explored further. It is worth noting that it is perceived depth and not simply the degree of connectedness of the context patterns that accounts for the effect.

9.5 Motion Detection

One aspect of vision where spatial and temporal factors are both important is in the detection, analysis and description of image motion on relative motions. In this section I shall describe two types of experiment that both lead to a similar conclusion about the initial image algebra stages of motion detection in human vision.

(i) Short-range Apparent Motion

Braddick devised an experiment to study motion. From a stimulus pattern of randomly placed dots, a central patch are all displaced together. By asking subjects to report whether the patch of dots that move forms a vertical or a horizontal rectangle, Braddick (1974) was able to assess the conditions under which a strong and reliable pattern of motion could be detected. Those dots that were not a part of the rectangle were moved randomly, i.e. incoherently, so that if the coherent motion could not be seen, then the form of the rectangle was not visible either. In the original experiment the percentage of errors and the time spent watching the stimulus until a response was made were both measured as a function of the distance that the dots within the rectangle were displaced through. The general finding, irrespective of the size of the random pattern elements, was that correct and rapid identification of the orientation of the rectangle depended on the displacement being no more than about 5 arc min. For displacements greater than about 15–20 arc min, subjects' responses were effectively at chance.

This finding, of a critical distance, $d_{\max}$, which is not dependent on dot spacing is rather suggestive of a spatial scale effect. The point is made more clearly by some experiments carried out by Cleary and Braddick (1990a, b). They blurred the stimulus so that the dots became blobs of irregular shapes.

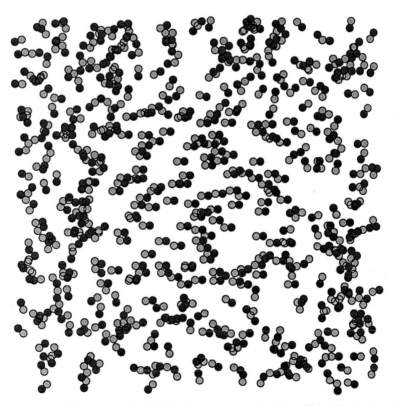

Figure 13. Schematic Braddick short-range stimulus. This illustrates the basic Braddick (1974) apparent motion stimulus. A small patch in the centre of the stimulus is displaced to one side, but all the dots remain. All other dots around are randomly moved.

Instead of using the rather complicated rectangle judgement, they simply required the subjects to say whether the patch moved upwards or down, and plotted per cent correct as a function of the displacement size. As the displacement increases, the percentage of correct responses rises until the subjects are able to perform without error. However as the displacement size increases further, the per cent correct falls down to chance again because the motion becomes difficult to see. This is the measure of d_{max} as before. For small amounts of blurring d_{max} is not altered, but as the blurring increases still further the value obtained for d_{max} also increases. For blurring that removes all spatial frequencies above about 4 cycles per degree or lower, d_{max} is inversely proportional to the highest spatial frequency in the stimulus.

Blurring removes detail from the stimulus. If we start with a very blurred stimulus, then the d_{max} that is measured is large. What the results of Cleary and Braddick show is that as detail is added to the stimulus, d_{max} is reduced in size. This is paradoxical: adding stimulus information makes performance worse. We have to think of blurring as revealing long-range spatial correlations in the stimulus. These correlations mean that the grey level of the stimulus does not vary very rapidly across space. For any blurred stimulus, a small displacement will cause each grey level to change just a little as a consequence of this. Moreover, if instead of an instantaneous shift, we were to continuously slide the stimulus through a short distance, then the direction in which the grey level changes will be consistent at any given point. Under these circumstances, motion detection is relatively straightforward and reliable. This means that the correlation length of the stimulus should determine d_{max}. In other words adding finer and finer detail should reduce d_{max} in proportion, as Cleary and Braddick found.

Unfortunately they also found that there comes a point, where the correlation length is of the order of 15 arc min, beyond which d_{max} is fixed and does not reduce still further with the addition of yet further detail. In

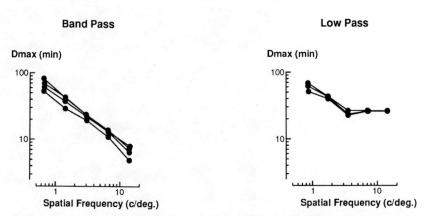

Figure 14. Cleary and Braddick results. This figure shows d_{max} as a function of the spatial frequency content of the filtered random dot stimulus. Data at the right for band-pass stimuli are taken from Cleary and Braddick (1990a); data from the left are taken from Cleary and Braddick (1990b).

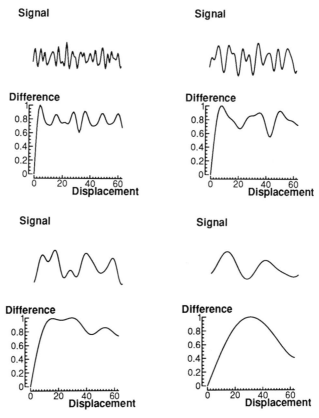

Figure 15. Correlation lengths. This figure shows one-dimensional luminance profiles, and a representation of how much the grey levels change as they are moved. The lower the spatial frequency content of the stimulus the further it can be moved before the changes become too large.

order to account for this finding, it is necessary to suppose that the visual system is itself blurring the target out over something around 15 arc min.

The situation is not so simple, however, because if the target were simply blurred in this fashion by the visual system to remove detail, then no motion should be visible in targets that had only the fine scale information, i.e. high pass spatial frequency filtered stimuli, because the target itself would be obliterated by the blurring. Cleary and Braddick found that motion is visible in such a stimulus and it is necessary to suppose a range of different filters exist.

(ii) Motion Interpolation

Following some earlier observations by others, Burr (1979) measured a rather novel form of Vernier acuity. Burr set up two situations in which a Vernier target of two vertical lines, one above the other, was seen to move across the display screen. In each case the movement was apparent rather than real: the targets were flashed in sequence at a series of discrete stations

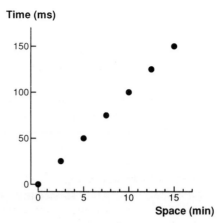

Figure 16. Motion interpolation stimulus. The two axes of this figure correspond to space and time. The space–time course of typical stimuli are shown.

separated from each other in space by intervals of 2.5 arc min. The flashes were separated in time by 25 ms, producing the phenomenal effect of a Vernier target moving at a velocity of 2.5/25 min ms^{-1} or 1.67 deg s^{-1}. By offsetting the upper line to the left or right of the lower line a psychometric function for judgements of Vernier misalignment was collected.

The interesting condition was the second where the same phenomenal effect of a moving Vernier target was produced as before. In this case the offset was created by delaying or advancing the upper line in time. The two lines were always displayed at spatial locations that were physically aligned, but the introduction of a consistent time delay caused one or other to lag behind. By varying the time delay and asking subjects to judge the spatial offset, Burr collected a second psychometric function that was very similar to the spatial psychometric function in form. The standard deviation of the spatial psychometric function was 10 arc sec, and the standard deviation of the temporal one was 2.7 ms. At a velocity of 6 arc sec ms^{-1}, this corresponds to a spatially equivalent offset threshold of 16 arc sec which is not radically different from the actual spatial offset threshold. These small figures for sensitivity imply that the visual system is interpolating along the trajectory of each line.

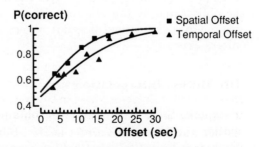

Figure 17. Motion interpolation psychometric functions. This figure shows the two psychometric functions for judgements of Vernier misalignment, one for a spatial offset in the motion trajectory and one for a temporal offset. Data from Burr (1979).

The result was extended in a painfully long series of measurements made by Morgan and Watt (1982). They repeated the experiment of Burr, adding in a check that the subject's eyes did not move during the target movement. They varied systematically the spatial distance between stations on the trajectory and independently, by varying the target velocity, the time separation between stations. The basic finding was that these parameters had no effect on sensitivity in the conditions where a truly spatial misalignment cue was shown, but that if the cue was presented as a time delay, then the stations had to be both less than about 5 arc min apart in space, and less than about 40 ms apart in time for the measured threshold to be equivalent to the spatial one. If the distance between the stations was greater than 5 arc min then the temporal threshold was poorer than the spatial threshold, although not very dramatically so.

The data obtained bear a striking resemblance to the measures of d_{max} that I have described above and it is tempting to suppose that some common mechanism underlies both. This point is further reinforced by an experiment carried out by Fahle and Poggio (1981), which measured the effects of stimulus blur on the interpolated Vernier task. Although they did not report many data on this issue, the indication is that a fairly large amount of blurring raises the critical distance for interpolation to a larger value of at least 15 arc min. This is very similar to the effects of stimulus blurring on the d_{max} measures.

Summary

All of the effects that I have described can be explained by supposing some form of spatiotemporal filtering of the stimulus. In the motion interpolation case, a filter which smoothed the target in time and space, with constants of about 40 ms and 5 arc min, respectively, would yield exactly equivalent images for the spatial and the temporal cue conditions. Equivalent offset thresholds would then be expected without having to make any assumptions about how the information for the task could be made explicit. If the time or spatial distance between stations on the motion trajectory were too great, then equivalent images would not be obtained, and different thresholds could be expected.

In the experiments concerned with d_{max} measurements, spatial filtering of the stimulus with a space constant of about 5 arc min cannot be used without further assumptions to account for the data. It is necessary to assume something about the motion detection device that follows this stage. The simplest such device is to compare the signs of the temporal and spatial derivatives. If they are the same then motion occurred in one direction; if they are different then it was in the opposite direction. This is then sufficient to explain the results that were obtained. The spatial filter is revealing spatial correlations in the stimulus that have the same length as the displacement itself, provided that the latter is 5 arc min or less. The effect of physically blurring the stimulus is to further lengthen these correlations, provided that the blurring is strong enough to have an effect over and above that of the visual machinery.

9.6 A Complete Task

I shall conclude this chapter with an account of an experiment conducted by Legge *et al.* (1985). They studied the visual aspects of reading in both normal subjects and also in people with low vision. I shall describe the data from normal subjects and urge the reader to follow this up by looking at the low vision results at source.

The basic stimulus material was a single line of text which was moved behind a window measuring 25 cm by 7 cm. At the start of a trial, the first letter of a line of text was visible to the subject at the right hand margin of the display. After a warning, the text began to sweep across the window from right to left at a fixed velocity. The subject was required to read aloud the line of text whilst the experimenter counted the number of wrongly read or missed words.

A form of psychometric function could be obtained by calculating reading rate (the rate at which words were correctly read), and plotting this as a function of the scanning velocity of the text. The psychometric function so obtained has reading rate and scanning velocity equal up to a value of about 200 words per minute. Beyond this velocity, reading rate falls precipitously because subjects start to make errors. The peak of this psychometric function thus provides a simple yet sensitive measure of how well a particular line of text can be read. This point is called the asymptotic reading rate.

Now, the interest lies not in this psychometric function, but in how it depends on the various spatial characteristics of the stimulus. Legge and colleagues varied many different parameters of the stimulus, of which I shall describe a few of general interest. The most obvious starting place, and indeed the first that the experimenters will have needed to consider in starting their studies, is the size of the letters and the number of letters visible at any one time.

The effect of letter size, from 6 arc min up to 10 degrees (a factor of 100) was measured for two sizes of display: 10 characters visible and four characters visible. The two functions obtained are virtually indistinguishable.

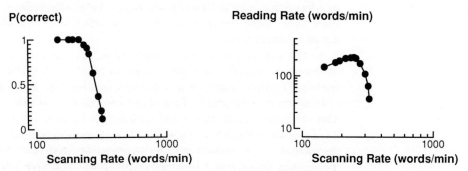

Figure 18. Reading psychometric function. This figure plots the performance on the reading task in two ways. It plots proportion of correctly read words as a function of stimulus presentation rate. It also plots the absolute number of correctly read words per time interval as a function of stimulus presentation rate. Data are taken from Legge *et al.* (1985).

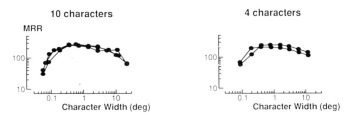

Figure 19. The effects of letter size on reading rate for two display sizes. Data are taken from Legge *et al.* (1985).

In each case, the greatest asymptotic reading rate occurs for letters that are about 20 arc min in width (centre to centre). If the letters are smaller than this then reading rate falls off very quickly; if the letters are larger then reading rate only falls off very gradually, so that for letters of width 10 degrees, reading rate is better than half of the optimum rate.

The effects of window size were also measured for various different character widths. Once again the two parameters were virtually independent. The finding was that if four characters are simultaneously visible, then performance is as fast as it ever will be. If less than four characters are visible, then reading rate falls off, but fairly gradually. If only one character width is visible at a time, then asymptotic reading rate is about half of the fastest rate; if only one-quarter width of a character is visible, then the reading rate is about one-fifth of the fastest rate. Don't be misled by these figures; the text is moving continuously behind a window and it is the window size that is being varied. This is not the same as presenting the text letter by letter.

In the context of the experiments that I have described in the earlier parts of this chapter, the next two stimulus parameters are particularly interesting. Legge and colleagues, having established the effects of relatively artificial factors like letter size and window width, set out to discover something of the visual mechanisms that might be involved. They measured the effect of blurring the target, and of replacing the letters by a matrix of discrete dots (i.e. of sampling the target). I'll start by describing the effects of blurring the target by placing a sheet of ground glass in front of the text. Compared with reading rate without any blur, reading rate is unaffected by modest amounts of blur which removes spatial frequencies above 2 cycles per character. For more severe blurring, reading rate is dramatically reduced. It is most appropriate to describe the blurring relative to the text because it was found that the effect of blur did not depend on the letter size when so expressed. This is an interesting finding because it suggests that different absolute spatial scales must be used for different sizes of text.

The effects of sampling follow from this general result in an interesting fashion. It is probable that the information that specifies which letter any particular form actually is, requires about 2 cycles per character. If this were the only factor, then the sampling theorem tells us that a sampling matrix of twice this frequency (i.e. 4 × 4 samples per character) will contain all the information. It is thus surprising to discover that for all character sizes, except the tiniest (6 arc min), considerably more samples are needed.

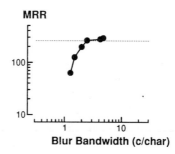

Figure 20.   The effects of blurring on reading rate. Data are taken from Legge *et al.* (1985).

For example, for a character size of 20 arc min (the optimum size), 8 × 8 samples are needed to allow optimal reading rate. Moreover, as character size increases, so too does the number of samples that are required, although not in proportion. This cannot be attributed just to the information content of the stimulus, but must also reflect some properties of human vision.

Legge and colleagues offer a simple account for this that has some interesting implications. Basically they point out that the samples themselves add fine scale detail to the image that is very different in structure from that that would be expected for the letter. At a fine scale of analysis, the form would not be that of letters, but of a matrix of dots. It is supposed that in some way this interferes with the coarser scale letter-true information. And indeed, this supposition is very reminiscent of the interactions between different spatial scales that I described above.

This set of experiments is very interesting, I hope you will agree. To a psychophysicist, the main message of them is that the standard types of stimulus manipulation and analysis can be applied with great success to tasks more complex than just button pressing. A reading rate of 300 words per minute implies that, on average, it takes 200 ms to read a word. On the basis of the data from Watt on coarse to fine scale scanning, the visual system might be expected to have reached a scale of about 10 arc min or 1 cycle per degree. Allowing two cycles per letter, this means that a letter size of about 20–30 arc min should be optimum, as was found. For smaller letters, the reading rate should decline in proportion, as was found. It would be interesting to know why, with larger letters, reading rate is not faster still.

9.7 Conclusion: Image Algebra in Human Vision

To conclude this chapter, I shall concentrate on how the experiments that have been described can be related to the principles of image algebra. As was pointed out at the beginning of this chapter, no experiment can be analysed solely in terms of image algebra, because image algebra has no mechanism for producing a response. The various operations of image algebra all produce images, two-dimensional functions, as their outputs. The logic in all of the experiments is to adopt the assumption that the processes that follow the image algebra remain fixed as the stimulus parameters are varied.

This is easiest to describe for the cosine-wave contrast detection experiments because the basic psychophysics of contrast detection has already been considered in the previous chapter in some detail. There is assumed to be a fixed process which examines the output of the image algebra stages to determine whether there is an optical signal present or whether it is just noise. The experimenter's task is then to take a set of data, such as the CSF, and find a way of expressing it so that, at threshold, all the images have the same characteristic.

Let us suppose, for a moment, that the variance of the values in the processed image is used by the fixed process and so that, at contrast threshold, this value is always the same. We are really assuming that the image is represented by its variance before the contrast decision is made. The variations in contrast threshold are then attributed to a series of image algebra processes which exert different degrees of attenuation in different spatial luminance patterns. We could take a simple Laplacian of Gaussian filter and calculate the variance of its response to cosine waves as a function of spatial frequency. The reciprocal of this is then the contrast of stimulus that is required to give a constant variance. In other words, for a particular filter (Laplacian of Gaussian) and a particular response measure (variance), we can predict how contrast should vary with spatial frequency.

The general problem with this logic is that it relies on two parts. If, instead of taking image variance as the measure to be used for determining response, we were to take something else, then the derived filter would be different. For response to cosine waves, the image variance is only proportional to the amplitude of the response which means that the predicted CSF is simply the Fourier transform of the filter. There are many response measures that are only proportional to the amplitude of the response, and would thus lead to equivalent deductions about the filter. However, I'll give two examples that are not equivalent.

Suppose that the response were based on the slopes of the zero crossings in the response image. These are proportional to the amplitude of the response and also proportional to the spatial frequency of the stimulus. This means that the CSF is given by the Fourier transform of the filter multiplied by spatial frequency. In order to derive the Fourier transform of the filter, each contrast sensitivity must be divided by the spatial frequency of the stimulus.

Suppose that the response were based on the zero-bounded mass of the response image. This is proportional to the amplitude of the response image and inversely proportional to the spatial frequency of the stimulus. The CSF is then given by the Fourier transform of the filter divided by spatial frequency. The Fourier transform of the filter is then obtained by multiplying the CSF by spatial frequency.

Unless there are independent grounds for preferring one particular response measure, then it is impossible to reach a firm conclusion, from a CSF, about the form of the filter. In the three cases above, the Fourier transform of the filter is given by the CSF, by the CSF multiplied by spatial frequency and by the CSF divided by spatial frequency. This remains a difficulty in interpretation for experiments which seek to measure directly the filter characteristics.

The same problem applies for interpretation of the experiments on gain adaptation, which entail two CSFs, one before and one after adaptation. The supposition is that the difference between these two is a Fourier transform of the impulse function of the individually adapted filter. Because one CSF is subtracted from the other, possible multiplicative factors of spatial frequency are not cancelled out, as they would be were it sensible to take the ratio of the two CSFs.

Paradoxically, less direct methods work better. In the motion experiments of Cleary and Braddick and of Morgan and Watt for example, the range of spatial frequencies involved can be assessed indirectly from measures of how blurring or sampling the stimulus changes judgements of motion directly. In effect, the experimenter is applying image algebra to the stimulus in advance of the visual system applying its own image algebra. The technique is to find what types of image algebra, such as blurring or sampling, and to what degrees can be imposed without performance being affected. The assumption is that if performance is not worsened by a stimulus degradation, then the critical information remains intact in the stimulus. The same assumption is also used successfully in the reading experiments of Legge.

References

Independent Filters

Blakemore C. and Campbell F.W. (1969) On the existence of neurones in the human visual system selectively sensitive to the orientation and size of retinal images. *J. Physiol.* **203**, 237–260.

Campbell F.W. and Robson J.G. (1968) Application of fourier analysis to the visibility of gratings. *J. Physiol.* **197**, 551–566.

Legge G.E. and Foley J.M. (1980) Contrast masking in human vision. *J. Opt. Soc. Am.* **70**, 1458–1471.

Interactions Between Filters

Andrews D.P., Butcher A.K. and Buckley B.R. (1973) Acuities for spatial arrangement in line figures: Human and ideal observers compared. *Vision Res.* **13**, 599–620.

Henning G.B., Hertz B.G. and Broadbent D.E. (1975) Some experiments bearing on the hypothesis that the visual system analyses spatial patterns in independent bands of spatial frequency. *Vision Res.* **15**, 887–897.

Nachmias J. and Rogowitz B.E. (1983) Masking by spatially-modulated gratings. *Vision Res.* **23**, 1621–1629.

Watt R.J. (1984) Towards a general theory of the visual acuities for shape and spatial arrangement. *Vision Res.* **24**, 1377–1386.

Watt R.J. (1988) "Visual Processing: Computational, Psychophysical and Cognitive Research". Lawrence Erlbaum Associates, Hove, UK.

Watt R.J. and Morgan M.J. (1984) Spatial filters and the localization of luminance changes in human vision. *Vision Res.* **24**, 1387–1397.

Watt R.J. and Morgan M.J. (1985) A theory of the primitive spatial code in human vision. *Vision Res.* **25**, 1661–1674.

Westheimer G., Shimamura K. and McKee S.P. (1976) Interference with line-orientation sensitivity. *J. Opt. Soc. Am.* **66**, 332–338.

Dynamic Factors

Kelly D.H. (1972) Flicker. In: D. Jameson and L.M. Hurvich (eds), "Handbook of Sensory Physiology", VII/4, pp. 273–302. Springer-Verlag, New York.

Moulden B., Renshaw J. and Mather G. (1984) Two channels for flicker in the human visual system. *Perception* **13**, 387–400.

Watt R.J. (1987) Scanning from coarse to fine spatial scales in the human visual system after the onset of a stimulus. *J. Opt. Soc. Am.* **4A**, 2006–2021.

Williams M. and Weisstein N. (1981) Spatial frequency response and perceived depth in the time course of object superiority. *Vision Res.* **21**, 631–674.

Wong E. and Weisstein N. (1983) Sharp targets are detected better against a figure, and blurred targets are detected better against a background. *J. Exp. Psychol. Human Percept. Perform.* **9**, 194–202.

Motion Processing

Braddick O.J. (1974) A short-range process in apparent motion. *Vision Res.* **14**, 519–527.

Burr D.C. (1979) Acuity for apparent vernier offset. *Vision Res.* **19**, 835–837.

Cleary R. and Braddick O.J. (1990a) Direction discrimination for band-pass filtered random dot kinematograms. *Vision Res.* **30**, 303–316.

Cleary R. and Braddick O.J. (1990b) Masking of low frequency information in short-range apparent motion. *Vision Res.* **30**, 317–327.

Fahle M. and Poggio T. (1981) Visual hyperacuity: spatiotemporal interpolation in human vision. *Proc. Roy. Soc. Lond.* **B213**, 451–477.

Morgan M.J. and Watt R.J. (1982) On the failure of spatiotemporal interpolation: a filtering model. *Vision Res.* **23**, 997–1004.

Reading

Legge G.E., Pelli D.G., Rubin G.S. and Schleske M.M. (1985) Psychophysics of reading—I. Normal Reading. *Vision Res.* **25**, 239–252.

Suggested Further Reading

Burbeck C.A. and Yap Y.L. (1990) Spatial-filter selection in large-scale spatial interval discrimination. *Vision Res.* **30**, 263–272.

De Bruyn B. and Orban G.A. (1989) Discrimination of opposite directions measured with stroboscopically illuminated random-dot patterns. *J. Opt. Soc Am.* **A6**, 323–328.

Graham N. (1977) Visual detection of aperiodic spatial stimuli by probability summation among narrowband channels. *Vision Res.* **17**, 637–652.

Graham N. and Nachmias J. (1971) Detection of grating patterns containing two spatial frequencies: a comparison of single-channel and multiple-channels models. *Vision Res.* **11**, 251–259.

Graham N., Robson J.G. and Nachmias J. (1978) Grating summation in fovea and periphery. *Vision Res.* **18**, 815–825.

Kröse B.J.A. and Julesz B. (1989) The control and speed of shifts of attention. *Vision Res.* **29**, 1607–1619.

Mather G. (1987) The dependence of edge displacement thresholds on edge blur, contrast and displacement distance. *Vision Res.* **27**, 1631–1637.

Morgan M.J. and Watt R.J. (1982) Mechanisms of interpolation in human spatial vision. *Nature* **299**, 553–555.

Nakayama K. and Mackeben M. (1989) Sustained and transient components of focal visual attention. *Vision Res.* **29**, 1631–1647.

Sagi D. and Hochstein S. (1985) Lateral inhibition between spatial adjacent spatial-frequency channels? *Percept. Psychophys.* **37**, 315–322.

Weisstein N. and Wong E. (1986) Figure-fround organization and the spatial and temporal responses of the visual system. In: E.C. Schwab and H.C. Nusbaum (eds), "Pattern Recognition in Man and Machine". Academic Press, New York.

Exercises

1. At the heart of any model of the spatial effects of contrast detection are assumptions about the noise source and assumptions about the detection mechanism. What assumptions are usually made, and what happens if these assumptions are varied? If you have access to a computer, it is worthwhile trying to simulate the experiments to find out the importance of the details of filter shapes and bandwidths, the noise spectrum and the detection process. Use additive noise (add constant amplitude random variables to the filter outputs) and multiplicative noise (add noise to the outputs in proportion to their local amplitudes).

2. Think about the overall picture of the dynamic effects on spatial scale. What happens during the first second after a stimulus appears? Bear in mind the possibility that eye movements of various kinds can occur during this time scale.

3. What is the evidence that the initial processes in human vision are not fixed in their actions, but respond to stimulus and to task demands? Where does visual memory fit into the scheme?

4. What happens when a target moves across the visual field? What is the nature of time in this situation?

5. Why are we so slow at reading?

10

Psychophysics and Visual Descriptions

All of the experiments that I described in the previous chapter could be accounted for in terms of image algebra processes such as filtering. Although a full analysis of any experiment must entail the conversion of image information into response information, and must therefore entail image descriptions or visual descriptions as well, to a large extent these could be ignored in analysis of the experiments described in the previous chapter. A great deal of the psychophysical research literature comes naturally into this category, and there are rather fewer interesting experiments that give an insight into the visual descriptions level of understanding. As previously, I have made a selection that is intended to show some of the ingenuity with which the basic psychophysical techniques have been used, and also to give a view of the range of topics that are being studied.

It is important to grasp the nature of explanation at this stage and in particular to distinguish between an understanding of some visual process and its implementation in a visual mechanism. The distinction is between what is done, step by step, and how it is achieved within a specific physical system. The experiments that I describe in this chapter all require the various concepts of visual description in order that they may be completely analysed to discover what the visual system is doing in each case.

For some of the experiments, this understanding is uncomfortably close to an older type of explanation that has not proved particularly helpful. An instance of this older explanation is provided by the sterile debate about whether human vision has "curvature detectors". It has long been assumed that human vision has, as an early stage in the sequence of processing, a collection of feature detectors each of which recognizes and signals the presence of its own particular feature in the optical image. This assumption has proved rather resistant to experimental test, and usually for the good reason that the term "feature" and the concept of a "detector" are too ill defined. What is a detector supposed to do? I could convince myself, with an appropriate 2AFC design, that my visual system is very sensitive to the curvature of a line. Does this imply the existence of curvature detectors? I don't know. Traditionally it has been supposed that if my visual system could be shown to exhibit curvature-specific adaptation and after effects, then it must have curvature detectors. In this case it is likely that, psychophysically, our vision is very sensitive to curvature of lines and yet, on this physiological criterion, does not have curvature detectors. The difficulty lies in identifying adaptation with feature detection.

The concepts of visual description and symbolic sentences are not defined by quasi-physiological criteria, nor are they defined by psychophysically operational criteria. They are defined by the logic of mapping from image to response. In this chapter, all the experiments require some use of these logical criteria in order to explain adequately how variations in subjects' responses are generated.

10.1 Descriptions of Smooth Lines

Watt and Andrews (1982) conducted a series of experiments that were concerned with how line curvature could be discriminated in human vision. Although the work is not yet complete, there are several interesting conclusions to date. The basic paradigm was to show subjects two curved lines and ask them to report which line was more curved. By varying the curvatures, a psychometric function for line curvature could be obtained and a measure of sensitivity calculated. Watt and Andrews went further and compared the sensitivities obtained for a variety of line lengths and line curvatures with the sensitivities of a notional ideal device, thereby deriving a relative efficiency in each case. Be careful because the result can be easily misunderstood. An increase in efficiency doesn't just mean that performance is improving; it means that performance is increasing faster than expected. Two clear results were obtained.

First, if the various efficiencies for all the conditions of line length and curvature were plotted as a function of the orientation range of the stimulus (the difference between the two extreme orientations), then a single function emerged. Efficiency, which was generally high anyway, rose gradually as orientation range was increased from 0° to about 40°. It then fell precipitously. In fact, the fall in efficiency could be accounted for by the proposition that only that part of the stimulus line that lay within the orientation range of 40° was being used: it was as if the rest of the target did not exist. The rise in efficiency from 0° to 40° remains something of a mystery.

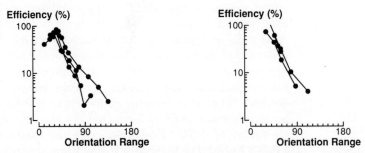

Figure 1. Efficiency for curvature discrimination is plotted as a function of the orientation range of the stimulus arc. The data are taken from Watt and Andrews (1982).

The second result, published in a second paper by Watt (1984a), concerned the effects of line length on the sensitivity to curvature. For a fixed orientation range, it was found that efficiency remained constant and high for line lengths up to about 30 arc min, the extent of the central fovea. For lengths of line greater than this, efficiency falls because the sensitivity of the visual system is not improved. It is not simple to interpret this result because of the effects arising through parts of line being presented away from the fovea. The constant efficiency for shorter lengths is another way of saying that differential curvature sensitivity rose in proportion to the square of line length: a doubling of line length causing a fourfold rise in sensitivity. This is interesting because it indicates that the visual system is using the information available to it in the best possible way: the ideal device behaves similarly. A square law of this form suggests that curvature is being performed by a process that is very similar to the curved principal axis analysis that I described in Chapter 5.

There is a dynamic component in the story. Foster (1983) has examined a similar situation where curvature discrimination judgements are made. Brief exposures were used and four short line stimuli were presented to the subjects rather than two. Subjects were required to identify which of the four had the greatest curvature. Under these conditions the function relating discrimination sensitivity to curvature is quite non-monotonic. It has several peaks of sensitivity, separated by troughs of insensitivity. Foster accounts for this find by suggesting that an incrementally improving representation of curvature is being calculated. The idea is that initially, only a small number of discrete values for line curvature are available, and that as time proceeds the representation is refined. Foster gives an analogy with a device called an analog-to-digital convertor (ADC). This device is used in computer equipment to sense the value of a voltage or current and record the value as a binary number. The device works by producing a voltage from a given

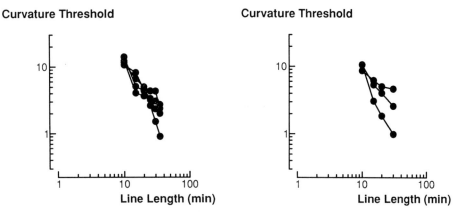

Figure 2. Effects of line length on curvature discrimination. The figure plots curvature discrimination thresholds as a function of line length for several different reference line curvatures. The results do not markedly depend on the reference line curvature, but show a square law effect of line length. Data taken from Watt (1984a).

binary number and comparing it with the voltage that is to be measured. If the produced voltage is low, then the binary number is increased and a new voltage tried. The bits of the binary number are set in sequence from the most significant to the least significant so that as time proceeds the number of potential states increases.

This analogy is useful because it makes a point that can be easily overlooked. The limitation on performance of the ADC is representational. The accuracy with which the voltages are compared does not improve with time. Similarly the results of Foster's experiment seem rather to indicate a similar limitation on representation rather than on accuracy of measurement. An important aspect of the design in Foster's experiment is that from trial to trial the various conditions are randomly interleaved so that the subject does not know which curvature will be presented next. This raises the possibility that the peaks in sensitivity, which separate discrete, stable states of curvature representation, might be placed at locations that are determined by the range of curvatures that are being encountered. This would be rather similar to the concept of error-correcting codes that I described in an earlier chapter.

The benefit of using a least squares or principal axis method for measuring line curvature is its great sensitivity to curvature plus its great stability in

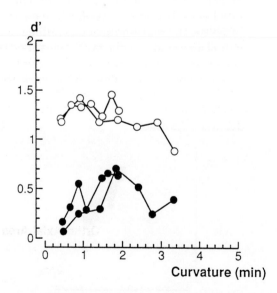

Figure 3. Categorical perception of line curvature. The data, taken from Foster (1983), show the effects of brief presentation and a large number of targets on the discrimination performance for curvature (filled circles) compared with a small number of targets and longer presentation (open circles).

the presence of noise. The cost however is that it is a relatively inflexible measure, not particularly appropriate for measuring the shape of lines that are not parts of the circumference of a circle. The limit on orientation range of around 40° can be seen as an attempt to provide more flexibility. A long arbitrary shape can be described piecewise as a series of overlapping or adjoining lines, each restricted to an orientation range of 40°. An orientation range of 40° is a rather mild curve, and a circular arc may well provide a reasonable description for most such lines. This is particularly true if the description can be improved by noting where and how it is inadequate.

A set of experiments conducted by Watt and various colleagues (Watt and Morgan, 1983; Watt *et al.*, 1987) has established one way in which the description of a line can be enhanced. If a principal curved axis is drawn through some arbitrary shaped line, then there will be places where the axis and the line do not coincide and are not in good agreement. Subjects were shown a stimulus that was straight except for a small wiggle. The subjects were asked to judge whether the line was bent to one way or the other. In this way, psychometric functions for various different wiggles were obtained. By measuring sensitivity to the presence and direction of departures from collinearity for a wide range of different shapes, it was established that at threshold, all conditions had the single common property that the largest of the various areas enclosed by the target and its principal axis was always the same at 0.4 arc min^2. For a typical target, the principal axis intersects it at a small number of places. Between each two adjacent intersections, the target is consistently on the same side of the axis. The area that target and axis enclose is a sensitive measure of how the axis is deficient as a description. A tentative conclusion from the psychophysical data is that departures from the principal axis are described as localized bulges. Of course, one could then have bulges on bulges and so on.

It is worth pointing out that the area cue that I have just described is exactly the same, formally, as the sequence description techniques of Chapter 5. It has the benefits of high sensitivity and stability, once again at the cost of flexibility.

We do not yet know how arbitrary smooth lines are described by human vision, but these experiments are a starting point.

Ortho-Axial Area

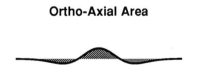

Target

Figure 4. Ortho-axial area. This figure illustrates the shape cue that is used to detect when a line is not straight.

10.2 Corners and Line Intersections

Curvature and smooth shape has been discussed in the context of experiments that have treated it as an attribute of something else, such as a line. I now turn to consider some experiments that are concerned with qualities in descriptive sentences. The qualities are corners in lines and intersections between lines.

The first experiment is due to Watt (1985), who reasoned that a discrete event like a corner or an intersection between lines might be used to break an outline shape up into pieces, each of which could then be analysed and described independently. If this is the case then curvature sensitivity, which depends so markedly on the length of the target line, should be reduced by the presence of a corner or intersection along the target.

The logic was checked by taking a target line and actually breaking it in two places, displaying the three parts at random places on a screen and then measuring curvature sensitivity. By varying the distance between the breaks in the line it was possible to check that the sensitivity was indeed much reduced by breaking the line, and exactly in line with an expectation based on the performance achievable with the longest of the three parts alone. The next step was to leave the target line intact but to add over it two crossing lines, so that it was potentially broken into three places as before, but this time by the line intersections. Of course, physically the target line was untouched, and sensitivity might be expected to remain unaltered. In fact, the pattern of results was virtually identical to that obtained when the target was physically broken into three parts and the conclusion drawn is that line intersections cause a block on the integrative processes of curvature measurement. A number of control experiments ruled out the most uninteresting alternative explanations.

It was then an easy matter to make a list of line configurations that cause this blocking of curvature integration, and another list of some that do not. Intersections between lines, sharp corners and line ends all have the effect; variations in line intensity, discontinuous changes in curvature and dotted sections of line do not. So, what does this indicate? It is tempting to suppose that the proper understanding of this result is to conclude that corner sentences are being created. But this is not entirely warranted: it might be that smooth, continuous lines are described by sentences, not corners. The answer to the question of which must await some more detailed results indicating how the corners are found.

A start in this direction has been made by Zucker and various colleagues. Link and Zucker (1987) made some measurements of subjects' ability to judge whether a change in orientation was smooth or abrupt. Their stimuli were a little different from the line stimuli that I have described so far in this chapter. Each stimulus was an image containing 600 dots. These 600 dots were displayed in small groups that formed short dotted lines randomly distributed across the screen. All the lines were nearly horizontal, but those on the left of the screen were oriented so that they were slightly inclined to the right and those on the right of the screen were slightly inclined to the left. Thus orientation changed down the centre of the screen. Lines that

Amplitude Threshold (sec)

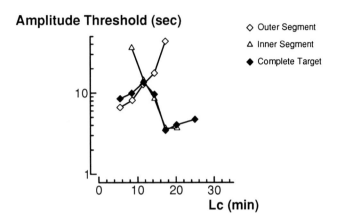

◇ Outer Segment

△ Inner Segment

◆ Complete Target

Lc (min)

Amplitude Threshold (sec)

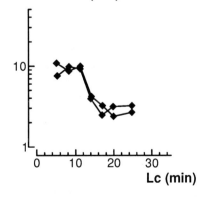

Lc (min)

Figure 5. Two sets of data illustrating the paradigm used by Watt (1985) to examine the segmentation of lines.

Figure 6. Some sample stimuli from the experiment by Link and Zucker (1987).

straddled this midline had an orientation change at the point that they crossed the midline. The change in orientation could be either a discontinuity (a sharp corner) or a smooth change of orientation. Subjects were asked to state which of these two they could see in each stimulus. The angle at which the two orientation patterns met was varied from 0° to 33°. At 0° the task is impossible, at 33° it is readily done. Link and Zucker were thus able to obtain psychometric functions relating the percentage of correct responses to the size of the angle cue.

The experiment was done as described, but with the 600 dots arranged into lines that were 2, 3, 5, 7 or 15 dots in length. The question was whether the length of the lines has an effect on the subject's sensitivity to the corner. The finding was that for lengths greater than 5 dots there was no effect; for shorter lengths sensitivity was poorer, very much so for a length of just 2 dots.

The experiment shows that a row of at least three dots is needed to be able to detect a discrete change in orientation pattern. This is not

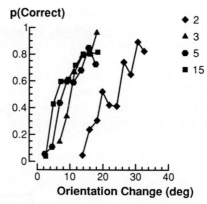

Figure 7. Psychometric functions for flow corner detection. The psychometric functions for detecting a discrete change in orientation flow in random dot patterns are plotted. Proportion correct as a function of the magnitude of orientation change are given for path lengths of different extents (2–15). Data are taken from Link and Zucker (1987).

particularly surprising: three points are needed to specify a curvature. That there were only slight improvements in sensitivities with increasing length of dot paths suggests that a rather crude mechanism may be involved.

10.3 Distance between Two Points

It is surprising, but certainly true, that no one yet has any clear idea of how the distance between two points is measured in human vision. There is a catalogue of ideas and experimental data, but no firm agreement. In this section I will describe a few of the more interesting findings, each rather briefly and with just a little commentary.

It has been known for a long time that judgements of distance, such as of line length, can be very accurate, but that sensitivity is inversely proportional to the length of the line. A Weber's law holds for distance so that distance difference thresholds are proportional to distance. This has been confirmed by Andrews *et al.* (1974), by showing subjects two lines and requiring them to report which was the longer. By varying the difference in lengths, psychometric functions were obtained from which line length thresholds could be calculated. The basic finding was that Weber's law holds for lengths up to at least 5 arc degrees. They also showed that the fall in sensitivity with increasing length that this finding implies could not be attributed to the decreasing acuity of increasingly eccentric vision. Interestingly, even though technically it is the end points of the line that hold all the information about the length of the line, if the subjects were shown two clearly visible dots instead of each line, then distance thresholds were poorer.

Westheimer and McKee (1977) added two further very interesting results to the picture. First they found that the Weber's law breaks down at short distances of 5 arc min or less. Their stimulus was a pair of vertical lines, the separation of which provided the distance cue to the subjects. For separations less than 5 arc min, threshold rises as the separation becomes less. Watt (1984b) has subsequently shown that this result is to be expected if the stimulus is filtered with a medium size filter, of space constant about 3 arc min. The second, and more profound, finding was that subjects do not need a reference stimulus. The experiment, as carried out by Westheimer and McKee, worked as follows. Subjects were shown a single pair of lines and asked to judge whether their separation was more or less than an implicit standard. Each response was followed by feedback to indicate whether it was right or wrong, so that subjects could learn what the implicit standard was. The subjects appeared to do this without any difficulty and the thresholds reported are as low as any others that have been reported. In effect, subjects are learning to compare each test presentation with a population of distances. A measure of central tendency, such as the mean separation, could be used in these circumstances as the standard separation.

A number of attempts to explain the high precision of the task have been made. Most rely on there being some filtering mechanism of a critical size that just blurs the two lines together if they are closer than the standard.

Difference Threshold (sec)

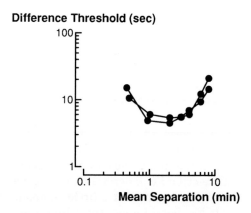

Mean Separation (min)

Figure 8.   Weber function for spatial separation. This plots the variations in
spatial separation sensitivity as a function of the separation. Data are taken
from Westheimer and McKee (1977).

The cue is either whether or not the critical size filter can resolve the dots
or alternatively how strong the response of the filter is. These accounts do
not explain the finding of Morgan and Ward (1985) that separation
judgements are not influenced by the presence of randomly placed lines
either beyond or within the space between the two target lines. Any filtering
explanation would predict that the random lines would add variability to
the filter response from trial to trial thereby adding variability to the
subjects' responses and causing measured sensitivity to fall.

A radically different hypothesis has been forwarded by Craven and Watt
(1990). It has been known for a long time that systematic errors of distance
judgements can be very reliable. These are best exemplified by a phenomenon
that goes variously under the name of the Botti illusion or the Oppel–Kundt
illusion. Basically an interval that is filled with lines appears to have a
greater width than an empty interval of the same physical width. The illusion
has been parametrically studied by Rentschler *et al.* (1981) who found that
compared with an interval delimited by just two lines, the apparent extent
of an interval filled with extra lines increases as the number of lines is
increased up to about 10 lines and then slowly falls again as more lines are
added.

The account offered by Craven and Watt is that the visual system counts
the number of zero-bounded responses in the outputs of filters of various
scales. At any scale, measured distance is then proportional to the product
of scale and number of responses. By averaging this measure across scales
a surprisingly accurate estimate can be obtained. Further the estimate is
without bias for a luminance profile that is fractal or has at least the same
statistics. The test figures in the illusion do not have these statistics, and
Craven and Watt were able to show that the data could be matched very
well to the model. They also repeated the experiment of Rentschler and
coworkers, but used a fractal luminance pattern as the reference distance
rather than the empty interval. They found that, just as the model predicts,

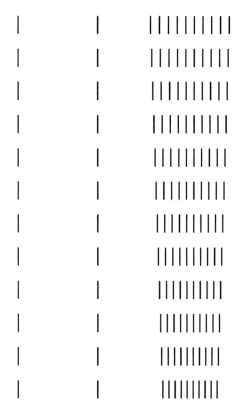

Figure 9. Oppel–Kundt illusion. In examining this figure, try to decide visually which interval on the left is the same as the filled interval on the right. Then test your visual perception with a ruler! This effect is known as the Oppel–Kundt illusion.

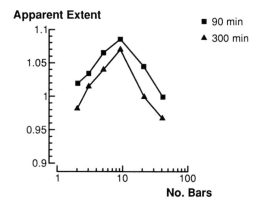

Figure 10. Measurements of the Oppel–Kundt illusion. Estimates of the bias or point of subjective equality in the Oppel–Kundt illusion as a function of the numbers of bars in the filled interval. The data are taken from Rentschler *et al.* (1981).

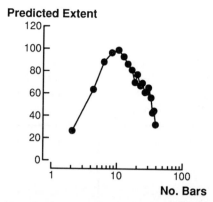

Figure 11. Oppel–Kundt illusion model. This shows the predicted variations in the magnitude of the Oppel–Kundt illusion as a function of the number of bars in the filled interval, from the hypothesis of Craven and Watt (1990).

empty intervals are underestimated in comparison with fractal patterns, and filled intervals are overestimated.

An earlier result from Regan and Beverley (1983) adds another piece to our understanding of this problem. They measured thresholds for changes in spatial frequency between two cosine-wave grating patterns. This has been known for some time to yield roughly equivalent results to those from other distance judgements when expressed in terms of the period of the grating. Regan and Beverley reported their experiment as a function of spatial frequency, both before and after adapting to a cosine wave stimulus with a frequency of $4\,\mathrm{c\,deg^{-1}}$. Recall that detection thresholds are elevated at and near the adapting frequency. Regan and Beverley found that frequency discrimination thresholds actually fell at the adapting frequency. Even more intriguingly, they were elevated at frequencies about 1' octaves either side of the adapting frequency.

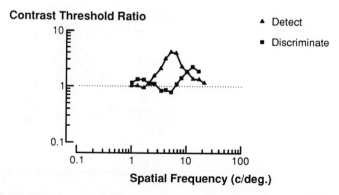

Figure 12. Effects of spatial frequency adaptation on discrimination of distance. This shows the effects of adaptation to a cosine wave of frequency $5\,\mathrm{c\,deg^{-1}}$ on contrast detection thresholds, and size (or spatial frequency) discrimination thresholds. The two effects are quite different. Data are taken from Regan and Beverley (1983).

This result follows from an error-correcting metric account of distance. The adaptation to a particular spatial frequency is obtained by prolonged exposure to a stimulus in which the population of distances is very restricted. For an error-correcting metric, this will stretch the metric at that distance and therefore compress it on either side. Stretching will improve sensitivity, in physical terms, and compressing will worsen sensitivity, both of which effects were found.

It still is a challenge to know how distances are judged. Whatever the final answer, it clearly won't be done by using a ruler or by using Pythagoras' theorem.

10.4 Motion Direction

In the previous chapter, I described some experiments that provided some insight into the image algebra stages of motion detection. There was no need to make any strong assumptions about how the motion was itself to be measured, but now I will pick up that strand and describe one of the many experiments that concern more directly the processes of motion analysis beyond simply filtering.

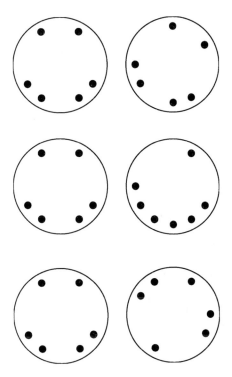

Figure 13. Three possible pairs of frames from the experiment of Allik and Dzhafarov (1984). At the top, the stimulus rotates one step between frames (left to right). In the middle, half of the discs reverse their contrast during the rotation. At the bottom, all the discs reverse their contrast.

The basic experimental design used by Allik and Dzhafarov (1984) was as follows. The stimulus comprised 12 discs equally spaced around the circumference of a circle. Each disc was either on, i.e. bright, or off, i.e. dark. After 100 ms the pattern of luminances was rotated clockwise or anticlockwise by one element. This rotation was repeated at 100 ms intervals for up to 12 times in successive frames. The subjects were required to judge whether the display had been rotated clockwise or anticlockwise. This task is easy, but what made it more difficult was that at each rotation, the pattern of luminance could be changed. On any one trial the probability that a disc, after being shifted, would retain its new value, light or dark, was varied. With the probability set to 1.0, so that all discs retained their new value, subjects could identify the direction of movement without difficulty. As the probability decreased so that more and more of the pattern was changed, the task becomes harder. When the probability was set to 0.5, so that roughly half of the discs were changed from whatever they should have been, light or dark, to the opposite, subjects were nearly responding at chance. As the probability was reduced still further, so that most discs changed, subjects' responses showed reliable preferences, so when the probability was close to 0.0 and all the discs were changed after the rotation, subjects nearly always responded with the same response. But it was the wrong one: subjects in this condition reliably saw motion in the opposite direction from that which was supposed to have taken place.

This phenomenon, called reversed phi motion, had been reported before by Anstis. A simple account for it can be constructed, by supposing that the direction of motion is given by comparing the signs of the spatial derivative and the temporal derivative. Normally, if these two have the same sign then the motion is one way, and if they have opposite signs, then the motion is the other way. (Which way depends on the direction in which the spatial derivative is computed and how its sign is assigned.) A moment's thought will show that this works for the normal case, at least for small displacements with respect to the spatial scale of the image. A moment more, and you will realize that in the case where the luminance is inverted, en route, it is hard to know what spatial derivative to take, that before or that after the inversion. These two alternatives have opposite signs and so the choice is not arbitrary. The least arbitrary approach is to add the images of the two frames together and take the spatial derivative of this. It will be found that this does indeed tend to produce reversed motion.

The Allik and Dzhafarov experiments are interesting, not so much for the reversed motion, which was already known to occur, but for what happens at intermediate probabilities of luminance inversion and how this depends on the number of frames of rotation that the subjects saw. For each condition of the number of frames parameter, Allik and Dzhafarov plotted a psychometric function of probability of (technically) correct response against the probability of maintaining luminance value. These functions all range from zero up to one and all can be fitted by smooth sigmoid curves. The steepness of the curves, i.e. the sensitivity of the observers, increases as the number of frames rises.

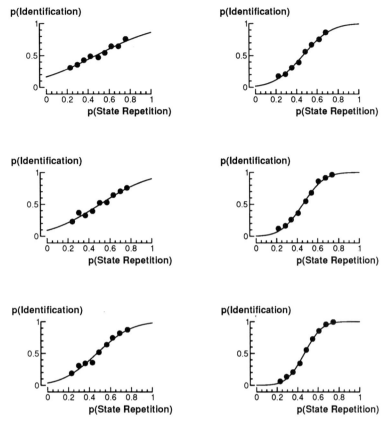

Figure 14. Psychometric functions giving the proportion of trials where the actual rotation was reported, as a function of the probability that any disc would not be changed in polarity. Several curves for different numbers of frames are shown (increasing down the left and then down the right). Data are taken from Allik and Dzhafarov (1984).

So far as the visual system knows, each disc could have been moved to any of the 12 locations and from any one of them. Take two locations, A and B: each had an intensity before and each has an intensity after the event. These four intensities can be used as evidence for three types of event: movement from A to B; no movement; movement from B to A. If we draw up all possible combinations of these four intensities, we see that: four combinations are consistent with just A to B motion; four are consistent with just B to A motion; two are consistent with either A to B, or B to A, or with no motion; two are consistent with either A to B or B to A, but not with no motion; two are only consistent with no motion; and two are not consistent with any shift. We can imagine each possible pair of locations (a dipole) voting for the motion(s) that it has evidence consistent with. That motion with the most votes is then accepted as the verdict.

In practice we only need to consider dipoles comprising adjacent pairs of discs. When the probability of an intensity change is zero, then half of

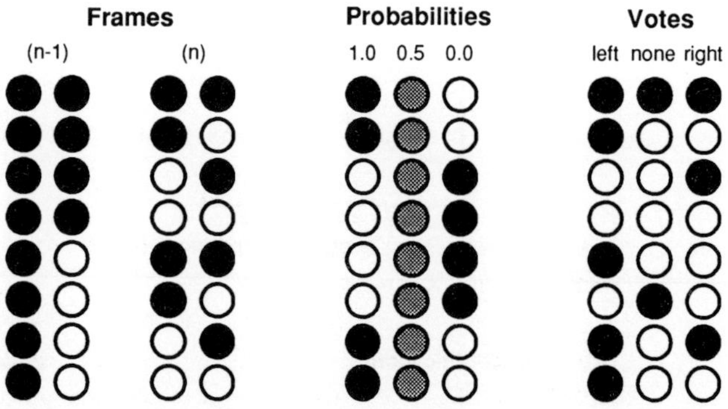

Frames

(n-1)   (n)

Probabilities

1.0   0.5   0.0

Votes

left none right

Figure 15. Voting procedure. There are 16 possible dipole combinations for two frames. Eight of these are shown, the other eight are identical subject to a reversal of contrast polarity. For each possible combination, its probability of occurrence in a leftwards motion is shown for three different probabilities of contrast change. Each is classified according to the votes to which they would give rise. Only the case where no discs change in contrast is considered here. The reader can construct similar figures for other cases.

these dipoles will place a vote for motion only in the correct direction. One-quarter will vote for motion in the correct direction and motion in the wrong direction. One-quarter will vote for motion in the correct direction, in the wrong direction, and for no motion. Votes will be in the ratios

correct direction	1.0
no motion	0.25
wrong direction	0.5

The overall verdict is correct. Note that these do not sum to 1.0 because some dipoles make more than one vote.

Now, when all the intensities are changed after the motion, what happens? If we examine how the votes are changed, we see that all dipoles that voted exclusively for the correct direction of motion will now vote exclusively for the wrong direction of motion. The dipoles that would have voted for both correct and incorrect direction will now vote only for no motion. The dipoles that would have voted for all three motions, now do not vote at all. The votes will be in the ratios:

correct direction	0.0
no motion	0.25
wrong direction	0.5

The overall verdict is in favour of motion in the wrong direction.

In the same way we can consider the case where half of the intensities are changed after the movement. In this circumstance, it works out that voting will be in these ratios

correct direction	0.5
no motion	0.25
wrong direction	0.5

Under such circumstances, the overall verdict will be at chance, as indeed were the subjects' responses.

Using a model that is equivalent to this one that I have described, Allik and Dzhafarov are able to produce very good predictions for the psychometric functions obtained. Because the number of void votes and votes for only no motion increases with increasing probability of intensity change, the model is asymmetric and thus accurately predicts the small asymmetry in the psychometric functions that was obtained.

The psychometric functions indicate that there is a sort of counting process taking place. Allik and Dzhafarov describe how, by counting the different types of dipoles that the stimulus offers, an estimate of motion can be obtained. This makes the important point that the overall direction of motion has to be obtained by some form of average or summary statistic. An alternative would be to compute the mean of the local directions obtained by comparing spatial and temporal derivatives. The finding that the psychometric function steepens with number of frames also implies some form of averaging over time. The steepness varies approximately in proportion to the square root of the number of frames as would be expected for simple averaging.

10.5 Structure in Texture

There have been a great many experiments reported on texture perception. Most of them have been demonstrations that some kinds of texture differences can be seen rapidly whereas others require a little longer. As demonstrations, these are interesting, but since rigorous psychophysical techniques have not been used, it remains difficult to draw conclusions about the mechanisms involved. A rather distinct issue from the detection of texture differences is the detection of structure and pattern within textures.

The first experiment I shall describe, by Bergen and Julesz (1983), used a technique which has become fairly standard. Subjects are shown a stimulus display with many short line segments distributed over 15 arc degrees. The display is displayed for only 40 ms, too short a time for the eye to move. After a variable delay a masking pattern of lines is then displayed. It is probable that this masking pattern has little effect other than to prevent the persisting retinal image from being used. If this is the case, then varying the delay until the mask is presented is equivalent to varying the exposure duration of the target, without the complication of eye movements.

Bergen and Julesz showed subjects a pattern in which all lines were oblique except that one, randomly located within the array, could be vertical. The subject's task is to decide whether the vertical line is present or not.

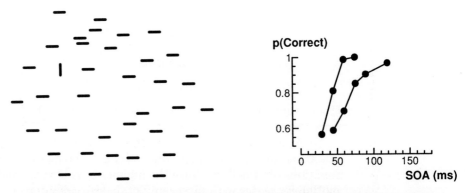

Figure 16. A typical stimulus from the Bergen and Julesz (1983) experiment is shown. Beneath this are plotted some psychometric functions for detecting the target vertical line as a function of the mask delay. Different orientations of background elements distinguish the different psychometric functions.

Bergen and Julesz measured the variation in the percentage of correct responses as a function of mask delay. When the oblique lines were actually horizontal, subjects could reliably detect the vertical line with a mask delay of just 60 ms.

The experiment was repeated for a range of different orientations of the oblique lines, ranging from 90° to the vertical down to 10° to the vertical. This variable has little effect on the percentage correct versus mask delay curve until the orientation difference is less than about 30°. The process of detecting the target is clearly slower for small orientation differences.

Nothdurft (1985b) has reported a comparable set of results. He used a presentation time of 30 ms, but had no mask afterwards. Subjects were required to identify the form of a region defined by having lines of a different orientation from the background. A measure of discriminability, which takes into account guesses, was plotted as a function of the length of the line segments at various orientation differences between target area and background. Once again there is little change in the data for orientation differences greater than about 30°, but for smaller orientation differences, a larger length of line is required for reliable discrimination.

In a second experiment, Nothdurft (1985a) compared the effect of line length on the form judgement with its effect on subjects' sensitivity to the orientation itself. In the first condition, a target region which was either a horizontal or a vertical rectangle was made of lines differing from the background by 90°, and subjects were required to say whether the form was the horizontal or the vertical rectangle. In the second condition all lines had the same orientation and subjects were required to judge this. The finding was that, for most subjects, the line orientation judgement required shorter line lengths than did the region for judgement.

The final experiment that I shall describe in this section was reported by Sagi and Julesz (1987). The experiment also involves arrays of line segments, most at one orientation but one line segment, the target, at right angles to this orientation. The stimuli were presented for 30 ms and then

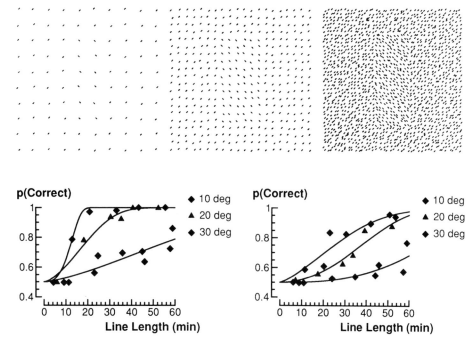

Figure 17. The effects of line length on texture discrimination are plotted for various orientation differences between target and the background. The data, taken from Nothdurft (1985b), are similar to the data of Bergen and Julesz above. It is tempting to relate this to the effects of exposure duration on orientation judgements from Watt (1987).

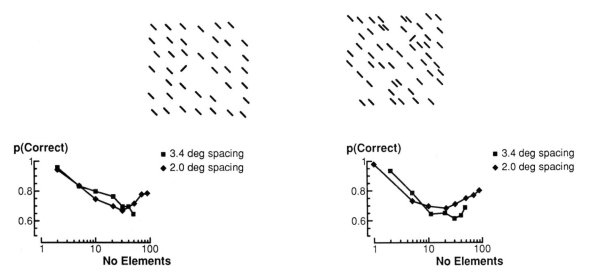

Figure 18. A typical stimulus is shown. Beneath is shown the proportion of correct responses in detecting the add line target as a function of the number of background elements. Two different display sizes are shown, and these have different effects. Data are taken from Sagi and Julesz (1987).

masked and the subjects had to detect the presence of the target line. Percentage correct responses was measured as a function of the number of elements in the background and for two conditions where the lines were spaced at minimum intervals of 3.4° and at minimum intervals of 2°. In the larger spacing condition, the results are as expected: percentage correct decreases monotonically as the number of background elements increases. However, in the closer spacing condition after an initial steep fall in correct responses, performance improves with further increases in the number of background elements. This pattern of results would be expected if the target were being detected as a result of pairwise comparisons between each line and its neighbours, within a radius of around 2 arc degrees.

It is clear that it is not yet possible to say how texture patches of the types that have been used in these various experiments are actually described in the visual system.

10.6 A Complete Task

As a final experiment in this chapter, I will describe one of a series of experiments conducted by Lee and colleagues, each of which is concerned with a detailed analysis of actions, rather than psychophysical judgements. The experiments are all investigations of how a simple statistical summary of an image can be used to control visually the timing of actions.

Lee *et al.* (1982) measured how athletes control their run up to the take-off board when making a long jump. For the athlete, the best jump is obtained when the foot lands on the take-off board rather than in front or behind it. The purpose of the run up is to place the athlete on this board at a peak velocity, and the athletes train to achieve this. The expansion of the image of something as it approaches or as it is approached can be used to provide information about the remaining time to contact. The results of the investigations are consistent with the suggestion that it is time to contact information that is being monitored and used to control the stride length as the take-off board is approached.

Lee and colleagues filmed athletes as they made long jumps and from the frames of the film they could measure the position and timing of each footfall and thereby the length and duration of each stride. They found that during the run up, the stride length changed systematically, increasing in length with time. The variability in stride length did not change with time until the last two or three strides. Obviously variability in stride length will cause variability in foot position to accumulate during the run up, so that, in order to land on the take-off board, some correction of stride length becomes necessary. Indeed the final two or three strides were very much more variable in length than the preceding ones, indicating corrections. By measuring variability of footfall location, rather than stride length, Lee was able to show that the increasing length variability was dramatically reducing footfall location variability.

This correction of striding must be under visual control and the next question was to ask what visual information is being used. Lee and his

SD(location)

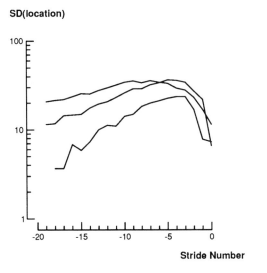

Stride Number

SD(length)

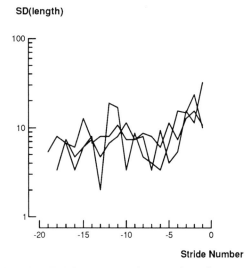

Stride Number

Figure 19. The variability in stride length (right) and in footfall location (left) are plotted as functions of the approach to the take-off board for a long jump. The data indicate that the athlete is making adjustments during the last few steps in order to land on or as near before the board as is possible. Data from Lee *et al.* (1982).

colleagues argued that it could be distance from the board or it could be time from contact with the board that was being used. If distance was being used, then the most natural consequence would be changes in stride length, whereas if time to contact was being used, then it is most likely that stride duration would be adjusted. They analysed the various different aspects of a stride which could be adjusted by the athlete, the duration of flight, the length of flight, the length of reaching with only one foot in the air and others. The finding was that flight time correlated very highly with the stride length, but the spatial distance parameters were not highly correlated with it. From this they conclude that time to contact is the most likely source of visual control of the behaviour.

Lee has shown that time to contact can be obtained from the image rather directly. Time to contact, for a constant velocity, is given by the reciprocal of the rate of dilation of the image, in this case of the take-off board. A simple visual description could provide all the necessary information to control the athlete's run up.

10.7 Conclusion

In this chapter, I have described a set of experiments that are all concerned mostly with parts of the visual mechanism that are most easily understood in the terms of visual descriptions. In each case, one has to suppose that image algebra of various kinds is also being used, but that the major experimental variations are not due principally to this. The intention in this chapter has been to illustrate how psychophysical techniques can be used to gain some insight into the visual descriptive stages in our understanding of human vision. I conclude this chapter with a consideration of the logic that requires the use of visual description rather than just image algebra to account for the experimental results.

Recall that in the previous chapter, the variations in performance that were obtained could all be attributed to image algebraic processes that precede putative descriptions for response. The use of descriptions to explain how subjects produce responses was necessary even in that chapter, it was just the case that the experimental manipulations and results required only the most general assumptions about the form and content of the descriptions. In this chapter, the logic is somewhat reversed. The experiments that I have now described rely on very general assumptions about image algebra, and the variations in performance have to be attributed to structures that are described in the terms of visual descriptions.

It would be possible to produce a mechanism that relied solely on image algebra followed by an image statistical summary that was able to perform the curvature discrimination experiments that I described. The amplitude of the response to a line of a Laplacian of Gaussian filter, for example, depends on the curvature of the line. So, the image could be differentiated in time so that all the stationary background was invisible and only the targets were in the image (albeit only at their onset and offset). Then the result could be filtered by a Laplacian of Gaussian and the result of that rectified, i.e. set to be positive whether it was actually positive or negative. The resultant image would have an overall centroid that was above or below the image centre depending on whether the more curved line were correspondingly above or below.

Such an account is not satisfactory for two reasons. The first one is a kind of thought experiment. The curvature response mechanism I have just given could be completely disrupted by randomly varying the relative intensity of the two lines from trial to trial. I doubt whether subjects would show the same degree of disruption. For any equivalent proposal there would be an equivalent control experiment, and the chances are high that the proposal would be refuted. My confidence arises from the second reason why an image algebra account is not satisfactory.

The data show a square law effect of line length on curvature sensitivity. This is indicative of a process that is forming response via a mechanism that is computing a second order polynomial coefficient of some variety. There are two implications here. The first is that the response depends on an explicit representation of the line curvatures rather than some by-product of them. Second, it implies that a statistical summation process is being used and this in turn requires that a set of points has been isolated.

These two implications are both symptoms that a visual description is needed to account for the results. Curvature is an attribute of something, and if curvature has been calculated then the thing has been described. Most statistics, and all of the ones that I have described, rely on summation over sets of values. If these sets have to be subsets of the whole image, then the mechanism of visual description is needed.

Similar arguments apply to the motion experiments that I have described in this chapter. These can be compared with those of the previous chapter to see where and why the two sets of experiments are in different chapters. Remember that it is not how the perception of motion is supposed to occur that determines whether an experiment is explained in terms of image algebra or of visual descriptions. We are concerned with accounting just for the variations in performance as the stimulus conditions are changed.

The main difference between the experiments in these two chapters lies in the actual stimulus changes. The experiments in the previous chapter were concerned with the effects of filtering or sampling the stimulus, image algebra operations. The experiments in the present chapter require something analogous to visual description merely to explain the experimental parameters. This means in turn that the effects obtained require equivalent explanatory domains.

As with the curvature results, the simplest account of the Allik and Dzaharov results involves computing a statistic by summation rather than other possibilities. As I have argued, this also necessitates a visual description explanation. The same is not true of the experiments in the previous chapter.

The long-jump data of Lee was accounted for by a description of a time-to-contact value for the target take-off board. The nature of the description has a subtlety that can be overlooked. Suppose that the image of the take-off board is a horizontally elongated rectangle. As the athlete approaches the board its image is isotropically expanded. So far as vision is concerned this expansion is equivalent to motion of each of the edges away from the centre of the image of the board. If the athlete is fixating the centre of the board, then this will not have any image motion, and the edges will have velocities that are proportional to their distance from the centre of the image. However the eyes are unlikely to be held so stable that the board image has no overall translation motion, and so this has to be subtracted from the edge motions.

We might be able to propose an image algebraic process that will create an "image velocity" image where the value at each point is a measure of the velocity in the original image. We cannot, however, subtract the motion of the centre of the board from this image, without identifying the image of the board. With image algebra, we can identify the centre of expansion of an image, but in the present case this need not be the centre of the board, but is more likely to be some point above it on the horizon.

Another problem if we try to use just image algebra to account for the computation of time to contact is that the velocity of each edge has to be divided by the distance of the edge from the centre of the image of the board. These distances cannot be calculated from image algebra except in the case where the centre of the board's image corresponds to the centre of the entire image of the scene.

These two difficulties arise because in image algebra there is no mechanism for dealing with special parts of the image separately from all the other parts. Instead we need to use a blob sentence to describe the image of the board. This sentence will have records of the position within the image of the blob, and of its length and width. Moreover, it could be easily extended to include the time derivatives of these quantities. This information is then sufficient to add a time-to-contact parameter to the description.

References

Shape

Foster D.H. (1980) Visual discrimination, categorical identification, and categorical rating in brief displays of curved lines: implications for discrete encoding processes. *J. Exp. Psychol. Human Percept. Perform.* **9**, 785–806.

Watt R.J. (1984a) Further evidence concerning the analysis of curvature in human foveal vision. *Vision Res.* **24**, 251–253.

Watt R.J. (1985) Image segmentation at contour intersections in human focal vision. *J. Opt. Soc. Am.* **2A**, 1200–1204.

Watt R.J. and Andrews D.P. (1982) Contour curvature analysis: hyperacuities in the discrimination of detailed shape. *Vision Res.* **22**, 449–460.

Watt R.J. and Morgan M.J. (1983) The use of different cues in vernier acuity. *Vision Res.* **23**, 991–995.

Watt R.J., Ward R.M. and Casco C. (1987) The detection of deviation from straightness in lines. *Vision Res.* **27**, 1659–1678.

Distance

Andrews D.P., Webb J. and Miller D. (1974) Acuity for length comparison in continuous and broken lines. *Vision Res.* **14**, 757–766.

Craven B.J. and Watt R.J. (1990) The use of image statistics in the estimation of lateral extent. *Spatial Vision*, **4**, 223–240.

Morgan M.J. and Ward R.M. (1985) Spatial and spatial-frequency primitives in spatial interval estimation. *J. Opt. Soc. Am.* **A2**, 1205–1210.

Regan D. and Beverley K.I. (1983) Spatial-frequency discrimination and detection: comparison of postadaptation thresholds. *J. Opt. Soc. Am.* **73**, 1684–1690.

Rentschler I., Hilz R., Sütterlin C. and Noguchi K. (1981) Illusions of filled lateral and angular extent. *Exp. Brain Res.* **44**, 154–158.

Watt R.J. (1984b) Towards a general theory of the visual acuities for shape and spatial arrangement. *Vision Res.* **24**, 1377–1386.

Westheimer G. and McKee S.P. (1977) Spatial configurations for visual hyperacuity. *Vision Res.* **17**, 941–947.

Motion Direction

Allik J. and Dzhafarov E.N. (1984) Motion direction identification in random cinematograms: a general model. *J. Exp. Psychol. Human Percept. Perform.* **10**, 378–393.

Texture

Bergen, J.R. and Julesz, B. (1983) Rapid discrimination of visual patterns. *IEEE Trans. Systems, Man Cybernet.* **SMC-13**, 857–863.

Link N.K. and Zucker S.W. (1987) Sensitivity to corners in flow patterns. *Spatial Vision* **2**, 233–244.

Nothdurft H.C. (1985a) Orientation sensitivity and texture segmentation in patterns with different line orientation. *Vision Res.* **25**, 551–560.

Nothdurft H.C. (1985b) Sensitivity for structure gradient in texture discrimination tasks. *Vision Res.* **25**, 1957–1968.

Sagi D. and Julesz B. (1987) Short-range limitation on detection of feature differences. *Spatial Vision* **2**, 39–49.

Watt R.J. (1987) Scanning from coarse to fine spatial scales in the human visual system after the onset of a stimulus. *J. Opt. Soc. Am.* **4A**, 2006–2021.

Long Jumping

Lee D.N., Lishman J.R. and Thomson J..A. (1982) Regulation of gait in long jumping. *J. Exp. Psychol. Human Percept. Perform.* **8**, 448–459.

Suggested Further Reading

Cornilleau-Pérès V. and Droulez J. (1989) Visual perception of surface curvature: psychophysics of curvature detection induced by motion parallax. *Percept. Psychophys.* **46**, 351–364.

Ike E.E., Ruddock K.H. and Skinner P. (1987) Visual discrimination of simple geometrical patterns: I Measurements for multiple element stimuli. *Spatial Vision* **2**, 13–30.

Legge G.E. and Gu Y. (1989) Stereopsis and contrast. *Vision Res.* **29**, 989–1004.

Mather G. (1984) Luminance change generates apparent movement: implications for models of directional specificity in the human visual system. *Vision Res.* **24**, 1399–1405.

Mayhew J.E.W. and Frisby J.P. (1981) Psychophysical and computational studies towards a theory of human stereopsis. *Artif. Intell.* **17**, 349–385.

Rogers B. and Caganello R. (1989) Disparity curvature and the perception of three-dimensional surfaces. *Nature* **339**, 135–137.

Wilson H.R. and Richards W.A. (1989) Mechanisms of contour curvature discrimination. *J. Opt. Soc. Am.* **A6**, 106–115.

Exercises

1. Under what circumstances, i.e. for what tasks, are judgements of relative distance a prerequisite? Are there situations where anything other than "greater than", "equal to", or "less than" are actually necessary? How might one set out to assess the nature of the metric for distance, in human vision?

2. Is it possible to write down a full description of the way in which an arbitrary curve in two dimensions might be represented by human vision? How is a circle represented? How about a spiral? What further information do we need to know, and how could that information be obtained?

3. Implied in the discussion of the apparent motion experiments of Braddick and Cleary and Braddick in the previous chapter and the role of correlation length is a notion of the way in which direction of motion is deduced. Relate the ideas of Allik and Dzhafarov to those experiments, to produce a more complete picture of motion processing in human vision. What is still missing?

4. Are the texture experiments that have been described really concerned with texture?

11
Psychophysics and Visual Interpretation

This is the last chapter on understanding human vision and it deals with those aspects of vision that are conceptually furthest away from the image itself. For this reason it is not always straightforward to construct parametrically varying stimuli to use the full power of psychophysical techniques. Nevertheless it is possible as the experiments that I describe will demonstrate. As in previous chapters, no attempt has been made to cover the literature and instead I have described in some depth a small number of experiments. The first two sets of experiments are concerned with the matching processes that are involved in the discovery of bilateral symmetry and in the calculation of stereoscopic disparity. The third set of experiments explores the mechanisms and processes that allow people to judge that two patterns are the same or not, subject to a range of geometric transformations. The fourth set of experiments is rather different in that subjects are taught the discrimination task, which itself is rather arbitrary. The main interest in the experiments is the learning process that subjects demonstrate.

The experiments that I describe here are all very artificial, involving either stimuli that have convenient statistical or geometric descriptions, or tasks that are somewhat bizarre. My own opinion is that such experiments do provide information about human vision in general and that it is not sensible or parsimonious to suppose that there are specific "channels" or "modules" or "units" or "pathways" or whatever through which artificial stimuli are processed. Artificial experiments and tasks tend to stress the visual components of a task, leaving the contextual and semantic aspects relatively uninfluential. The role of context is very interesting, but it is as well to know what vision is capable of on its own before speculating too much on the effects of semantics.

In the final section of this chapter, I describe an area of research that is important in everyday life. Lip reading is a skill that all sighted people share to some extent. The visible information about speech complements the acoustic information, so that it can be used to solve ambiguities in what is heard. I describe some work, mathematical, physical and psychophysical, that is discovering how we can lip read.

11.1 Organization in Random Dot Patterns

We have seen in Chapter 7 how symmetry can have a powerful organizing role in visual interpretation. As a phenomenon it is both compelling and intriguing and there have been many studies of its perception. An experiment by Barlow and Reeves (1979) measured sensitivity d' for the presence of symmetry in random dot patterns. From these measures, efficiencies could be calculated and were found to be surprisingly high. Under some circumstances, efficiency was 25%, which places symmetry detection among the highest efficiency tasks.

The basic experiment worked as follows. The stimulus was a pattern comprising 100 dots. A certain proportion of these dots were paired and placed in equivalent locations on opposite sides of a vertical axis so that they had bilateral symmetry. The remaining dots were placed individually in random locations. Obviously when the proportion of paired dots was zero, a wholly random dot pattern is obtained. Two different proportions of paired dots were selected, and the subject was shown a number of examples of each in order to form an impression of the two populations. A sequence of 100 trials then followed with the subject being required to discriminate on each trial the population to which the stimulus belonged. In the simplest case, one of the proportions would be zero and the subject's task was simply to detect if any symmetry was present or not. Another simple case would be where one of the proportions was set to one, so that the subject's task was to detect if any unpaired dots were present.

Values of d' discriminability for detecting the presence of symmetry were obtained as a function of the number of paired dots. The function obtained is a positively accelerating function. A similar function was obtained for the detection of unpaired dots as a function of their number. These two functions, $d'(0.0/X)$ and $d'(X/1.0)$ appear to be the same positively accelerating function.

One of the benefits of the d' measure is that, under certain circumstances, it is additive so that

$$d'(C|A) = d'(C|B) + d'(B|A)$$

The expression $d'(C|A)$ means the d' for discriminating C from A. If we take the case where one proportion of paired dots is zero, then d' takes a

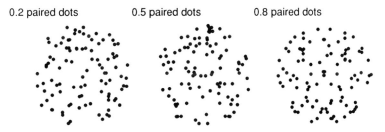

| 0.2 paired dots | 0.5 paired dots | 0.8 paired dots |

Figure 1. The stimulus used by Barlow and Reeves (1979) to measure the efficiency with which symmetry can be detected.

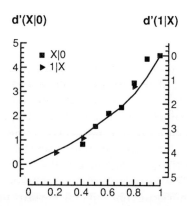

Figure 2. The cumulative d' function for symmetry detection as a function of the proportion of paired dots. Data are taken from Barlow and Reeves (1979).

value of 1.0 for the condition where the second proportion is about 0.3. Beyond this, d' would be difficult to measure accurately because a great many trials would be needed to catch the small error rate that would be expected. Instead, Barlow and Reeves measured d' from discriminating a proportion of 0.4 from 0.2; 0.6 from 0.4, etc. By accumulating (adding) the d' values that are obtained, one single function can be obtained. The resulting function that was calculated matched the original positively accelerating function quite closely.

Barlow and Reeves then went on to assess the degree of positional accuracy that is needed to allow the judgement of symmetry. The stimuli were as before, except that the paired dots were all plotted with independent random errors in their positions. Subjects were asked to discriminate between two stimuli in which either all dots were paired or no dots were paired. Discrimination performance was measured as a function of the positional error with which the dots were plotted. The results obtained show a considerable degree of tolerance for spatial error: 75% correct judgements when each dot is plotted anywhere within a square of side 24 arc min, which is one-fifth of the total width of the pattern. Performance, expressed as percentage of correct responses, falls more or less linearly with increasing spatial error until the chance performance of 50% at around a spatial error of $1°$.

This high degree of tolerance for spatial error is a useful piece of information that gives some clues about the mechanisms that might be involved. Barlow and Reeves show how a very crude model can perform at roughly the same levels as human subjects and with the same tolerance of spatial error. Suppose that the target area is split up into 16 smaller squares and the number of dots in each square counted up. If the numbers of dots in symmetrically placed squares are the same, then the pattern itself may well be symmetric. The notion of counting dots within regions is rather similar to the operation of smoothing, if all the dots have the same luminance. So another way of describing the results is to state that they are compatible with a relatively coarse scale analysis.

Maloney *et al.* (1987) report an experiment concerned with how subjects can detect the structure in Glass patterns. These patterns, named after Glass who first described them, can be easily generated. Take a set of randomly placed dots and then duplicate every dot at a fixed distance and direction away. The resultant image has a number of paired dots that could be joined by a line which would then indicate the distance and direction transformation used to generate the pattern. Maloney and colleagues measured how discriminable a Glass pattern is from a random pattern for a 150 ms exposure. The random pattern was constructed by placing dot pairs in random orientations in the image, whereas the Glass pattern had dot pairs in coherent orientations. To each pattern a further number of unpaired dots was added as noise to make the judgement more difficult. The local dot densities of the two patterns were the same and the only way that the subject could distinguish them was by the orientation of dot pairs.

Discriminability, d', was measured for these patterns as a function of the number of paired dots and the number of unpaired, noise dots. For three different types of Glass pattern, the results obtained could be expressed as a function relating d' to the ratio of the number of noise dots to the number of paired dots. Discriminability was decreased as the ratio of the number of added noise dots to the number of dot pairs was increased. A d' value of

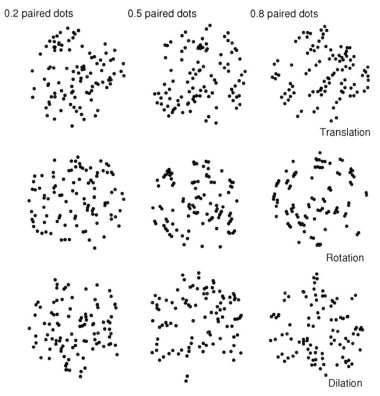

Figure 3. The stimuli used for assessing the detection of Glass pattern structure are shown by Maloney *et al.* (1979).

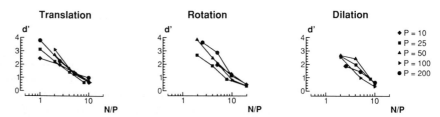

Figure 4. The discriminability of a Glass pattern from a random dot pattern is plotted as a function of the ratio of number of unpaired dots to the number of paired dots. Data are taken from Maloney *et al.* (1979).

1.0 was obtained when this ratio had a value of between 5 and 10, depending on condition. If the number of noise dots is, say, eight times as great as the number of dot pairs and the dot pairs are themselves relatively dense, then it is increasingly likely that any one of any dot pair will have as its nearest neighbour a noise dot rather than its paired dot.

The results imply a fairly local process of calculating orientation dipoles and an averaging process to extract the global mean orientation which then describes the pattern structure. In this instance, it is apparently the case that dipoles beyond the nearest neighbour have to be considered as well because discrimination is still reliable even when the number of noise dots far outweighs the number of dot pairs.

11.2 Stereoscopic Matching

One instance of the general problem of matching may be found in a relatively basic visual process, namely stereopsis. In stereoscopic visual systems, the two eyes or cameras are set apart so that each obtains a slightly different view of the scene. The differences can then be used to aid reconstruction of the three-dimensional structure of the scene. In a mathematical sense, the further apart the two eyes, the greater the differences in the two views and the more reliable the distance reconstruction. However, from a computational point of view, the greater the difference between the two views, then the more complex the matching process to determine which parts of the two images correspond.

In stereopsis, two discrete images are obtained from which one single representation of the scene is to be obtained. The difference in position of a particular identical feature in the two images, its *disparity*, is a function of how far in front or behind the object in the scene is from the plane at which the observers' eyes are converged. In order to compute distance from the observer, the separation of the two eyes and their lines of sight must also be known. The general problem in stereopsis is the matching process of deciding which image parts from one image correspond to which image parts in the other. This is quite equivalent to the high combinatorial problem of matching a visual description to a model description, and it is obviously necessary to exploit as many potentially time-saving strategies as possible.

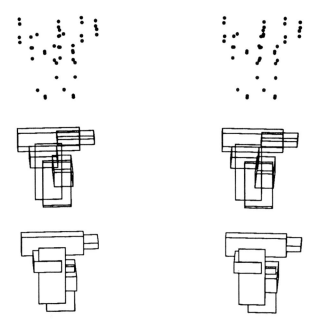

Figure 5. The stereo matching problem. What processes are required to determine which parts of one image match with which parts of the other image?

There have been many experimental analyses of stereopsis, and it continues to be a favourite research topic in psychophysics. For this reason alone, it might be expected that a great deal would be known about the matching process in stereopsis. In fact, rather little is known about the actual matching process itself, although there is rather more evidence concerning the nature of the image algebra and visual descriptions that are used.

A series of experiments was carried out by Mitchison and McKee (1987) to examine the matching process itself. They used two test stimuli that were rectangular arrays of dots, one for each eye and viewed stereoscopically (see Figure 6). The observers thus saw one array of dots, but at a depth that depends on the details of the two eyes' images. A comparison stimulus, a single dot, was displayed centrally beneath the array in each eye's image. The disparity of the comparison dot was varied from trial to trial, and the observers were required to report whether it appeared in front of or behind the centre of the test array of points, after an exposure of 160 ms. Psychometric functions could then be obtained, from which estimates of sensitivity and bias were calculated. The bias is a measure of the difference between the perceived distance of the array and its actual difference as physically specified by its disparity.

In the first experiment the leftmost column of dots was shifted slightly to the right in the left eye's image and the rightmost column of dots was shifted slightly to the left in the right eye's image. This would change the disparities of the outer columns and result in them being seen as moved nearer to the observer, leaving all the other dots where they were. If each

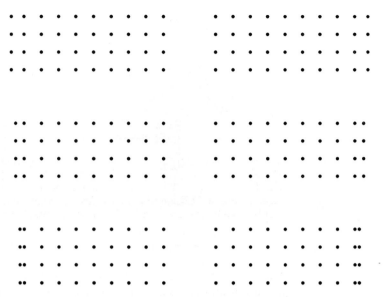

Figure 6. The two stimuli to the two eyes from the Mitchison and McKee (1987) experiments are drawn beside each other. Several different conditions are given.

outermost column had been moved so far inwards that it merged with its neighbour, then a different percept would be expected. On a dot-to-dot basis the whole array should appear nearer to the observer by an amount corresponding to a disparity of one intercolumn spacing. So, as the actual disparity of the outer columns is gradually increased, the perceived depth of the central columns should flip suddenly between two stable states. In the terms of psychometric functions relating responses to the disparity of the comparison spot, the bias corresponds to the perceived depth and thus should also change quite suddenly as the shift of the outer columns is increased.

Mitchison and McKee report that, for large spacings between columns (7 or 14 arc min), the bias does occur at, or very close to, zero disparity for all conditions where the outer columns are displaced inwards by less than half of the intercolumn spacing. For larger inwards displacements, bias is at, or very close to, the intercolumn spacing. These results are as expected. However, for smaller intercolumn spacings, this is not what they found. Instead the bias follows a more gradual change with the disparity of the outer columns, implying that the depth of the central rows is being interpolated between the two extreme disparities. Taking one of the more closely spaced stimuli that yielded interpolated depth, they then repeated the experiment with exposure durations of $\frac{1}{2}$, 1 and 2 s. The result was that the interpolation effect is reduced with increasing exposure, being effectively abolished in one subject after 2 s.

Mitchison and McKee argue that the results, although there clearly is a spatial scale factor in that the distance between columns is important, cannot be accounted for by spatial scale alone. They demonstrated their

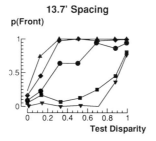 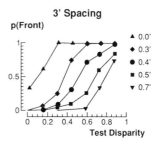

Figure 7. The psychometric functions for the relative depth judgements in the Mitchison and McKee (1987) experiments. Two different spacings between the lines are shown. The different curves at each spacing are for different displacements of the end points in the stimulus grid. Notice that the depth is continuously interpolated for the small spacing, but not for the large spacing.

argument by making a small, fine scale change to the stimulus with closely spaced columns and showing that a different depth percept results. The change was to move one of the central columns rightwards by a small amount in both eyes' images. This caused the centre of the pattern to appear nearer to the fixation plane. A filter which is of fine enough scale to resolve this small difference in the finest scale pattern will also be fine enough to resolve the individual columns when they are separated by 5 arc min. The deduction is that an account of the result simply in terms of spatial filtering cannot be adequate and that the phenomenon is due to the matching process.

Mitchison and McKee make the suggestion that the matching process first deals with unambiguous points such as the end columns, and then matches the ambiguous inner columns. The inner columns are initially assigned a disparity by interpolation between the disparities of the end columns, and then are matched individually, so that the individual disparities are all as close to the interpolation as possible.

11.3 Spatial Relations

We have already seen in the discussion of experiments and visual descriptions, that simple tasks such as judging the distance and orientation between two points can be done with high precision, but we still do not have any clear idea how they might be done. In this section, I shall now describe some intriguing experiments that give some information about how such spatial relations are used and interact with a pattern-matching task.

In the original experiments, Foster (1978) showed subjects two patterns made up from a number, seven or ten, of randomly arranged dots. The dots were exposed for 200 ms, and afterwards the subject was required to report whether the two patterns had been the same or different. If the two patterns were the same, they may have been subjected to either a rotation about the centre of the pattern or a reflection about a vertical axis. The main finding was that the percentage of correct same responses was strongly dependent

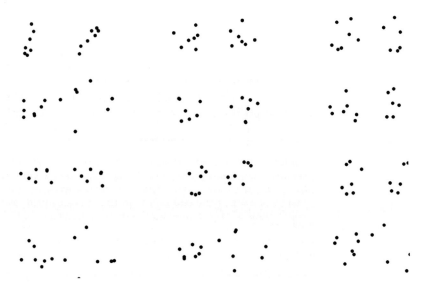

Figure 8.   Foster stimuli. Sample random patterns subjected to a range of rotations are shown. Some pairs are similar subject to a rotation and some are quite different. Which?

on the angle through which the patterns had been rotated, being best for 0° and 180° rotations.

Further experiments by Kahn and Foster (1981) confirmed the finding that recognition is best for patterns that have been rotated through 0° or 180° rather than intermediate values. They also examined the effects of the relative positions of the two patterns in the visual field. As before the two patterns were each made of 10 randomly placed dots and were presented for 100 ms after which subjects were required to state whether the two patterns were the same or different. The patterns could either be completely different, or the same subject to one of four transformations: identity (no

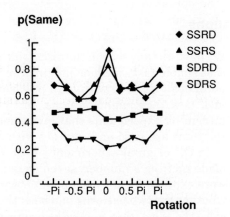

Figure 9.   The effects of pattern rotation on the proportion of same responses for patterns that were the same shape (SSRS), or the same number of dots (SSRD), or not the same shape (SDRS, SDRD). Data taken from Foster (1978).

transformation); mirror inversion; rotation through 90°; and rotation through 180° (point inversion). Each pattern was shown at one of five positions: centred at the fixation point; half a degree left or right of fixation; or one degree left or right of fixation.

Kahn and Foster analysed the performance of subjects for a range of different positions for each of the two patterns. With five locations and two patterns, there are 25 possible combinations, but only a subset of these was examined. The general finding was that the relative position of the patterns has an effect on performance, but one that is different for the different transformations. Once the effects of eccentricity (on acuity for example), per se, have been accounted for, the performance for identical patterns is best when the two patterns are presented at the same site and deteriorates with separation between the patterns. On the other hand, performance for point inverted patterns is best for locations that are symmetrically placed either side of fixation, and deteriorates with distance from symmetry rather than distance between the patterns. The mirror reversal transformation was broadly similar to the point inversion but showed a slight separation effect in addition. For the 90° rotation patterns the only differences in performance were due to the mean eccentricity of the patterns.

These results can be accounted for by postulating restrictions on the ways in which the visual descriptions of the patterns can be treated for matching comparisons. Suppose that each pattern is represented by a visual description which records relative locations of the dots with respect to the mean location of the pattern (local position) and also records the latter with respect to the point of fixation (global position). In order for a same response to be generated, these two descriptions have to be equated by transforming one until it is as near as possible to being the same as the other. In the identity case, the patterns are to be matched for local positions but not global position. This means that only the global positions have to be transformed. The effect of separation implies some loss of information in the process. In the point inversion condition, the local positions of all the dots in one of the patterns have to be inverted before being matched. If we suppose that all spatial relations, local and global, must be inverted together in one step, then this result follows. The point inversion condition is then performed by a complete inversion of the pattern followed by a transformation of just the global position, hence separation has its effect.

An interesting further experimental analysis was carried out by Bischof *et al.* (1985). Their basic design was similar to the experiments just described, except that the dot patterns were constructed from randomly placed subpatterns, each a cluster of 3 or 4 dots, of a determinate shape. This allows the possibility of transforming the whole pattern or just the subpatterns within the pattern. Four different transformations were used: (i) identity transformation; (ii) position point inversion, where the positions of the subpatterns were point inverted about the centre of each pattern, but the subpatterns themselves were not reoriented; (iii) local point inversion, where the subpatterns were point inverted about their own centres, but left at the same positions in the pattern; and (iv) global point inversion, where the whole pattern was point inverted.

As a further complication, instead of just having as a "different" pattern one that is wholly unrelated to the other, they added a number of other patterns to be regarded as different. "Different" patterns could be wholly different; have different subpatterns but at the same positions or at point-inverted positions; or they could have the same subpatterns or their point inversions, but at different positions within the pattern.

The results showed that identity transformations are detected with greatest sensitivity; local and global point inversions are also well detected; and position point inversions are least well discriminated. Within the general framework used to account for their earlier results that I have just described, the present results can be accommodated without undue difficulty. Bischof and colleagues start by noting that the poorest condition, position point inversion, is formally equivalent to an application of a global point inversion followed by a local point inversion (or local followed by global). If, indeed, the matching comparison were being done in this way, then the poorer performance could be expected. So why should the matching process be done this way?

A speculative answer is that these patterns are represented hierarchically, so that the subpatterns are identified and their intrinsic spatial relations are represented. Above this, the spatial relations between the subpatterns are also represented. If spatial relations between subpatterns are modified, then the equivalent relations within each subpattern have also to be modified. In other words, changes in a descriptive hierarchy must be propagated from the level at which they occur down to the bottom.

11.4 Learning Categories

I now describe an experiment conducted by Caelli *et al.* (1987) in which subjects had to learn how to categorize a set of stimuli according to a rule that was given by example and experience rather than by instructions. The interest in the experiment concerns the extent to which the human visual system can derive prototypical stimuli from a set of exemplars rather than having a fixed set of prototypes that cannot be modified. This will be clearer once the experimental procedure has been described.

The stimuli were all gratings made from two components modulated within a Gaussian contrast envelope. Each grating had the same fundamental component, a cosine wave of fixed phase and amplitude, and a third harmonic of variable phase and amplitude. This third harmonic can be described as the sum of a cosine and a sine wave. The sum of these two, which differ in phase by 90°, has a phase and amplitude which depends on their relative amplitudes. Thus each member of the set of stimuli can be described as having a location in a two-dimensional space where the dimensions correspond to the amplitude of the odd-symmetric component (sine wave) and the amplitude of the even-symmetric component (cosine wave) of the third harmonic. There were 15 such stimuli, each assigned to one of three categories.

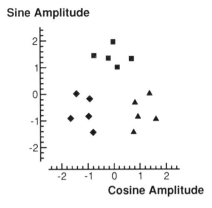

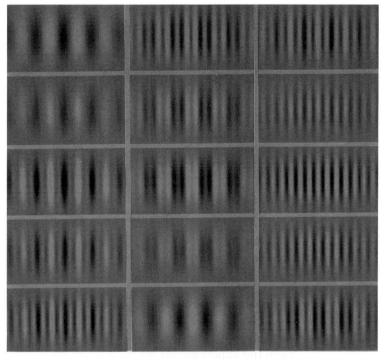

Figure 10. Fifteen training stimuli from the study of Caelli *et al.* (1987). The positions of these stimuli in a two-dimensional space defined by the amplitudes of the even- and odd-symmetric components are shown in a plan of the space.

Subjects were shown each of the 15 training stimuli for 200 ms and told to which class it belonged. This was then repeated twice more, so that in all the subjects saw 45 training stimuli. Then each training stimulus was presented once more as a test stimulus and the subject was required to classify it into one of the three classes. This whole learning and test procedure was repeated up to 15 times until the subject had learnt the classification. Cumulative classification performance, a measure of the learning rate, for each of the 15 patterns was then calculated.

Caelli and colleagues used four sets of 15 stimuli, varying in the extent to which the classes were separated and in their relative positions in the two-dimensional stimulus space. At one extreme there was considerable overlap of the classes, whereas at the other extreme each exemplar was always nearest to another member of its own class. Naturally, the ability of subjects to learn the classification depends on this variable.

The simplest analysis of the data is to suppose that a prototype is constructed for each class by computing the centroid in the stimulus space of the exemplars, and that each test pattern is then compared with the three centroid prototypes. The probability of identifying it as belong to class i can then be predicted from its distance d_1, d_2, d_3 to the three prototypes according to the formula

$$p(\text{class i/sample}) = \frac{\dfrac{1}{d_i}}{\left(\dfrac{1}{d_1} + \dfrac{1}{d_2} + \dfrac{1}{d_3}\right)}$$

This formula was found to provide a good prediction of the actual probabilities of assignment to classes obtained in the experiment.

As a further test, a second experiment was carried out, once again using 15 training stimuli and testing with these stimuli until 100% correct classifications could be obtained. Then, however, a new set of 30 novel stimuli were shown, one by one, to the subjects who had to classify these new stimuli into the three classes. The new stimuli were randomly distributed across the stimulus space. This is accordingly a test of how the learning can be generalized. Once again an analysis in terms of centroid prototypes and distances from these prototypes was found to provide a good account for the subjects' behaviour.

The general conclusion from this experiment is that categories can be learnt from examples and experience. The implication is that a set of arbitrary prototypical model descriptions can be created and subsequently used for classification.

11.5 A Complete Task

Finally, I will describe a body of research that is concerned with understanding lip reading. There are many different approaches to this phenomenon, and a good general introduction will be found in the book by Dodd and Campbell (1987). I have selected the areas that are most directly concerned with the visual rather than the linguistic parts of the phenomenon. The knowledge that has accumulated over the past few years concerns three different perspectives. There are now data available on the physical stimulus: measurements have been made of the movements of various parts of the face during speech production. There are also studies of the gross performance of lip reading; how good is lip reading in general and in what circumstances? Recent studies have begun unravelling the specific facial cues that are used by speech watchers.

The basic relevant facts about lip reading are that it is physically possible to obtain information from the visual appearance of various parts of the face that would be useful in deciding what a speaker is saying. Moreover, some of this information is used by listeners to some benefit in nearly all circumstances. The lips, tongue and teeth appear to be particularly salient and useful. It is now possible to define models of the facial shape and even to build effective computer simulations. It is not known exactly which cues are actually used or how they are calculated from images.

The visual skill of lip reading starts with the isolation from images of the parts that are relevant, such as the lips. The shape, spatial relations and movements of these have then to be described. From the descriptions that are obtained, some information about the speech can be interpreted.

(i) Gross Performance

Before examining the details of lip reading cues and performance, it is obviously sensible to establish whether lip reading actually occurs, and if so under what circumstances.

In a comprehensive study, Erber (1974) measured the percentage of words that could be correctly lip read by profoundly deaf children as a function of viewing distance, viewing angle, and illumination of the face. The percentages correct ranged from over 80% under optimum conditions at 2 m to around 40% under the worst conditions at 7.4 m. At such a distance, lip movements of 20 mm subtend a visual angle of 9 arc min. The direction of illumination had little effect on performance. Viewing direction had more effect. Changing from being full-face to a three-quarters view (45°) made no appreciable difference to performance. Performance on a profile view (90°) was however consistently worse, with percentage correct dropping from 80% to just over 60% at 2 m. This is equivalent to the change in going from 2 m to 7.4 m distant.

Walden *et al.* (1977) trained hearing-impaired adults to lip read. They then measured the confusions that their subjects tended to make in identifying consonants. An interesting result was obtained. The least confusable consonants, visually, tended to be those that are most confusable acoustically and vice versa. There is a degree of complementarity between the two modalities of information.

This complementarity suggests that lip reading might be of general use in hearing subjects as well as in the deaf or partially deaf. MacLeod and Summerfield (1987) demonstrated this by measuring the benefit accrued from seeing a speaker. Taking a group of normal subjects and a set of test sentences they measured the accuracy of reporting the sentences. The sentences were presented either auditory alone or audio-visual presentations. The auditory presentations had a variable quantity of noise added and a psychophysical technique was used to measure a signal-to-noise ratio threshold for correctly hearing each sentence. By comparing these thresholds with and without visual information, the effective contribution of lip reading could be calculated.

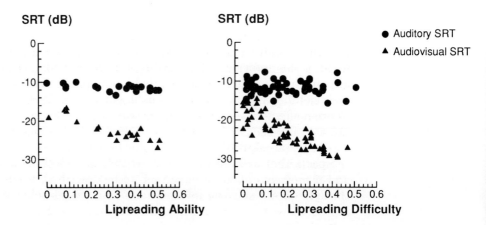

Figure 11. The two graphs show the two speech reception thresholds for recognizing sentences either with or without visual cues (lips). The panel on the left shows the data plotted as a function of the lip reading ability of the individual subjects, giving an impression of the range of benefit across the population. The right panel shows the same data, but plotted according to the benefit per sentence, giving an impression of the benefit across a range of different utterances. Data are taken from MacLeod and Summerfield (1987).

Lip reading information is roughly equivalent to an 11 dB signal/noise ratio improvement. This is considerable. Moreover, by comparing the improvement with lip reading performance without any sound, it was found that the degree of benefit is correlated with how good the subject is generally at lip reading without sound and also with how easy the sentence is to lip read. These findings clearly suggest that lip reading is a daily benefit to all.

(ii) The Physical Stimulus

Obviously, the visible parts of our speech-producing apparatus, the lips, tongue, and lower jaw, all move during speech. However it is not obvious how those movements are related to the different parts and sounds of speech. To obtain this information, it has been necessary to make direct measurements of the movements. In making the measurements, the natural interest lies in how different the movements are for different sounds.

The first study was by Fromkin (1964) who used an array of techniques to obtain measurements of the width and height of the open mouth whilst the 12 standard vowel sounds were made. Fromkin found that the height did vary somewhat between vowels, ranging from 5 mm to 15 mm. For a single speaker the variability in mouth height for a given vowel sound could span 5 mm and was normally between 3 and 5 mm in range. Variability between different speakers was about twice as great as this. On its own, mouth height does not distinguish between the vowels. Mouth width ranges from around 15 mm up to around 45–50 mm for different vowels. Variability is of the order of 5–10 mm within one speaker, and around 10 mm between different speakers.

When the two dimensions, width and height, are taken together, then a consistent pattern emerges. For any one speaker, there is a set of vowels for which width and height are proportional and another set for which width is maximum and does not vary. Individual differences in mouth size are obviously going to obscure this pattern, and it is necessary to normalize each individual's measurements to their own mean and standard deviation. These results have been replicated by Montgomery and Jackson (1983), who went on to relate the measurements to actual lip reading performance as we shall see below.

Speaking is a dynamic process, and it may well be misleading to treat vowel production as if it involved a fixed mouth shape. Several studies of the dynamics of the process have been made. Kelso *et al.* (1985) had subjects repeat the same syllable over and over again, but using it to replace the syllables of a proper sentence. They give as an example:

"when the sun light strikes rain drops in the air"

ba   ba **ba** ba   **ba**   **ba**   ba   ba ba **ba**

Speakers were asked to repeat the sentences at a conversational and at a fast rate while the position and velocity of the lower lip was measured. The basic finding was that the mean periods in the conversational and fast speaking rates were 211 ms and 167 ms, respectively. They found that the amplitude of lip movement was proportional to the duration of the movement, implying a fixed velocity. Smaller amplitudes tended to occur for fast speaking rates and for unstressed sounds.

The most sophisticated set of measurements was made by Brooke and Summerfield (1983). They used video recordings obtained with a shuttered camera (thereby obtaining brief exposures and sharply focused images). Subjects were filmed full faced and in profile simultaneously whilst pronouncing vowel–consonant–vowel syllables. The two-dimensional locations in the images of 12 references points over the face and particularly around the mouth were obtained. From these coordinates from the two viewing directions, and assuming that certain points around the eyes and on the nose were not in relative motion, the three-dimensional trajectories of 11 points around the lips and one on the chin could be computed.

Not unnaturally, there are considerable correlations between the motions of the various points. The centres of the two lips move in opposite directions; typical amplitudes for the upper lip are 3 mm and those for the lower lip are 15 mm. The mouth tends to open by vertical movement of both lips. For the vowel sounds that were used, the outer extremities of the lips tend to move downwards and outwards in phase with the lower lip. The vertical movements have amplitudes of around 5 mm and outwards of around 1 or 2 mm.

Finally, Browman and Goldstein (1984), as part of a study of the dynamics of lip motions, obtained acoustic and visual traces simultaneously. The acoustic waveform can be compared with the vertical trajectory of the lower lip. There is a clear relationship between the two.

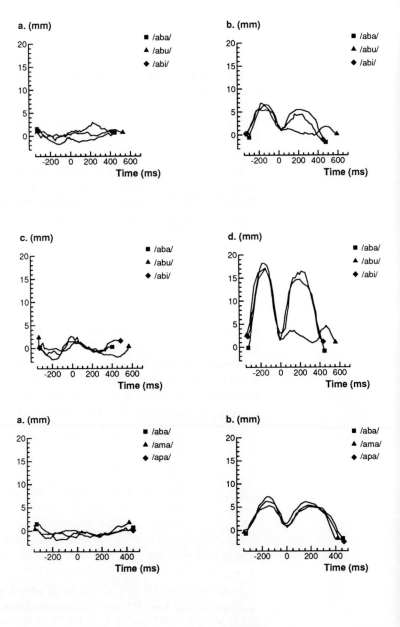

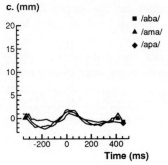

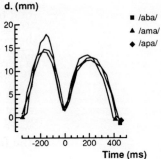

Figure 12. Traces for lip movements. These traces, taken from Brooke and Summerfield (1987), show the movements of the lip corners (a: horizontally; b: vertically) and the lip centres (c: upper lip, vertical; d: lower lip, vertical). Several different consonants are compared with several different vowels.

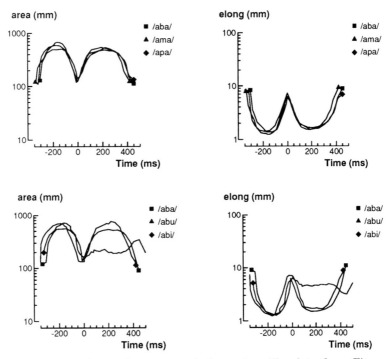

Figure 13. Mouth opening area and elongation. The data from Figure 12 were used to compute the mouth dimensions for the utterances.

(iii) Specific Cues

There have been a few studies that have sought to identify the roles of the various potential cues in lip and mouth changes during speech perception. All of the studies have used essentially the same technique, each new one adding a further sophistication to the design. I shall describe one of the most recent studies, conducted by McGrath *et al.* (1984), which is different in using normally hearing subjects and also in comparing real videotapes with computer-drawn caricatures. This latter aspect provides the ability to control the stimulus parametrically.

From the subject's point of view the experiment involved watching a number of displays of faces each of which was saying a syllable of the form b-vowel-b (e.g. bib). There was no sound cue. There were 11 different syllables and the subject was required to say for each presentation which syllable had been spoken. The response was a forced choice, and so subjects had to guess if they were unsure. There were three basic stimulus conditions. The first was a condition where the subjects saw a full-face video recording of a person speaking the syllables. In the second, the video recording was made so that only the lips and teeth were visible. This was done by painting them with fluorescent dye and recording under UV light. In the third condition only the lips were visible. Amongst a number of further conditions that were also tested, two involved computer line drawings which caricatured the face and lips, or face, lips and teeth.

The percentage of correct responses for each vowel and in each condition were calculated. These varied from around 20% at worst to around 90% at best, with an average of about 50% correct. For 7 out of the 11 vowels tested, the proportion of correct responses was the same for natural and for synthetic faces. The synthetic faces led to a pattern of correct scores that was very similar to the condition where only natural lips and teeth were visible. This would seem to indicate that in normal lip reading there is another source of information in the face. For both the natural and synthetic faces, the presence of teeth had a large effect in identification of the vowel E.

Instead of obtaining a psychometric function for the results, McGrath and colleagues drew up a confusion matrix for each condition. This is a matrix which records the number of each of the 11 responses for each of the 11 stimuli. It thus has 11^2 cells, those down the identity diagonal (i.e. top left to bottom right) being the correct responses, all others being errors. There is a statistical treatment of such matrices, called multidimensional scaling (MDS), which can be used to summarize the pattern of confusions.

MDS takes a matrix of confusions and attempts to find a way in which the cells can be placed in space so that the distance between any two cells in this space is proportional to the discriminability of the two conditions that the cells represent. The position of a cell in a matrix is arbitrary, the matrix does not have metrical dimensions and it is only a convenient way of encoding the data. Suppose we had three stimuli, each of which was equally discriminable from each of the others. In this case the three points could be placed at the corners of an equilateral triangle in a two-dimensional space and all the distances would correspond to discriminability. If we then added a fourth that was also equally discriminable from each of the other three, then there is no point in the plane of the triangle at which it could be placed. We would need to add another dimension so that the four points lay at the vertices of a tetrahedron in three-dimensional space. A further point also equally discriminable from all others would require a fourth dimension, and so on.

If we were to start with n points and measures of how discriminable each was from each of the others, then an $(n - 1)$-dimensional space will always provide an exact solution. If we restrict the number of dimensions to a number less than $(n - 1)$ then an exact solution is unlikely and each point will be placed at a compromise position. The extent of compromise can be quantified by comparing the metrical distances with the discriminabilities. The trick is to find the minimum number of dimensions that will provide an acceptable degree of compromise.

Once a solution has been obtained to an acceptable compromise it is interesting to interpret it. The number of dimensions is a measure of the number of independent variables determining the discrimination performance. For any multidimensional space, the directions of the axes or dimensions are only constrained to be mutually orthogonal (i.e. to be pairwise at $90°$ to each other in their common plane). The whole axis system can be rotated arbitrarily. The next step in MDS is to decide which direction of axes to use. The criterion that is used is to select the direction of axes which lie along the directions that have the greatest dispersion of points. It is then up to the experimenter to decide what physical variables these abstract dimensions actually correspond to.

In the McGrath experiments, MDS found an acceptable solution using three dimensions. The three dimensions could be described as corresponding to (i) the degree of elongation vs roundness of the mouth, such as the ratio of opening width to height; (ii) the extent to which the mouth is opened, such as the product of mouth width and height; and (iii) the temporal duration of the opening.

Summary

In this section I have described a range of experiments that together provide a considerable understanding of the process involved in lip reading. Some experiments have demonstrated the general utility of lip reading. These have considerable practical significance. The paper by Erber which examined the effects of viewing angle and illumination direction on the ability of deaf children to lip read, ended with a simple and valid specification of how classrooms should be laid out with the teacher opposite the window and the children placed so that all could see at least a three-quarters view of the teacher's face.

The physical examination of the cues in lip reading is obviously incomplete so far, but already appears to match the psychophysical data rather well. It is clear that there are a number of significant cues available to help lip reading and that not one of them on its own is sufficient. The MDS approach is actually rather analogous to the formal representation of the visual model and interpretative processes that the experiments elucidate.

11.6 Conclusion

This chapter has dealt with a few experiments which have been analysed at the levels of visual interpretation. The four different sets of experiments are quite different from each other in subject matter and in experimental design. Each of them has as a core the idea that it is important to give subjects tasks to perform rather than just have them report experiences. The precision and the bias with which these tasks are performed provide the scientific insights into the nature of the processes involved.

Most psychologists will object that nearly all of the corpus of knowledge about higher level and cognitive aspects of vision has been omitted from the account. I would offer two reasons for this omission. The first is that the techniques employed are rarely rigorous enough for quantitative conclusions to have any utility. The second reason is that all those missing experiments were all conceived within a type of framework for understanding of vision that I have not adopted and further have not found useful. Both reasons involve a judgement about how useful an experiment is, not how good or how clever, or even how surprising its result is. Ultimately experiments, frameworks and theories lead to new experiments. Each of the experiments that I have described in this book has left me wanting to do further research myself along similar lines. That is why, for me, these are the most useful experiments.

References

Organization in Random Dot Patterns

Barlow H.B. and Reeves B.C. (1979) The versatility and absolute efficiency of detecting mirror symmetry in random dot displays. *Vision Res.* **19**, 783–793.
Jenkins B. (1983a) Spatial limits to the detection of transpositional symmetry in dynamic dot textures. *J. Exp. Psychol. Human Percept. Perform.* **9**, 258–269.
Jenkins B. (1983b) Temporal limits to the detection of correlation in transpositionally symmetric dynamic dot textures. *Percept. Psychophys.* **33**, 79–84.
Maloney R.K., Mitchison G.J. and Barlow H.B. (1987) Limit to the detection of Glass patterns in the presence of noise. *J. Opt. Soc. Am.* **A4**, 2336–2341.

Stereopsis

Mitchison G.J. and McKee S.P. (1987) Interpolation and the detection of fine structure in stereoscopic matching. *Vision Res.* **27**, 295–302.

Spatial Relations

Bischof W.F., Foster D.H. and Kahn J.I. (1985) Selective internal operations in the recognition of locally and globally point-inverted patterns. *Spatial Vision* **1**, 179–196.
Foster D.H. (1978) Visual comparison of random-dot patterns: evidence concerning a fixed visual association between features and feature-relations. *Q. J. Exp. Psychol.* **30**, 637–654.
Kahn J.I. and Foster D.H. (1981) Visual comparison of rotated and reflected random-dot patterns as a function of their potential symmetry and separation in the field. *Quart. J. Exp. Psychol.*, **33A**, 155–166.
Kahn J.I. and Foster D.H. (1986) Horizontal-vertical structure in the visual comparison of rigidly transformed patterns. *J. Exp. Psychol. Human Percept. Perform.* **12**, 422–433.

Visual Learning

Caelli, T., Rentschler I. and Scheidler W. (1987) Visual pattern recognition in humans. I: Evidence for adaptive filtering. *Biol. Cybern.* **57**, 233–240.

Lip Reading

Brooke N.M. and Summerfield Q. (1983) Analysis, synthesis, and perception of visible articulatory movements. *J. Phonetics* **11**, 63–76.
Browman C.P. and Goldstein L.M. (1984) Dynamic modelling of phonetic structure. In: V. Fromkin (ed.) "Phonetic Linguistics". Academic Press, New York.

Dodd B. and Campbell R. (1987) (eds) "Hearing by Eye: the Psychology of Lip Reading". Lawrence Erlbaum Associates, London.

Erber, N.P. (1974) Effects of angle, distance and illumination on visual reception of speech by profoundly deaf children. *J. Speech Hearing Res.* **17**, 99–112.

Fromkin V. (1964) Lip positions in American-English vowels. *Language Speech* **7**, 215–225.

Kelso J.A.S., Vatikiotis-Bateson E., Saltzman E.L. and Kay B. (1985) A qualitative dynamic analysis of reiterant speech production: phase portraits, kinematics and dynamic modelling. *J. Acous. Soc. Am.* **77**, 266–280.

MacLeod A. and Summerfield Q. (1987) Quantifying the contribution of vision to speech perception in noise. *Br. J. Audiol.* **21**, 131–141.

McGrath M., Summerfield Q. and Brooke M. (1984) Role of lips and teeth in lipreading vowels. *Proc. Inst. Acoustics* **6**, 401–408.

Montgomery A.A. and Jackson P.L. (1983) Physical characteristics of the lips underlying vowel lipreading. *J. Acous. Soc. Am.* **73**, 2134–2144.

Walden B.E., Prosek R.A., Montgomery A.A., Scherr, C.K. and Jones C.J. (1977) Effects of training on the visual recognition of consonants. *J. Speech Hearing Res.* **20**, 130–145.

Suggested Further Reading

Buckley D., Frisby J.P. and Mayhew J.E.W. (1989) Integration of stereo and texture cues in the formation of discontinuities during three-dimensional surface interpolation. *Perception* **18**, 563–588.

De Bruyn B. and Orban G.A. (1990) The role of direction information in the perception of geometric optic flow components. *Perception and Psychophysics* **47**, 433–438.

De Bruyn B. and Orban G.A. (1990) The importance of velocity gradients in the perception of three-dimensional rigidity. *Perception* **19**, 21–28.

Hogben J.H., Julesz B. and Ross J. (1976) Short-term memory for symmetry. *Vision Res.* **16**, 861–866.

Jenkins B. (1982) Redundancy in the perception of bilateral symmetry in dot textures. *Percept. Psychophys.* **32**, 171–177.

Jenkins B. (1983) Component processes in the perception of bilaterally symmetric dot textures. *Percept. Psychophys.* **34**, 433–440.

Pavel M., Sperling G., Riedl T. and Vanderbeek A. (1987) Limits of visual communication: the effect of signal-to-noise ratio on the intelligibility of American Sign Language. *J. Opt. Soc. Am.* **A4**, 2355–2365.

Ronacher B. (1984) Human pattern recognition: evidence for a switching between strategies in analyzing complex stimuli. *Biol. Cybern.* **51**, 205–210.

Ronacher B. and Bautz W. (1985) Human pattern recognition: individually different strategies in analyzing complex stimuli. *Biol. Cybern.* **51**, 249–261.

Exercises

1. Many of the experiments described in this chapter involve random dot stimuli. Whilst these have a certain type of neutral status, this cannot be guaranteed, and inspection of the figures will persuade you that there are local configurations of dots that are useful in the various tasks, and others that are not. Form an informal list of the configurations that appear to help, and then design experiments to test whether they do.

2. In this book, I have only described one experiment on stereopsis. Work back through the other levels of visual analysis, and discover what is known about the filtering stages and the matching primitives.

3. Design a perceptual learning experiment that uses stimuli that co-vary on three or more dimensions. What are the problems here? How are distances across dimensions that are not intimately related (such as those of space are) to be treated in such an experiment?
4. What other complete tasks can be examined in the way that lip reading has been already? How would you set about organizing a full study of them?

12
Postscript

In this book, I have described a way of understanding vision. I have put together the various elements that I will need in order to claim to understand vision. I have also indicated the types of experiment that provide me with further insights into human vision. Understanding is a very personal affair, and in this final, brief comment, I will draw a few of the important characteristics of my understanding.

12.1 Basics Of Understanding Vision

Vision starts with the light array, which is a multidimensional function of space, time and wavelength. Vision ends with a decision or an action or the readiness to act (i.e. a memory). These outcomes are all described by a quality, such as type of action, and a vector quantity, such as grip strength or movement length. At the simplest level, vision can be seen as a process which maps a huge multidimensional function onto one or more vectors in a space of different dimensions.

The image is a multidimensional real-valued function. There are many processes that can be usefully applied to images to remove unwanted, irrelevant variations and to render more salient or more explicit the relevant information. These, taken together, I have described as image algebra, and chief amongst them are the processes of smoothing and differentiation. Any filter that has a smooth or a continuous impulse function can be regarded as applying one or both of these processes.

Once an image has been appropriately processed using the techniques of image algebra then it is ready for description. In creating an image description, the domain is changed from the image to a set of descriptive sentences. The sentences are constructed ideally using stable yet sensitive measures of the image patterns that they describe. I have described how the low order central moments are very suitable for describing zero-bounded blobs in the image. At this stage, the explicit information is still image based.

Within the domain of descriptive sentences it is possible to combine sentences to form more complex sentences, such as creating a corner sentence from two line sentences. It is also necessary to bring subsets of sentences together to form visual descriptive structures because the object of most actions will involve various related parts of the image. The two most useful relationships between sentences that can be used are neighbourhood and similarity. As we have seen, neither of these is as simple as might be supposed. By now, the explicit information is visual rather than image based because the nature of the relationships between sentences within such a structure are relatively abstract from the geometry of the image.

A great many actions are possible with this level of visual processing, but there are also many more that require the combination of visual information with information stored in memory. The circumstances in which this is appropriate are specified by a model which contains a set of conditions that the visual description must meet. Because the circumstances are specified in a three-dimensional world and the visual descriptions refer to two-dimensional images, the matching process is far from trivial and can be combinatorially explosive.

To avoid the combinatorial explosion, it is very useful to impose an ordering or a partial ordering on the descriptive structures. Hierarchical graph structures which contain partial ordering are particularly useful because different branches of the tree can correspond to different views of the same object.

In the last chapters of this book I have described a wide range of psychophysical research and results. The understanding of vision that I have developed can be used quite naturally for accounting for the results of the experiments. There is a preponderance of research aimed at the image algebra levels and much less at the higher levels.

12.2 Gaps in Knowledge about Vision

In writing this book, I have become aware of a number of real gaps in our knowledge of vision. The following topics are ones where there do not seem to be serious conceptual difficulties. It is knowledge rather than understanding that is lacking.

(i) Structural Descriptions and Matching

The process of matching visual and stored descriptions has not really been considered in any detail. The ways in which structures in descriptions, on the one hand, and noise or uncertainty, on the other, will interact with each other and with the matching process itself need to be examined. The prevalent view seems to be that keeping descriptions concise, by reducing redundancy, is a good thing. The normal reason given is that the brain has a limited capacity. One might equally well argue that redundancy is vital in a numerically ill-behaved process such as matching, and that structures such as symmetries that emphasize the redundancy present are similarly vital.

(ii) Ecological Physics

Another area where much more knowledge is required concerns the physical and statistical structure of the environment. Vision depends on knowing, at a procedural level, what it is possible to see. Given this, an understanding of vision is similarly dependent on a good body of knowledge about the environment and how it appears in images.

(iii) Implementations and Neural Networks

Throughout this book, I have been concerned to draw a distinction between a formal understanding of the processes of vision and a discussion of how those processes might be implemented. At present there is no theory of implementation. The vision systems that have been implemented in computers fall into two broad categories. One class of implementations has strictly sequential translations of a task specification that is similar to the terms of this book so that image processing and symbol manipulation are coded more or less directly and independently. The other class involves taught neural networks where the programming effort is minimal and the network learns a mapping from image to response by experience from multiple instances with feedback.

Neither approach to implementation is very satisfactory from a practical point of view, and neither has yet added to our understanding of vision. The first, sequential approach works, and given certain conditions of illumination or whatever, can be specified to work. It is fairly standard engineering. However, it is almost certainly very inefficient both of resources and of time. To date most systems have sophisticated image algebraic processes and then relatively crude description structures and interpretative matching processes. Such systems do not require that resources be used efficiently, except for the image-wide algebra, for which special purpose hardware is available. A simple clue to the problems yet to be faced is the absence in any common scientific or engineering compiled computer languages of a comprehensive implementation of set algebra.

Neural networks are also very unsatisfactory. They appear to be all powerful, capable of learning seemingly difficult problems. Unfortunately neural networks, at least as presently structured, are also unable to implement set algebra, and this places a serious limitation on their scope. It is not clear that neural networks can be proved to work to a particular specification of performance, and this, from an engineering point of view, is most unsatisfactory. It seems to me that wild claims are made for what particular networks can or cannot do, but usually by people other than their inventors.

The greatest risk with neural networks is that they will cause a widespread confusion between the ability to do something, or to mimic a process, and the claim to understand a process. The possession of a network that can do some process does not help at all in understanding that process. It is instructive to wonder why. In the end, it is the absence of a theory of implementation that bars a relationship between understanding something and doing it. Paradoxically, it could be that research into neural networks will provide such a theory.

12.3 Gaps in Understanding Vision

Next I turn to some areas where there are, at least in my opinion, serious conceptual difficulties, so that it is difficult to know how they might be understood.

(i) Memory

The relationship between vision and memory seems fairly obvious at first sight. Vision can produce more results than could be acted upon at any one time; memory exists to hold the results until such time as they can be acted upon. As a statement, this implies a great deal about the world that we inhabit, and implies a great deal about the results of vision. Our own mental model of the world that we live in carries most of these implications. The world is stable. We see objects and the relationships between objects. Wrong, both times?

The idea is to hold the information that is necessary for actions until those actions will be executed. But the world is not perfectly stable: we will need information that is correct at the time of the action, not at some time earlier. So, the memory really ought to hold the best prediction of what is likely to be the useful information at the time the action will be executed. This time itself cannot be predicted, and so it becomes difficult to predict what information is likely to be useful at that time. As time passes, the fidelity of the prediction weakens, and so too should the memory. The core of what memory can hold for a longer time is simply a set of possible types of action plus a rough guide to where in space they should be directed.

(ii) Consciousness

Throughout this book, I have warned against being confused between the subjective phenomenology of vision, the experience of visual consciousness, and the objective, action-controlling side of vision. In order to give some justification to this, let me offer an idea of what the functional role of consciousness might be. In a sentence, our experience of vision might be a representation of the potential actions that we could make in the scene that we find ourselves. This representation must involve memory, for the reasons that I have given above.

It seems quite possible that the visual system delivers directions to whatever effector organs are in use, quite independently of phenomenology. To me, this is the real vision, the flow of information from the sensor to the effector, controlling actions. What we experience is a synthesis of vision and memory. If this is true, then whether a line looks sharp or not depends on what is being predicted on the basis of memory for similar situations, as well as what is happening at the eye. So long as this is a possibility, it pays to be extremely cautious of subjective experience.

12.4 Last Word

I have completed my task of trying to discover what understanding vision might involve. The title of this book is deliberately ambiguous—I am fascinated by the process of understanding vision and by the product: an understanding of vision. This area of research is the one in which we are nearest yet to a breakthrough in the most challenging scientific realm: understanding our brains and our minds.

Index

action 3, 13, 22, 57–58, 97–103, 120, 133–137,
    161–165, 264, 293–296
  action commands 4
  action description 15, 133–135, 161–164, 188
  catching 5, 98
  control of 4, 10, 13, 57, 133–136, 164, 264–265, 296
  grasping 4–5, 135–136, 159–165
  lifting 5, 135–137, 159–161
  touching 4, 133–136, 159–161
alerting 6
algorithm 11
aliasing 59–60
athletes 264
attention 6, 243
auto-correlation 85–86

brightness 7, 13–16, 20, 100

categorical perception 248
centroid 15, 17, 99–103, 114–118, 126, 129–130,
    152, 155, 177
colour 2, 6, 30, 136
consciousness 211, 296
contrast
  contrast sensitivity function (CSF) 220, 241–242
  detection 201–203, 213, 218, 221–224, 228, 241, 256
  discrimination 203–205
  Michelson 54, 64, 201
convolution 15, 22, 81, 84–85, 93–95, 223
corner 1, 5, 18–20, 25–26, 74, 111, 139, 142,
    157–158, 167, 183–184, 250–252, 288, 293
crease 1, 5, 9, 20, 26, 30, 32, 37, 40–43, 47, 74
cross-correlation 86
curvature 9, 16, 25, 43, 74, 112, 129–131, 142–144,
    182, 266
  curvature detectors 245–246
  curvature discrimination 209–211, 230,
    246–248
  Gaussian 28–30, 37–39, 70
  mean 29–30, 70

normal 28
principal 28–30, 70

decisions 13, 57, 100, 107, 120, 133, 140
  decision description 161–168, 174, 188
decision function 192–198, 214
descriptive sentence 17–23, 133–138, 149–154,
    167–168, 250, 293
  action description 15, 133–135, 161–164, 188
  decision description 161–168, 174, 188
difference of Gaussians (DoG) 84
differentiation 22, 68–74, 81, 84, 90, 98, 110–111,
    266, 293
d_{max} 233–237
dynamics 1, 213, 217, 228, 247, 285
d' 205–206

edge 1, 9, 19–20, 27, 31–32, 43–47, 63, 72, 84, 114,
    142–144, 150, 211, 223–228, 267
efficiency 142, 209–213
error 16, 120–127, 131, 146–149, 158, 166–167,
    173
  subject's response error distribution 196–198
experience 2–3, 191–192, 212, 289, 296–297
eye 21, 24, 52–55, 164, 285
  movements 44, 244, 261

faces 10, 19–20, 66, 161–164, 282–288
filter 81–85, 181, 217, 220–242, 254, 266, 293
Fourier transform 56, 86, 220–221, 241–242
fractal 31, 48, 254, 256

gain adaptation 220–221, 242
Glass patterns 273
grammar 9, 141–142, 157

H transform 62–65

illuminance 32–64
illumination 7, 19, 32–50, 59–64, 71, 74, 163–164,
    182–188, 283–289, 295
illusions 201, 211, 254
image algebra 15–16, 57–96, 217–244, 265–267,
    275, 293–295
image description 16–18, 97–132, 245, 293
image summary 13–17, 97, 122
integration 78, 89
invariance 20, 146, 167

Laplacian 69–74, 91
Laplacian of Gaussian 82–84, 99, 241, 266
learning 280
length 9, 104–113, 138, 146, 182–184, 201, 210, 230,
    247, 252–253, 262, 266
light sources 24, 32, 35, 41, 47
line 9, 16–26, 47, 106, 138–140, 149–150, 157–158,
    167, 183–184, 226–235, 246–254, 261, 266
    curvature 16, 25, 111, 209, 246, 249
    orientation 25, 211
lipreading 282–289
locomotion 5
log transform 62–63
long jump 264
luminance 17, 22, 41–50, 59–64, 71–76, 142, 201,
    211, 218–220
    profile 74–75, 235

mass 5, 8, 44, 103, 114, 121–123, 129–134,
    241
match 161–188, 211–212, 270–280, 294–295
    qualitative 167–168, 174
    quantitative 167, 173–174
medial axis 114
memory 19, 162, 195, 293–297
Method of Adjustment 192
    Constant Stimuli 192
    Two Alternative Forced Choice (2AFC) 192
metric 143–151, 209, 257
    city block metric 146
    Euclidean metric 146
    Minkowski metric 146
model 20–23, 142, 161–166
    description 161–173, 184–185, 274, 282
modulation transfer function (MTF) 55–56
moments 66, 115–116, 130, 258, 293
motion 44–47, 122, 156, 180, 188, 217, 232–237,
    257–260, 267, 282–286
    short-range apparent motion 232
motion parallax 161, 165
movement of bodies 43
movement of observer 5, 13, 16, 43–45, 97, 100,
    133, 165, 183
multidimensional scaling 288

neighbour 25–26, 76–79, 105, 136, 144–152, 173,
    214, 274–276, 294
neighbourhood operation 57, 67–68
neural networks 295–296
noise 17, 59–61, 66, 99, 116, 121–123, 208, 213,
    243, 249, 294
    intrinsic 206–214, 229
    photon 49, 63, 219

object 4–16, 135–137, 153–165, 185, 188, 294–296
occluding contour, occlusion 9, 18, 31–32, 41,
    46–48, 74, 114, 142, 165, 183–184
operations
    binary 57, 66
    global 57, 85
    point 57, 68
    unary 16, 57
Oppel–Kundt illusion 254–256
optical image 3–9, 21–22, 48, 54, 57–59, 62, 68, 71,
    87, 97–98, 103, 137, 184, 188
organization 107, 129, 175–182, 188, 271
orientation 9, 25, 226, 230–233, 246–252, 262–263,
    273–277
    discrimination 207, 230
outline 105–113, 128

patch 9, 23–27, 32, 41, 43, 76, 207–209, 264
pattern 9, 17, 21–25, 30–31, 42, 48, 56, 59
phenomenology 296
photometry 24, 48–49
planning 6, 161–164
point of subjective equality 199
principal axis 116–119, 124–126, 129–132, 138, 249
probability summation 223
psychometric function 192–209, 212–214, 236, 238

quantity 8, 57, 134, 140–148

reaction time 212–213
reading 238–240
recognition 19, 161, 167, 245, 278
reflectance 42, 47–51, 59–64
region 17, 100–118, 124, 130–139, 152
relationship 21, 85, 108, 137–186, 294
    spatial 9, 25, 107, 167, 185, 277–283
representation 8–9, 17–22, 97, 108, 113–114, 142,
    163–168, 184–185, 247, 266, 274, 289, 296

sampling 59–60, 89–95
scale-space 180–182
scene 1–13
second order statistics 119–120
segmentation 100–103, 121, 251

self-similarity 31, 176
shading 161, 165
shape 1, 4–5, 10, 19–25, 30–35, 41, 47–48, 74,
    105–109, 163–167, 182–188, 233, 249–250, 268,
    279–285
similarity 19, 22, 149–159, 167–169, 173, 294
size 7, 20–21, 30, 47–48, 58–59, 108, 113, 136, 142,
    153, 164–167, 170, 179–183, 218–219, 238–240,
    285
slant 26–29, 37, 41, 70
smoothing 77, 80–81, 84, 93, 109, 180–181, 272, 293
spatial frequency 54–56, 85, 219–227, 234–235,
    241–242, 256–257
spatial scale 78, 81–85, 102, 124, 137, 176,
    180–182, 220–223, 228–239
specularity 42–43, 48
standard deviation 61, 66, 72, 90, 98–100,
    115–123, 129–131, 138, 196, 199, 201, 206, 208
statistics 15, 75–79, 98–99, 103, 114–120, 129, 254,
    266
  mean 13–16, 61, 72–84, 90, 98–115, 123, 126,
    201, 208
  standard deviation 61, 66, 72, 90, 98–100,
    115–123, 129–131, 138, 196–201, 206, 208
stereopsis 161, 165, 191, 270, 274–275
surface 1–8, 18–25, 29–37, 41–43, 47–50, 59, 64,
    72–76, 136–137, 153, 164–168
  curvature 26, 27

extrinsic properties 59
intrinsic properties 59
normal 26, 27, 32, 49, 70
orientation 26, 30, 37, 43, 70
symbol 8–9, 12, 17–23, 140–142, 168, 246, 295
symmetry 73–74, 84–86, 164, 175–180, 270–272

texture 8, 30–31, 41–42, 48, 59, 75–81, 136, 165,
    169, 207–208, 261–264
things 3–10, 19–20, 25, 44–48, 134, 161–163,
    188
tilt 27–29, 37, 70

Vernier 226, 235–237
visual description 18, 22, 133–160, 245–269,
    274–279, 294
visual model 23, 161–166, 186–189, 289

Weber's Law 205, 253
Weibull function 203
weighting function 15, 79–84, 95

zero-crossing 108, 112, 114, 180–182